Understanding the Psychology of Internet Behaviour

For Carol, Daniel and Nicholas

Understanding the Psychology of Internet Behaviour

Virtual Worlds, Real Lives

Adam N. Joinson

First published 2003 by
PALGRAVE MACMILLAN
Houndmills, Basingstoke, Hampshire RG21 6XS and
175 Fifth Avenue, New York, N.Y. 10010
Companies and representatives throughout the world

PALGRAVE MACMILLAN is the global academic imprint of the Palgrave
Macmillan division of St. Martin's Press, LLC and of Palgrave Macmillan Ltd.
Macmillan® is a registered trademark in the United States, United Kingdom
and other countries. Palgrave is a registered trademark in the European
Union and other countries.

ISBN 0–333–98467–6 hardback
ISBN 0–333–98468–4 paperback

This book is printed on paper suitable for recycling and made from fully
managed and sustained forest sources.

A catalogue record for this book is available from the British Library.

A catalogue record for this book is available from the Library of Congress.

10   9   8   7   6   5   4   3   2   1
12 11 10 09 08 07 06 05 04 03

Printed in Great Britain by
Creative Print & Design, (Wales), Ebbw Vale

Contents

List of Figures

List of Tables

Preface

Early in January 2001, I was waiting in a barbershop in Glasgow when an article in the local newspaper caught my eye. It explained the case of a pair of young lovers who had never met. Instead, they had courted using Morse code and signal lamps across the Clyde Estuary when both were signal operators during the Second World War. She was land-based, while he was posted on an American ship anchored offshore. Although she tried to convince her superiors that they should be allowed to meet, they were forever to remain apart. After the war, she made great efforts to track her sweetheart, but to no avail. This tale only made the news because they were reunited after fifty years.

At the time, I was also reading about similar occurrences amongst telegraph operators towards the end of the nineteenth century. Simultaneously, the 'content is king' model of e-commerce was found to be badly lacking, while seemingly any technologies that enabled text-based communication (for example, mobile phone text messaging and 'chat' sites) were booming.

This book is an attempt to integrate these varied phenomena – although the focus of the book is the Internet, the analysis draws heavily on other forms of technologically mediated communication. This is not to say that just because an interaction is 'mediated' the form of that mediation is not important – quite the opposite. What I intend to argue is that the interaction between the tool, the person and the context leads to predictable patterns of behaviour. An eye on the past also invariably leads to a look to the future. In the final chapter, some time is spent looking at future Internet developments, and their potential psychological and behavioural impact. It is argued that behaviour can effectively be designed in (and out of) the Internet. Future Internet developments that stress, say, accountability or identifiability will change the nature of Internet behaviour, not necessarily for the better.

The division of the book also indicates the tendency for research that investigates psychology and the Internet to reflect either positive or negative outcomes of Internet use. Although this division is somewhat arbitrary (quite a number of studies straddle both good and bad outcomes), in the main, dividing research this way was surprisingly easy. Although more 'neutral' studies exist, there were not enough to justify a separate chapter. These studies thus tend to be intermingled in the positive and negative chapters.

Although the division into positive and negative outcomes could be characterised as unduly technologically determinist (that technology exerts an effect independently of the user), this is deliberate. The model outlined in Chapter 7, and the conclusions in Chapter 8, argue that although both positive and negative outcomes of Internet use are identifiable, these depend very much on how we view interaction via technology, the assumptions we bring vis-à-vis reality, and the user themselves. It is further argued that both positive and negative outcomes associated with Internet use depend upon essentially the same processes, and that many attempts to regulate what is termed the negative will also impact on the positive.

I am grateful to the Institute of Educational Technology at the Open University for allowing me the time on study leave to write this book, and to my family for providing the support actually needed to write it. I am also indebted to a number of colleagues for their insight provided through collaboration and debate, specifically, Mark Griffiths, Phil Banyard, Tom Buchanan and Beth Dietz-Uhler. I am grateful to a large number of colleagues who have assisted by providing copies of their published and unpublished work, including Andrea Baker, Azy Barak, Pam Briggs, Beth Dietz-Uhler, Karen Douglas, Della Drees, Christian End, Jeff Hancock, Katelyn McKenna, James Pennebaker, Tom Postmes, Richard Sherman and Russell Spears. Finally, my thanks go to my editor, Frances Arnold, and to John Suler and Tom Buchanan for their feedback and comments on the draft version of the book.

ADAM N. JOINSON

Acknowledgements

The author and publishers are grateful to the following for permission to reproduce copyright material:

Figure 2.3: Spears, R., Lea, M. and Lee, S. (1990) De-individuation and group polarization in computer-mediated communication. *British Journal of Social Psychology*, 29, p. 129.

Figure 2.4: Spears, R. and Lea, M. (1992) Social influence and the influence of the 'social' in computer-mediated communication. In M. Lea (ed.), *Contexts in Computer-mediated Communication*. London: Harvester Wheatsheaf, pp. 30–64.

Figure 3.1: Davis, R. A. (2001) A cognitive-behavioural model of pathological Internet use. *Computers in Human Behavior*, 17, p. 190, Copyright © 2001, reprinted with permission from Elsevier Science.

Figures 4.1 and 4.2: Nie, N. H. and Erbring, L. (2000) *Internet and Society: A Preliminary Report*. Stanford, Calif.: Stanford Institute for the Quantitative Study of Society. Available on-line at http://www. stanford.edu/group/siqss

Figure 5.1: McKenna, K. Y. A. and Bargh, J. (1998) Coming out in the age of the Internet: identity 'demarginalization' through virtual group participation. *Journal of Personality and Social Psychology*, 75, p. 683, Copyright © 1998 the American Psychological Association, reprinted with permission.

Table 3.2: Morahan-Martin, J. and Schumacher, P. (2000) Incidence and correlates of pathological Internet use among college students. *Computers in Human Behavior*, 16, p. 17, Copyright © 2000, with permission from Elsevier Science.

Table 3.3: Castellá, V. O. *et al*. (2000) The influence of familiarity among group members, group atmosphere and assertiveness on uninhibited behaviour through three different communication media. *Computers in Human Behavior*, 16, p. 150, Copyright © 2000, with permission from Elsevier Science.

Table 3.4: Cornwell, B. and Lundgren, D. C. (2001) Love on the Internet: involvement and misrepresentation in romantic relationships in cyberspace vs. realspace. *Computers in Human Behavior*, 17, p. 207, Copyright © 2001, reprinted with permission from Elsevier Science.

Table 6.1: Pew Internet and American Life, March 2000 Poll: Rainie and Kohut, 2000. Available on-line at www.pewinternet.org

Case Studies on page 80 and 82–3 are reprinted with the permission of copyright-holder www.saferdating.com

Every effort has been made to trace all the copyright-holders, but if any have been inadvertently overlooked the publishers will be pleased to make the necessary arrangement at the first opportunity.

List of Abbreviations

AA	Alcoholics Anonymous
BIRGing	Basking in reflected glory
CEO	Chief Executive Officer
CES-D	Centre for Epidemiological Studies Depression Scale
CFO	Cues filtered out
CMC	Computer-mediated communication
CORFing	Cutting off reflected failure
CSCW	Computer supported co-operative work
DSA	Dual self-awareness
EPI	Eysenck's personality inventory
ESG	Electronic support group
FAQs	Frequently asked questions
FtF	Face to face
FTP	File transfer protocol
GSM	Global System for Mobile communication
HTML	Hypertext mark-up language
IAD	Internet addiction disorder
ICQ	I seek you
IP	Internet Protocol
IRC	Internet Relay Chat
IRE	Initiation–response–evaluation
ISP	Internet Service Provider
MMS	Multimedia Messaging System
MUDs	Multi-user dungeons/dimensions
NWM	Nowheremom
PIU	Pathological Internet users
RL	Real life
RSC	Reduced social cues
SIDE	Social identity explanation of de-individuation effects
SIQSS	Stanford Institute for the Quantitative Study of Society
SIT	Social Identity Theory

SMEE	Strategic and motivated user, expected and emergent effects
SMS	Short Messaging System
VLEs	Virtual learning environments
VR	Virtual reality
WAC	Writing across the curriculum
WAP	Wireless Application Protocol
WELL	Whole Earth 'Lectronic Link
WWW	World Wide Web
XML	Extensible mark-up language

Putting Psychology and the Internet in Context

1

An on-line friendship developed between John Stansbury, who was posted to a rural outback, and 'Mat' during a lonely summer. They chatted regularly, and even developed plans to go on a joint holiday and fishing trip. However, 'Mat' changed plans, and decided instead on a trip to New Mexico that involved passing through Stansbury's area. At the time, Stansbury was taken ill with a fever, and can only recall being 'vaguely aware of gentle womanly hands and a kindly presence in my sickroom'. Suffice it to say, 'Mat' turned out to be the handle for a woman, and the couple were married soon after.

Familiar? Of course. The Internet has, quite apart from everything else, led to a large number of news pieces about on-line romance, entrapment and disinhibited behaviour. However, the report above was published in a 1891 article in the *Western Electrician* (and retold by Standage, 1999, pp. 127–8), and our young lovers were telegraph operators, not Internet chat-room users.

Tina Huish sent the text message 'Feel like talking?' to a phone number almost identical to her own. The message appeared on the phone of Andrew Baldwin, 140 miles away. He replied, and the two hit it off immediately. The couple spent hundreds of pounds on text messages and phone calls, and within six months, Baldwin had moved to Somerset to be with Huish. According to press reports, they planned to marry in the near future. (Ananova.com, 20 July 2001: 'Random text message leads to marriage')

Two key elements of the above tales are worth noting. The first is that such occurrences still receive press attention and a fair degree of wonderment. The second is that they provide a clue that to understand psychology and the Internet, we need to look not only at the present, but also the past. This is not to say that the specific tool used to mediate communication is unimportant (it clearly is), but rather that the act of mediating communication can have effects that transfer across time and media.

Tools and the psychology of the Internet

In the 1980s I was studying for my first degree in Psychology, and took a computing course. All the computers we learnt on were DOS-PCs – to do anything you needed to use the command line interface.

To use the word processing software, you needed a long piece of card placed across the top of the 'F' keys on the keyboard. When correctly aligned, this card told the user what combination of key presses to use to achieve a specific result (e.g. to make a word emboldened). But, the package couldn't give any feedback as to whether or not your goal had been achieved – a screen of plain text always sat in front of you. Formatting a document in these seemingly simple ways was seen as such an achievement that it actually formed a substantial part of the assessment of the course.

*Around the time I flunked the computing course because I couldn't 'do' subscript (someone stole my stick-on card), an Apple Macintosh appeared in the corner of the computer lab. I never saw anyone touch it. So I tried. But all I could see was a blank grey screen with a tiny icon in the top right corner labelled 'Macintosh-HD'. I could move the 'Macintosh-HD' icon around the grey screen, but nothing else. It never occurred to me to 'double click' (why would it?), and the idea that there might be something **inside** that tiny icon was ludicrous.*

Two years later my brother bought a new Apple Macintosh, and installed it in his flat. The experience was both bewildering and intoxicating. The interface felt like it had real depth – as if you could really open items and delve and explore. I had become an Apple Mac convert.

The point I would make from this experience is this: tools are more than just something to make a task easier. They change your way of thinking, of approaching a task (and indeed the nature of the task itself), and can reap unimagined wider social changes.

To take each point in turn, a task (e.g. to remember the shopping) is fundamentally different if we use a tool (e.g. a shopping list) or use our own memory. In the former, the task becomes 'match the shopping in your basket to that on the list (and remember to use the list)'. In the latter, the task is to remember the shopping you need to buy. The development of tools, right from the earliest alphabetic and numbering systems, has radically transformed not only the task, but also human capabilities. Vygotsky (1978) called this 'mediation', and argued that tools (as well as other people) allow for the extension of human capabilities.

When communication is technologically mediated, for instance, by using the telephone or the Internet, the task is similarly changed. The tools we have traditionally relied on to communicate, say, turn-taking or nodding to signify agreement, become obsolete. Body language, while not extinguished (who hasn't smiled when reading an e-mail?), becomes irrelevant to the communication of interpersonal affect.

More importantly, it is questionable whether or not the outcomes of a mediated and non-mediated communication are the same. When we write down a shopping list or alternatively memorise it, and assuming that we have a fairly good memory (or a short shopping list), the outcome (food in your fridge) is likely to be the same. However, when our communication is mediated it is possible that the outcomes are likely to be quite different than in a similar encounter face to face. This is the crux of cyberpsychology. We need to understand the psychological processes that underpin mediated communication to predict and explain not only how the task differs, but also how the outcome might differ, and the reasons for this. It is the differences in outcomes, rather than just how we complete a task, that is important, that begins to explain the phenomenal growth of the Internet, and that predicts wide social changes from a seemingly simple task.

A brief introduction to the Internet

The roots of the Internet can be traced to a US Defense Department initiative in the mid-1960s to develop a distributed network of computers. Originally perceived as a method for sharing data only, the original intention of the Internet (at the time called Arpanet) was to provide links between computers rather than people. However, e-mail was developed relatively early by the users of Arpanet as a means of person-to-person (as opposed to computer-to-computer) communication. With the advent of the World Wide Web in the early 1990s, and the commercial release of web browsers in 1993–4, the Internet began to expand rapidly, and to attract increasing numbers of commercial organisations and private users. For the study of psychology and the Internet, it is worth separating eight different domains of Internet activity. These are:

- *E-mail* E-mail is *asynchronous* text-based communication, which can be one-to-one or one-to-many. E-mail-based discussion lists (also called Listservs after the name of a product that manages these lists) involve posting to a group whereupon the message is distributed to all members. As e-mail tools have developed, they have gained a number of new capabilities, including attachments (files added to the e-mail), and e-mail forms (tick boxes and so on integrated into the e-mail).
- *Chat* Chat software allows for synchronous (real-time) text-based communication, again either one-to-one or many-to-many (e.g. Internet Relay Chat or IRC). Chatting can be conducted over the World Wide Web (WWW) or using dedicated software (e.g. IRC). Other chat services include instant messaging, buddy lists (people you regularly talk to) and, in some cases, file sharing.
- *File sharing* File sharing was one of the earliest activities on the Internet. In its early format, file sharing on the Internet involved logging on to a remote server (using, for instance, file transfer protocol (FTP) or Gopher), and uploading and downloading files. In the late 1990s peer-to-peer file sharing (e.g. Napster, Aimster, Gnutella) allowed people to connect directly to other computers to share files, rather than share via a remote server.
- *Asynchronous discussion groups* Asynchronous discussion groups are many-to-many systems for exchanging messages. Examples include Usenet newsgroups or bulletin boards. They can be hosted and distributed by e-mail, WWW or using newsgroup servers and readers. Generally, a user subscribes to a particular group to read and post messages.
- *Multi-user dungeons/dimensions (MUDs)* MUDs are text-based virtual environments that developed out of role-playing games. They provide not only synchronous communication environments,

but also descriptions of environments and a series of commands for interaction with those environments and other participants.

- *Virtual worlds* Virtual worlds are effectively 3D MUDs (e.g. the Palace) where participants are represented graphically and interact with environments and other users in the graphical 3D environment. Participants are represented by 'avatars', graphical representations of their character. As more immersive virtual reality (VR) develops, the use of VR tools (e.g. goggles, suits) will most likely increase the 'reality' component of the virtual space.

- *Video/voice communication* As the price of webcams (video cameras for sending live video over the Internet) has dropped dramatically, so the use of videoconferencing has moved from a primarily commercial concern to being more common on the Internet. Applications like CuSeeMe effectively create chat rooms with either one-to-one, one-to-many (i.e. a webcast) or many-to-many voice, text and video links between users.

- *The World Wide Web* The World Wide Web accounts for much of the data transmitted on the Internet (although it is still behind e-mail as the most popular use). Although much is made of the WWW as a content delivery device, it is the use of hypertext links between pages that provides something unique to users. WWW pages are written using hypertext mark-up language (HTML), although the use of XML, JavaScript, Coldfusion and other scripting languages and applications allows for the design of 'dynamic' web pages.

The above list is not exhaustive, nor are the activities or tools mutually exclusive. A mailing list uses e-mail, but can be archived on the WWW (and in the case of newsgroups, posting can now be done via a WWW interface). File-sharing applications, particularly peer-to-peer ones like Napster, sometimes also include a chat function. As the technology develops, we may well see new Internet activities develop, particularly if we see convergence between media (e.g. interactive TV) and increasingly immersive virtual experiences.

The various different Internet activities and tools outlined above provide users with a range of benefits and shortcomings, many of which users are actively aware of, and with which users seek to advance their own goals (Mantovani, 1996). They also determine what a user can do, with whom, and, to a degree, how that behaviour will be enacted. It is this balance between the aware user and the effects a media exerts on behaviour or psychological state that is the domain of the study of the psychology of the Internet.

Talking without meeting: a quick look back at the psychological consequences of mediated communication

Gackenbach and Ellerman (1998) note, in a discussion of private radio, that from the 1920s through to the 1940s

> Dozens of scholarly books were written ... studying the ways in which the new technology was reshaping personal relationships, the structure of the family, the literacy of children, and the ability of people to think critically and express themselves. We have only to pass by the shelves of any bookstore to see this whole process repeating itself with respect to the Internet. (p. 14)

Gackenbach and Ellerman's argument is essentially that the Internet has led to many scholars essentially reinventing the wheel, along with similarly utopian (and dystopian) predictions of the social impact of a new technology. A study of old 'new technologies' can also teach us valuable lessons about the impact of technology on behaviour. First, there are often striking similarities between mediated behaviours that share certain characteristics, regardless of the technology doing the mediating. Second, there is evidence that earlier technologies influence the psychological impact, and behavioural norms, of later technologies. For instance, writing has its own impact both socially, historically and psychologically, but of course, when we think about computer-mediated communication we focus on the newer technology (the computer) rather than the older one (writing). I would argue that these two technologies are inseparable, and that to amply consider the psychological impact of text-based communication we also need to think about the impact of writing itself. Further, as technology develops, earlier technology use influences how we use later technologies. For instance, when radio began to replace the telegraph, radio operators used the same slang and acronyms as telegraph operators. This then influenced the norms and behaviour of amateur radio operators (radio hams), an influence still discernible today.

In the following section, five 'new' (and not so new) technologies – writing, the telegraph, the telephone, the radio and mobile phone text messaging – are discussed in a historical and psychological context.

Writing

It is easy to forget that writing, as opposed to oral communication, is a technology (Ong, 1986). Not only that, but it is a relatively new technology as far as human development is concerned. Although human oral communication is dated at about 50,000 years, the development of writing and alphabets is only around 5,000 years old.

Like other, more recent forms of mediated communication, writing requires its own specialised tools – whether that be slate and chalk, pen and paper or even the word processor. And, like the Internet and computers, writing was also railed against in its early days. In *Phaedrus*, Plato argues that writing is inhuman and artificial, that it destroys memory and 'weakens the mind' (Ong, 1982, p. 79).

Until medieval times, writing was very much a minority pursuit. Documents were handwritten on expensive parchment. It might take a copyist (usually a monk) a year to make a copy of a religious text (Burke, 1991). The vast majority of information was transmitted orally – by travelling poets or a network of messengers employed by the Church or a royal house. To the illiterate, writing held little value – unless a document had an official seal, there was no counting on its authenticity (and they were often faked). In law, it was the oral that counted – the court 'heard' evidence against charges read aloud to the defendant (a practice that continues to this day). Unlike today, writing was expected to be read aloud, and in most well-to-do households different people would occupy the role of the reader and writer of letters. To have meaning, the written would be spoken, rather like religious incantations and wills are spoken today.

A number of developments led to the rapid spread of literacy and writing – the (re)invention of the moveable type printing press by Gutenberg around 1450 removed the need for laborious copying by hand, while the availability of a cheap material for writing – paper – meant that the printing press could be used liberally. Paper was a Chinese invention that was discovered by the Arabs in the eighth century, and eventually exported as technology to Europe by the fourteenth century. Burke (1991) reports that in Bologna the price of paper had dropped by 400 per cent in the fourteenth century. The invention of the printing press in the 1450s 'destroyed the oral society ... and its effects were to be felt in every area of human activity' (Burke, 1991, p. 77).

According to Ong (1986), writing 'restructures consciousness', it separates the knower from the known and creates a distance between the author and the reader. Writing cannot answer questions, and is forever static (one of Plato's concerns). Ong (1986) even argues that writing may have a neuropsychological effect – encouraging left-hemisphere activity in readers of alphabetic scripts. There is an educational movement, writing across the curriculum (WAC), that has since the early 1970s attempted to use writing as an aid for student learning (Hilgers et al., 1999). Hilgers et al. (1999) interviewed students enrolled on an intensive writing course about their experiences. Hilgers et al. note that 'throughout the interviews, interviewees made summary and general statements about the perceived benefits of writing' (p. 341). Some of the quotes from their participants illustrate the potential perceived benefits of writing for understanding a topic, for learning and for formalising ideas (all from Hilgers et al., pp. 342–3):

When I just made the outline, the paper meant nothing to me and I thought this was going to be a hard paper to write. But as I was writing – I had read all the stuff and gone to all the classes and knew all the information – but as you're writing, you have these epiphanies and things come to you. It just all seems to fit together.

Writing helps me organise my thoughts ... Now, when I'm talking to someone, I tend to think 'Okay, what are the major points I want to make in this conversation?'

When you write an idea or concept or branch off from there into a full essay, it's very different from regurgitating facts because when you're writing something you need to think about how you connect things.

The specific technology used for writing can have an effect too. When writing was a time-consuming, difficult job, a scribe would often be used to put one's thoughts on to paper (so writing became more a transcription). While the printing press made entirely new uses of the written word possible (for instance, a newspaper), it also made text universally legible. However, it was not until the development of computer technology, and word processing packages in particular, that the written word was freed from many of its previous technological constraints.

The journalist Steven Johnson (1997) discusses how his use of a word-processing package changed his whole process of writing:

In the years when I still wrote using pen and paper or a typewriter, I almost invariably worked out each sentence in my head before I began transcribing it on to the page ... All this changed when the siren song of the Mac's interface lured me into writing directly at the computer. I began with my familiar start-and-stop routine, dutifully thinking up the sentences before typing it out, but it soon became clear that the word-processor eliminated the penalty that revisions normally exact ... I noticed a qualitative shift in the way I worked with sentences: the thinking and typing processes began to overlap. (pp. 143–4)

It is arguable that in one way computer technology has brought writing closer to its oral predecessor (Yates, 1996). When writing was transcribed and then read aloud, the register and protocol for writing were still based upon an oral tradition. However, perhaps as more people wrote (and read), and the technology for writing became easier, so writing itself moved to its own status. However, computer technology and the Internet have allowed us to type freely, without the need to carefully form sentences before we write. Plato complained that writing is always a facsimile of the mind, while the spoken word taps directly into consciousness. However, as the quote from Johnson illustrates, this need not be the case any more. In support of this contention, it has been noted by linguists that the register of synchronous computer-mediated communication shares many of the characteristics of verbal communication (Collot and Belmore, 1996). The Internet has seen an upsurge in written communication amongst groups who, only ten years ago, would have hardly written at all during a normal working day. This shift towards the written word, regardless of the register (or grammatical and spelling mistakes), may in itself have a large-scale impact on people's psychological processes.

The telegraph

While writing was perhaps the first form of technologically mediated communication, the telegraph (which translates as 'far writer') was certainly the immediate ancestor of modern electronic communication, including the Internet (Standage, 1999).

The ability to communicate quickly between two distant points offered commerce and governments a competitive advantage from the earliest stages of civilisation. For instance, in warfare, being able to get news from a battle, and relay instructions (and supplies) back, would give any army a substantial advantage over their opponent. Similarly, if a commercial organisation could gather information faster than their competitors about, for example, commodity prices, they stood to profit from that knowledge.

By the time of the Industrial Revolution in Europe, the need for the fast transmission of commercial and government information became more pressing. The search for a communication technology intensified. In 1791, Claude Chappe demonstrated an optical system that allowed the communication of a complex message to a point ten miles distant. His system was quickly adopted by the French government and expanded by Napoleon in 1804. The importance of his invention was recognised across Europe and by the early part of the nineteenth century, an optical telegraph system covered much of Europe. In the UK, fear of invasion (by variously the Spanish and the French) had led to an earlier system of beacons linking the south coast to London. These beacons were replaced with an optical telegraph system at the turn of the nineteenth century.

The development of an electric telegraph took a further fifty years of research and testing. Again, part of the problem was in developing a suitable protocol for communicating between the two points (after all, an electric current can only pulse, so the letters of the alphabet need to be represented some other way). It was 1841 before Morse could demonstrate his electric telegraph well enough to convince people of its value. By the end of the nineteenth century, the electric telegraph had revolutionised the speed of communication, and in turn the pace of life itself.

The telegraph serves to illustrate an important point about the nature of mediated communication. First, the importance of bandwidth and associated costs. Telegraph messages were charged by the word, so there was considerable incentive to make messages as short as possible, and where possible to use shorthand rather than full words. Although a trained operator could send up to 40 words a minute using Morse code, it was common for them to abbreviate some common phrases.

A second point worth noting is that an interesting communication phenomenon generally occurred 'off record' between operators, rather than between clients of the telegraph companies (although to be sure the CAPS used in telegraph messages, along with the shorthand, certainly lends them a sense of urgency). The cost and lack of privacy tended to inhibit personal communication between members of the general public using the telegraph. However, for the telegraph operators, the network provided an 'on-line community encompassing thousands of people, very few of whom ever met face-to-face' (Standage, 1999, pp. 122–3). The sense of community amongst telegraph operators was heightened by their own norms and customs, vocabulary, the use of short (usually two or three letters) signatures or 'sigs' and a sense of ownership of a particular 'line'. According to Standage, experienced operators could even recognise their on-line friends simply from their style of Morse code.

Because the wires (with the exception of rural outposts) were staffed continuously, during the quiet periods telegraph operators would engage in lively on-line interaction – swapping jokes, stories and opinions, which were, according to Edison (a one-time telegraph operator), far too rude to publish. Women formed a reasonably large proportion of this community (estimated at around a third), and were generally aged between 18 and 30 and unmarried. Although these women operators were usually physically segregated from the men, they were of course in contact with them daily on-line. It is perhaps not surprising then that romances between telegraph operators were widespread.

For instance, Ella Cheever Thayer's novel *Wired Love: A Romance of Dots and Dashes* was published in 1879. The plot of *Wired Love* was based around a romance on-line. An article in an 1891 edition of the *Western Electrician* titled 'Romances of the Telegraph' outlines a romance between two operators that led to marriage when they met. Standage quotes one operator from the 1880s saying that 'many a telegraph romance begun "over the wire" culminated in marriage' (1999, p. 129).

The evidence of an on-line community of telegraph operators, alongside the romances between distant pairs, led Standage to conclude that 'despite the apparently impersonal nature of communicating by wire, it [the telegraph] was in fact an extremely subtle and intimate means of communication' (Standage, 1999, p. 123).

The telegraph is also important in any consideration of mediated communication because the codes and norms developed by telegraph operators moved to radio when the operators moved, and were picked up by ham radio hobbyists, who a generation later were also some of the early enthusiasts of the Internet. In addition, many of the leading figures in the telegraph industry went on to similar roles in the developing telephone business.

The telephone

In 1876, Alexander Graham Bell's experiments to develop an enhanced 'harmonic' telegraph led to the patenting of what became known as the telephone (the original invention can be traced to Halian Antonio Meucci). The possibilities of the telephone were missed by many – when turning down the offer to purchase the patent for the telephone (and so monopolise the market), the President of the Western Union Telegraph Company asked 'What use could this company make of an electrical toy?'

Perhaps not surprisingly, considering many of the early 'telephone men' came from the telegraph industry, the marketing of the telephone in the early days stressed its business uses and the possibility of the telephone as a device for broadcasting rather than for one-to-one communication. For instance, future visions of the telephone involved the broadcasting of 'distinguished men' to remote audiences in various music halls (*Boston Transcript*, 18 July 1876) or even a 'dancing party [with] ... no need for a musician' (*Nature*, 24 August 1876). Advertising pitches to residential customers almost universally stressed the practical value of the telephone rather than its possible use for social interaction. Such 'practical' uses included the broadcasting of news, weather reports and sports results, for ordering goods and services, and in emergencies.

Fischer (1992) notes that telephone executives bemoaned frivolous use of the telephone in internal memoranda, and actively discouraged social uses of the telephone until the 1920s. For instance, in 1909 a local manager in Seattle listened in to calls on a residential exchange, and found that 30 per cent were 'purely idle gossip', his concern being how to reduce this 'unnecessary use' (Fischer, 1992). Similarly, at the turn of the century a telephone directory in Canada stated that 'It is, of course, well understood that business conversations cannot be limited as to time, but "visiting" can beneficially be confined to a reasonably short duration of time' (Fischer, 1992).

At the same time, both the telephone industry and popular press were concerned with abuse of the telephone. In 1884, *Electrical World* magazine warned that 'The serenading troubadour can now thrum his guitar before the telephone, undisturbed by apprehension of shotguns and bull dogs. Romeo need no longer catch a cold waiting at Juliet's balcony.' A series of cards developed by the Canadian Dominion Telegraph Company in 1877 to advertise their telephone service show a man speaking to, presumably, his wife on the telephone while she conducts a dalliance with a younger man. In another card, a husband explains to his wife that he 'can't come dear, too busy' while he gambles with friends.

According to Fischer, 'Many industry people complained of profanity, yelling and abuse on the telephone. Through notices, direct chastisement of customers by employees, and occasional legal action, the companies sought to improve telephone courtesy' (1992, p. 70). In some cases customers were cut off or even jailed for profanity. In 1910, Bell published an advert titled 'Dr Jekyll and Mr Hyde at the Telephone' to highlight misuse and abuse. As well as abuse of the telephone, the lack of etiquette was also a cause for concern. Until well into the 1920s, most social commentators bemoaned the use of the telephone to issue invitations, and telephone companies tried desperately to discourage the use of 'hello' instead of more 'proper' greetings. AT&T distributed the following to local companies for inclusion in their directories in 1910:

> Would you rush into an office or up to the door of a residence and blurt out 'Hello! Hello! Who am I talking to?' No, one should open conversations with phrases such as 'Mr. Wood, of Curtis and Sons, wishes to talk with Mr. White ...' without any unnecessary and undignified 'Hello's'.

From the 1920s onwards, the telephone industry effectively 'discovered' sociability, and began marketing the telephone as a technology for socialising as well as for practical uses. Around this time, adverts began to stress the use of the telephone to keep in touch with family and friends in a more 'intimate' manner than a letter. A typical advert around this time noted that: 'It's a weekly affair now, those fond intimate talks. Distance rolls away and for a few minutes every Thursday night the familiar voices tell the little family gossip that both are so eager to hear' (Bell Canada, 1921).

So, effectively for thirty years, the telephone industry was out of step with the actual uses of the telephone in residential households. The attempts by the companies to create uses for the telephone have echoes in early attempts to encourage households to purchase PCs to manage their accounts or to plan their garden. It was not until the discovery of sociability in the form of the Internet that these efforts desisted.

A further parallel with the development and spread of computer technology in the household is the early theorising on the social impact of the telephone. One concern, that I will return to in the following chapter, was that the telephone would replace face-to-face encounters with something less 'real'. Fischer (1992) exemplifies this concern when he states:

> Not even a telephone company publicist could assert that telephone calls capture the intimacies conveyed by eye contact and physical contact, or that telephone friendships can plumb the same depths as sharing meals, taking walks or just being together. (p. 239)

Indeed, McLuhan (1964) quotes from a 1906 copy of the *New York Telegram* the use of the word 'phoney' meaning the lack of real 'substance' inherent in a telephone conversation. Even relatively recently Berger (1979) claims:

> to use the phone habitually also means to learn a specific style of dealing with others – a style marked by impersonality, precision, and a certain superficial civility. The key question is this: Do these internal habits carry over into other areas of life, such as nontelephonic relations with other persons? The answer is almost certainly yes. The problem is: just how, and to what extent? (1979, pp. 6–7)

However, there is evidence that people use the telephone to develop relationships, and that they feel close to those they talk to regularly on the phone. A vast majority of telephone calls are directed to a relatively low number of people (typically five or six), suggesting that close relationships are maintained on the telephone. In the UK, British Telecom launched a 'Friends and Family' discount for five selected numbers, suggesting that they recognise this use of the phone. This does not, alas, suggest that telephones are always designed to support the user: the absence of off switches on standard land-line telephones has led to third-party devices (e.g. Caller ID) to manage the interaction (Brown and Perry, 2000). Mobile telephones that automatically answer when they are opened is another case of design impeding user control of the interaction. However, in late 2001 Samsung launched a mobile telephone with a window on the front that displayed the caller's number (or name if entered in the phone's memory), allowing the user to know who is calling before answering. The advertisements for this telephone stressed this use, with the television ads showing a female choosing from a selection of males, and the print advert with the tag line that it puts 'you' in control. The development of third generation (3G) mobile phones that allow multimedia messaging will no doubt lead to more unexpected, perhaps unwanted, uses of the telephone.

Radio communication

Following the development of radio by Marconi, most radio stations were staffed by ex-telegraph operators. As both the radio waves and telegraph used Morse code, it was not surprising that these new operators took with them the linguistic short-cuts used on the telegraph, and many of the social norms and etiquette.

By the end of the First World War, relatively large numbers of amateur radio enthusiasts had joined the airwaves. These amateurs were called 'hams' – which also happened to be the name given by telegraph operators to particularly slow (and usually rural) operators on the wires. The use of radio waves by 'hams' gave members of the public, for the first time, the experience of a global community linked by mediated communication. The following three decades were the 'golden age' of radio, although it also represented an increasing amount of regulation of the airwaves by governments, the military and commercial broadcasters.

Although the number of radio 'hobbyists' increased during the period between the wars, amateur radio, because of the restrictions on its use, was bound to remain a minority pursuit.

The introduction of 'citizens' band' radio (that does not require a licence) and computer technology has seen the number of radio hams reach a plateau and begin to reduce in recent years. However, one estimate at the turn of the twenty-first century puts the number of radio hams at 600,000 globally. In some places, the licence to operate as a radio ham still requires a knowledge of Morse code, limiting the number of likely users.

Amateur radio gave many people an 'Internet-like' experience (and to many, still does). According to one of the many radio FAQs, amateur radio is 'one of the most direct and personal means of communications between citizens of different countries, races, culture [*sic*] and believings' (http://www.qsl.net/iu0paw/curiosity.htm).

Ham radio, like the telegraph before it, also has its own customs and language. For instance, there is a considerable emphasis paid on radio ham Internet sites to establishing proper behaviour. One such site explaining 'repeater' etiquette (http://butler.qrp.com/~n9ynf/rprt-etiquette.html) states:

- Use the correct phonetic alphabet when identifying
- Don't call CQ, just 'your call listening'
- Use 'Break' only in emergencies
- To interrupt give your call sign between other stations' transmissions
- Brevity, be short and concise with your conversations
- Remember that nothing is private on the air
- No need for 'no contact' or 'nothing heard' or 'clear' after making a failed call. All the other stations heard you not make your contact.

Some of the language used by radio hams, such as 10-4, has passed into everyday understanding, while other codes (CQ for 'seeking', 88 for 'hugs and kisses', 73 for 'best regards') have not. Each user has their own unique call sign which is a combination of letters and numbers (e.g. N9YNF for the poster of the etiquette above). Although the call sign is usually provided by the registering authority, there is a considerable market in 'vanity' call signs.

Because most early radio operators were on board navy ships, they were predominantly male. Similarly, most of the early hobbyists were also young males. However, like the telegraph before it, there are some reports of romance between radio hams. For instance, one web site says: 'A growing proportion of radioamateurs are women, and it is fairly common for OM's (male amateurs) and YL's (young lady operators) to meet first over the air, then in person, get married and start raising their own future radio operators' (www.qsl.net/iu0paw/curiosity.htm)

However, this may be wishful thinking: the Electronics Museum Amateur Radio Club's 1996 newsletter reports that a request for information about radio romances led to no results, but does state that 'One does hear romantic chit-chat on the air from time to time. There is a real drama when a lady of certain years who happens to have a youthful voice is chatted up by a young man who thinks he has found a possible love interest who would not object to his hobby.'

The Amateur Radio Newsline (1998) does report on the marriage of Erin Burck and Don LaFreniere, who courted on-air. Although they used their own secret frequency, Erin says 'We had many interesting conversations on the air. We had a lot of people from both sides of the border who would love to tune in to us and tease us at appropriate times. Yea, it was an on the air soap opera.'

Mobile telephone text messaging

SMS or Short Messaging System was developed during the early 1990s as an addition to the new GSM (Global System for Mobile communications) system for mobile telephones. According to the web site mobilesms.com, 'SMS was an accidental success that took nearly everyone in the mobile industry by surprise'. The first text message was sent in 1992 by Vodafone between an engineer's computer and mobile telephone. The system allows mobile telephone users to send short text messages to other users using a difficult-to-master and slow-to-use interface.

At the same time, in Europe pre-pay mobile phones became popular during the late 1990s. A pre-pay tariff allowed young people to own a mobile telephone because they paid for their usage in advance (rather like an electricity meter that uses pre-paid keys to run). The ability of mobile telephones to send and receive text messages was little publicised and, at least initially, usage was not billed by the companies. For young people with limited funds, the ability of mobile phones to send free messages to friends was soon well-known, and SMS traffic increased exponentially. For instance, in August 2000, 560 million text messages were sent in the UK alone, according to the GSM Association, more than ten times the 50 million recorded in May 1999. Worldwide, the number of text messages sent to mobile phones in October 2000 reached 10 billion, compared with 1 billion in early 1999. The best-selling book in the UK immediately before Christmas 2000 was a guide to text messaging.

Because of the limited number of characters allowed in each message (160 for the Latin alphabet, 70 for non-Latin alphabets like Chinese), a new language reminiscent of early Internet communication developed. So 'see you later' became 'CU L8er'. It took several months for the mobile network operators to develop a system for billing SMS messages, by which time the use of text messages was well-established.

The phenomenal growth of text messaging has also led to a rash of media stories and reports of text message oddities, its use in romance and courting and, of course, the potential dangers of too much text. For instance, writing in the *Prague Post*, Kate Swoger (16 May 2001) reports the case of Donat who sends between 20 and 30 texts a day. Although he is reluctant to share the contents of his texts, he does show her one: it reads 'I want you'. Swoger also quotes Michal Cernousek of Charles University stating that text messaging is mostly used for banal, meaningless conversation, and that 'It is a medium of loneliness ... You must use it so as not to feel the loneliness of our modern world'. Swoger also quotes another academic arguing that SMS keeps intimacy at bay and encourages terseness: 'Personal moments have been vanishing from communication'.

This emphasis on courtship is similar to the increased use of the telephone during dating at the start of the twentieth century reported by Fischer. In his interviews with users of telephones between 1900 and 1920, Fischer notes that many recall increased use of the telephone to arrange dates and other courtship matters. One hundred years later, it would seem that the same use of the telephone, except SMS rather than talk, is taking place.

Similarly, concerns that SMS has a negative net social impact similarly echo earlier concerns that new technology, whether writing or the telephone, has a negative impact on people's well-being or social skills (there have even been reports of SMS-derived repetitive strain injury). As we shall see later, the Internet has encountered similar concerns.

Mediated communication – lessons from history

This somewhat brief look at technology and communication illustrates a number of points that will develop throughout this volume. One is that technology is, at least initially, seen as an artificial substitute for something more 'real'. Just as writing was bemoaned by Plato as lacking the direct link with consciousness that speech has, so the telephone was initially seen as a poor substitute for face-to-face interaction that could lead to misunderstandings or worse. The same pattern is repeated for mobile phone text messages and the Internet.

A second point is that tools do not simply translate a behaviour to a new medium without some impact on psychological processes. These psychological processes may occur both because of the unique requirements of the tool (e.g. writing), and out of the affordances and environment for communication a tool provides (e.g. telegraph operators). When a medium offers, for instance, limited bandwidth and exerts a cost on verbosity (e.g. SMS or Morse code), we would expect some form of linguistic adaptation, both to reduce word count and to express socio-emotional themes. However, this adaptation to the affordances of the tool will also carry with it a psychological effect. For instance, the abbreviations used in text messaging or indeed Morse code also serve to exclude certain groups who do not understand them. The need to express concisely might encourage candidness because 'beating around the bush' is not possible.

Sara Kiesler (1997) draws a distinction between technologies that amplify and those that transform:

> Some technological change is primarily amplifying, making it possible for people to do what they have done before, but more accurately, quickly or cheaply. In other cases, technology is truly transformative: It leads to qualitative change in how people think about the world, in their social roles and institutions, in the ways they work, and in the political and economic challenges they face ... Sometimes the amplifying effect is what we see first, never realising there is a later transformative effect to come, or that the amplifying technology is part of a larger social change. (pp. xii–xiii)

As Sherman notes (2001), it is a little too early to say whether the Internet is amplifying or transformative, but 'As history has illustrated, it is wise to remain open to all possibilities' (p. 68).

From Tools to Behaviour

2

It was argued in the previous chapter that technologies for mediating communication and interaction often bring with them unpredicted and unexpected social and psychological impacts. While in part the aim of research must be to map these differences between 'traditional' and new technologies, a crucial issue is why a particular technology (or suite of technologies) leads to different patterns of behaviour.

Characteristics of the tool and behaviour

The cognitive psychologist Gibson introduced the idea of affordances to explain his notion of direct perception. According to Gibson (1979), objects or environments have certain properties that lead to different types of behaviour. For instance, a solid, flat surface affords walking, while a vertical or boggy surface does not. This idea of objects affording certain types of behaviour was adopted enthusiastically by human–computer interaction researchers, most notably Don Norman (1988). Norman, in applying the notion of affordances to everyday objects, argues that affordances are the 'perceived and actual properties of the thing, primarily those fundamental properties that determine just how the thing could possibly be used' (1988, p. 9).

So, just as a flat smooth surface affords walking, so the telephone affords ('is for') talking, but not walking on. What is important about the idea of affordances is that they imply a direct, in some cases *designed*, link between the properties of an object, material or tool, and the uses to which it is put.

Just as importantly, whenever technology is used to mediate communication or behaviour in some way, the tool not only affords certain behaviours, but also removes the need for, or opportunity to conduct, other aspects of a behaviour.

So, in affording easy walking conditions, a pavement will also limit the possibilities of recreational climbing along the high street. Similarly, the Internet affords new patterns of interaction, but with the accompanying cost of, for instance, a loss of non-verbal cues during the interaction. So, at a very basic level, a model of the psychological impact of a technology on communication needs to take into account both the affordances of the technology, and the social–psychological consequences of those affordances.

Of course, different ways of mediating social behaviour will differ in their affordances. Although the number of ways in which they differ (or by the same token are similar) is virtually limitless (for instance, whether or not they allow for permanent records, the level of automation and so on), there are five key dimensions that are important in understanding the link between a tool and social behaviour:

- Synchronicity
- The cues transmitted
- Bandwidth and cost constraints
- The level and type of anonymity
- Exclusivity.

Synchronicity

Synchronicity refers to whether or not a discussion or conversation takes place in 'real time' or is spread over time. Media are usually divided into synchronous communication (e.g. the telephone) and asynchronous (e.g. the letter). However, this neat division is being blurred by newer communication technologies like e-mail and SMS, that are typically seen as asynchronous, but in some cases take on the characteristics of synchronous communication because of the speed of reply and networks. However, even in these cases, the psychological imperative to reply immediately (as you would need to in a conversation) is not there.

While I was on the fast train to London, a young man sat opposite, took out his mobile phone and read an SMS message. He suppressed a grin, and began to write a reply. Just before he sent the reply, I noticed a smile, and then a press of the send button. At first I was puzzled – why would you smile at your own reply? Then it struck me – he was smiling because he was pleased and amused by his own repartee. Using SMS, there was less likelihood of kicking yourself for missing the comeback – you have the time to construct an impression of yourself as the Oscar Wilde of the 7.45 to London Euston.

Synchronicity is important to understanding mediated communication because once the pressure to reply immediately is removed, the person has the opportunity to move scarce cognitive resources from the management of the conversation to the actual message. It also means that users have more time to develop a message (even if an asynchronous conversation is moving rapidly).

The cues transmitted

The amount of cues or social presence conveyed by a communication technology has been arranged along a continuum ranging from the lowest level (e.g. text-based formal modes such as a business letter) through to the telephone, videophone and eventually, at the highest level, face to face (Daft and Lengel, 1984; Short *et al.*, 1976). Although the assumption that lower-level cues invariably lead to less social communication is questionable, that different communication technologies provide different types of information and feedback throughout an interaction is generally implicated in many, if not all, theories of mediated interaction.

I would further argue that the impact of, say, voice versus text communication extends beyond the amount or type of information conveyed during interaction. Just as the acts of writing and talking are fundamentally different, and invoke different psychological processes, so the act of talking via the Internet and text-based communication will invoke those same processes quite separately from any differences in, say, the amount of social context cues conveyed during interaction. Thus, any study of the psychological processes involved in Internet use also needs to consider whether the interaction is text- or voice- or video-based.

Bandwidth and cost constraints

Another key consideration for psychology and the Internet is the cost, in financial and bandwidth terms, of the interaction. When cost is high then brevity will tend to be encouraged. For instance, the charging of telegraph messages by the word led to a specific type of communication. Similarly, mobile telephone text messaging developed in popularity because of its cost (initially free), but it also adds a band-width restriction in the form of the number of characters allowed per message. To a degree, bandwidth constraints in early e-mail use also led to a norm of brief messages and acronyms (which are also used extensively in chat environments). It is arguable that a tendency towards brevity has an impact on the type of message conveyed, and how it is perceived by the recipient. In the case of the telegraph, the brevity of the messages could be argued to add to a sense of urgency and a lack of normal conversational niceties. Although it is often difficult to disentangle the cost of bandwidth from the cues transmitted, I would argue for its value. For instance, letter writing and the telegraph both convey essentially the same cues, but the cost of sending a telegraph leads to a unique imperative towards directness.

Anonymity

When anonymity is referred to, it usually implies 'lack of identifiability' (say, when you are a member of a large crowd). However, computer-mediated communication (CMC) is usually conducted in a state of *visual anonymity* (you can't see the person you're talking to), but without *lack of identifiability* (you know their name from their e-mail address, unless the person is using a pseudonym to identify them-selves). Knowing someone's e-mail address, while providing a degree of identifiability, is not the same as if you met them face to face. Anonym-ity, in one form or another, is implicated in most, models of Internet behaviour.

Sender-recipient exclusivity

The final factor discussed here is whether or not a mediation technol-ogy allows for private communication between people. For instance, many early telephone installations used party lines, where a number of households shared a line. Although listening in to others' conversa-tion was actively discouraged, this did not stop at least some level of snooping (Fischer, 1992). Similarly, radio discussions are usually non-private, again, perhaps limiting the likelihood of intimate con-versations taking place. It might be expected that people will move to more private media for intimate communication. Thus, a chat room meeting might lead to e-mail, rather than other chat rooms (this also of course adds an asynchronous dimension).

| | | | Cost and | Anonymity – | |
Medium	Synchro-nicity	Cues/format	bandwidth constraints	type and level	Exclusivity
Table 2.1 Media and the five dimensions of mediation					
Letter	Low	Text	Low cost	Visual/Medium	Yes
Telegraph: Operators	High	Text	Low cost	Visual/Medium	Sometimes
Telegraph: Client	Low	Text	High cost	Visual/Low	No
Telephone	High	Voice	Early: High Later: Medium	Visual/Low	Sometimes – not party lines
Radio ham	High	Voice	Low cost	Visual/Medium	Not usually
SMS	Medium	Text	Low cost and physical constraint	Visual/Medium	Yes

Mapping media to the five dimensions

In Table 2.1, the media discussed in the previous chapter are mapped alongside the dimensions outlined above.

Affordances and the Internet

Like its forebears, the Internet also places various constraints, as well as new opportunities, on the actors in a mediated encounter. However, unlike most of the earlier technologies discussed, the various types of Internet mediation mean that its affordances differ by the types of software used (see Table 2.2).

When considering the impact of the Internet on psychological processes, we need first to identify what Internet behaviour we are observing. As we can see from Table 2.2, different types of communication on the Internet have quite different structural characteristics and affordances. If we follow the argument that it is these structural differences that lead to certain behaviours, then we must also take into account the form of the communication, as well as its environment.

Medium	Synchro-nicity	Cues/ format	Cost and bandwidth constraints	Anonymity – type and level	Exclusivity
Chat – 1-2-1	High	Text	High – cognitive load/low cost	Visual/High	Yes
Chat rooms	High	Text	High – cognitive load/low cost	Visual/High	No
Usenet	Low	Text	Low	Visual/Medium	No
E-mail	Medium	Text	Low	Visual/Medium	Yes
MUD/Moo	High	Text	High	Visual/High	Not usually
Video-conferencing	High	Visual voice/ Text	Low	Low/ Medium	Sometimes

Table 2.2 Internet communication and the five dimensions

Models of mediated communication

As we have seen, mediated communication imposes various constraints on communication (as well as affording new communication opportunities). Probably the most fundamental is that, at least with most CMC, you cannot see or hear the person you are communicating with. Not surprisingly then, models of the impact of technology on communication have tended to focus on the role of these visual and verbal cues in communication, and what happens when they are lost. These models have been termed 'technological determinist' (Markus, 1994) because they are grounded in the assumption that the features of the technology, for instance, visual anonymity, lead to specific psychological or behavioural outcomes. Technological determinist approaches can be further divided into two main sub-groups. The first, called 'cues filtered out', predicts that the lack of social cues in mediated communication leads to deregulated, depersonalised and de-individuated communication. The second, called here 'self-focus approaches', argues that the design of the technology leads to changes in self-focus (of either personal or social identity), which again has predictable psychological and behavioural effects.

Cues-filtered-out approaches

The first concerted attempt to understand mediated communication came about in the late 1960s and early 1970s when the psychology of telecommunication use became a topic of interest to a group of researchers based at University College London. Called the Communication Studies Group, these researchers were interested in the psychological processes involved in technological communication (primarily the telephone), a research area that culminated in a book called *The Social Psychology of Telecommunications* (Short *et al.*, 1976). The construct they developed to explain media differences was social presence.

Social presence

The Communication Studies Group focused on two key questions: what factors determine use of the telephone and what are the social psychological processes invoked by telephone communication? In common with many later theories of computer-mediated communication, the starting point of their research was what people *lost* when they communicated by telephone rather than face to face (FtF). Much of this effort was directed at the 'most obvious defect of the simple telephone – the fact that one cannot see the other person or group' (Short *et al.*, 1976, p. 43). Traditional social psychological literature tends to stress the importance of visual cues in communication – in, for instance, showing mutual attention, channel control (who speaks when), providing feedback, illustrations in the form of gestures, emblems (e.g. a nod of the head) and interpersonal attitudes, physical appearance, facial expressions, non-verbal communication using body posture and movement and the proximity between speakers (Short *et al.*, 1976). Although some of these non-verbal cues might be transferable to the telephone, the majority (e.g. gesture, body posture, facial expressions) are not.

The Communication Studies Group conducted a series of experiments to test whether the lack of visual cues had an impact on people's behaviour (Reid, 1981). Of most interest here, are the studies they conducted into group discussions and the resolution of conflict and person perception. John Short asked participants to argue a case, from a viewpoint provided by the experimenter (e.g. as a union rep or an employer), using only an audio channel of communication or face to face. In his first study, Short found that strong arguments were more persuasive in audio-only compared to face-to-face discussions. In a second experiment, Short manipulated whether the disagreement between participants was due to a difference of opinion or objective.

A difference of opinion was when the two participants held different attitudes to a topic, while a difference of objectives was when they were aiming for different, often contradictory, outcomes to the discussions (e.g. a pay rise versus a pay cut). He found that the stronger argument had more influence face to face when it was a difference of opinion, and more influence over audio only when it was a difference of objectives. A third condition, with two-way television screens (so the participants could see each other), showed no difference from the face-to-face condition. In a follow-up study Short found that, when discussing differences of opinion, his participants were persuaded more by strong arguments over the audio channel than face to face. These findings led Reid (1981) to conclude that 'the clearest and most consistent finding in this series of ... experiments using conflict tasks is the unexpected result that audio discussions produce more opinion change than do face-to-face discussions' (pp. 404–5).

The second series of experiments of interest addresses the accuracy and confidence of face-to-face and telephone judgements. For example, in general there is little difference in the accuracy of people's judgements of others across media, but face-to-face participants tend to express greater confidence in their judgements (Reid, 1981).

Williams (1972) found that participants evaluated their communication partner more favourably if they could see and hear them (a videophone) rather than just hear them. In a follow-up study, Williams (1975) had teams of four participants brainstorming topics selected by the experimenter either face to face, by video link or by audio link. In the two telecommunication conditions, the groups consisted of two people at each end of the line (so a group of four in total). Williams found that the two people stationed together tended to agree more with each other than with the distant members of their group, and that any dissent to an idea raised was significantly more likely to emanate from the other end of the line, not from the person next to them. Moreover, participants in the audio condition were significantly more likely to rate their fellow group members on the other 'node' as lower in both sincerity and intelligence.

Short et al. (1976) developed social presence theory to explain these findings. They began by arguing that interpersonal attitudes are primarily conveyed using visual cues, while the verbal channel contains only interparty, task-oriented, cognitive material. So, if the visual channel is removed (as in the case of the telephone), what remains is simply the capacity to transmit the task-oriented material, not the social, interpersonal information.

Short *et al.* go on to argue that the 'salience of the other person in the interaction and the consequent salience of the interpersonal relationships' is an objective quality of the medium of communication. They termed this quality social presence. What is meant by 'objective quality' is that social presence is a property of the medium (like its affordances), rather than just a user's reactions to the medium. According to Short *et al.*, the 'capacity to transmit information about facial expression, direction of looking, posture, dress and non-verbal cues, all contribute to the social presence of a communications medium' (1976, p. 65).

However, social presence also seems to have a phenomenological aspect, in that it relates to people's subjective responses to a medium. The social presence of different media like the telephone, e-mail and so on is measured by asking users to score them on a series of semantic differential scales labelled as, for instance, personal–impersonal, sociable–unsociable and cold–warm. A medium with high social presence would tend to be rated as more warm, personal and sociable than a medium with low social presence. Short *et al.* report that, using these types of measures, people rate non-visual communication (e.g. by telephone) as low in social presence, with face to face highest in social presence. Communication over a video link was reported as having relatively high social presence, but still less than face to face. Indeed, the only communication medium rated as having less social presence than the telephone was the business letter.

The social presence of a medium will, according to Short *et al.*, have implications for the intimacy of a communication. They predicted that the higher the social presence of a medium, so the greater the intimacy between users, all other things being equal. This prediction is based on Argyle and Dean's (1965) intimacy-equilibrium theory. This theory argues that people have an optimum level of intimacy during an interaction. Because intimacy can be communicated in many different ways (e.g. eye contact, proximity, self-disclosure), an increase in one form of intimacy will lead to a reduction in another to redress the balance and return the equilibrium. Thus, for instance, people reduce eye contact when they are about to discuss personal intimacies (Exline *et al.*, 1965). However, instead of arguing that the reduction in intimacy caused by the removal of many visual cues will lead to a compensatory increase in intimacy via verbal behaviour, Short *et al.* argue the opposite, that because eye contact is so important in intimacy, its removal may well lead to conflict rather than greater intimacy. So, in the case of the telephone, because visual cues are absent, we should, according to Short *et al.*, be less intimate on the telephone than face to face. Media with low social presence are, according Short *et al.*, best-suited for tasks such as information transmission and simple problem-solving. Indeed, Short *et al.* argue that 'telephone communication is intrinsically less sociable, more impersonal, and that, unless the task requires such psychological "distance", the mismatch is felt to be unpleasant' (1976, p. 81).

Reduced social cues

The earliest psychological studies of the Internet were actually studies of computer-mediated communication conducted in the late 1970s and early 1980s. During this time, a number of US universities had installed CMC systems for students' use, while some of the major computer companies were experimenting with text-based communication tools for staff. All these systems were based on either a bulletin board or e-mail system, where messages would be posted to a central server to be accessed by subscribers. In many of these early systems, bandwidth was severely limited, with computer memory being expensive, and networks slow.

Perhaps not surprisingly then, the earliest psychological theories of the Internet addressed the lack of social information, the reduced feedback and control when not communicating face to face, and the frustration inherent in electronic communication.

By far the most well-developed cues-filtered-out approach to CMC was developed by Sara Kiesler and her colleagues during the 1980s. The starting point of this model, rather like social presence before it, was what was lost when communication is technologically mediated. Sproull and Kiesler (1986) identify three types of variables that contribute to a social context for communication: geographic, organisational and situational. The cues that help people understand this social context can be organised into two main types. Static cues come from a person's appearance, environment and so on, while dynamic cues come from a person's non-verbal communication behaviour during an interaction – for instance, their nodding in agreement or frowning in disagreement.

Like social presence theory, Kiesler's argument is that social context cues allow people to manage their behaviour throughout an interaction, adjusting their behaviour according to the dynamics of the situation at any particular time. According to Sproull and Kiesler:

> All communications media attenuate to at least some degree the social context cues available in face-to-face conversation. The

telephone reduces dynamic and static cues by eliminating visual information about the communicators. Letters and memos reduce static cues by imposing standardized format conventions; they eliminate dynamic cues altogether. (1986, pp. 1495–6)

When these cues are removed during CMC Kiesler *et al.* (1984) predict that

Social standards will be less important and communication will be more impersonal and more free because the rapid exchange of text, the lack of social feedback, and the absence of norms governing the social interaction redirect attention away from others and toward the message itself. (p. 1126)

This model is illustrated in Figure 2.1. According to this model, the role of the media is in attenuating social context cues, which interferes with (or reduces) the cognitive interpretation of the social context, which in turn leads to certain communication behaviours. So, in the case of e-mail or computer conferencing within an organisation, it is reasonable to assume that users might lack information on the geographic location of others, possibly their status or place in the hierarchy and certainly situational variables, including the lack of norms for electronic interaction.

This attenuation or complete loss of social context cues reduces a person's ability to adjust the target, tone and verbal content of their communication in light of their interpretation of the situation. So, if social context cues are weak, as is the case in e-mail, people's communicative behaviour will tend to be weakly regulated, meaning more uninhibited behaviour. The implications of this model for explanations of flaming and communicative deviance are discussed in the following chapter.

It is also worth noting that another outcome of reduced social cues should be higher levels of extreme behaviour. Kiesler and her colleagues tested this using group discussions across various media. The general finding, in line with earlier work on telephone conferencing, was that groups shifted more to the extreme end of a decision-making scale (called group polarisation) when they discussed electronically and anonymously, compared to FtF.

Sproull and Kiesler (1986) examined the e-mail system of a large organisation in the USA to test whether or not electronic mail did lack social context cues. They studied the e-mail communication

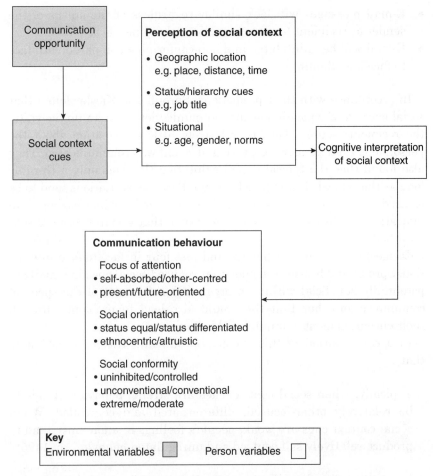

Figure 2.1   Reduced social context cues and communication outcomes

Source: Adapted from Sproull and Kiesler (1986).

of 96 staff, as well as collecting questionnaire responses. In accordance with their model (see Figure 2.1), Sproull and Kiesler predicted that:

- There will be fewer social context cues communicated by e-mail (e.g. geographic location, job category, age or sex)
- E-mail users will be self-absorbed rather than focused on the 'other' during communication

- E-mail messages will look similar regardless of the status of the sender or recipient (e.g. managers or subordinates)
- E-mail will be uninhibited and non-conforming compared with face to face (e.g. flaming).

In accordance with their predictions, Sproull and Kiesler found that social cues were typically low for communication from an unknown (to the recipient) source. That is, relatively little information about the person (e.g. their gender, age, race and so on) was communicated. They also found that the typical e-mail salutation (Hi) was only a third as long as the typical closing (bye for now). Because salutations tend to be focused on the other person (e.g. how are you?), while closings are indicative of a focus on the self, they argue that e-mail users are self-absorbed. E-mail users also reported seeing 33 flames (antisocial messages) on e-mail in a month, and just four in face-to-face interaction. Sproull and Kiesler conclude that reduced social cues in e-mail are potentially beneficial within an organisation (because of the speed of communication), but that they could also lead to problems through their encouragement of uninhibited behaviour.

In a continuation of this theme, Sproull and Kiesler (1986) note that

> Typically, when social context cues are strong, behaviour tends to be relatively other-focused, differentiated and controlled. When social context cues are weak, people's feelings of anonymity tend to produce relatively self-centred and unregulated behavior. (p. 1495)

In a series of studies, Kiesler and colleagues examined the influence of CMC in two main areas: uninhibited communication and group decision-making. Although uninhibited communication is dealt with in more detail later, suffice it to say that the general finding of the Kiesler *et al.* research programme was that anonymous CMC encouraged uninhibited communication in the form of flaming and self-disclosure.

The second focus of work from a reduced social cues perspective was on social influence in CMC. This work specifically focused on a phenomenon in social psychology termed 'group polarisation'. Group polarisation is the tendency for a group's consensus to become more extreme following discussion compared to the average pre-discussion opinions of the group's members. The general finding of this research was that group decisions became more extreme (i.e. polarised) when discussions were held over CMC systems compared with face to face.

Kiesler *et al.* (1984) explain these findings using reduced social context cues. The reduced cues inherent in CMC lead to more uninhibited, anti-normative behaviour, which leads to more extreme opinions being expressed, which leads to the group decision becoming more extreme. Thus, the basis for group polarisation during CMC is that participants voice more extreme opinions during CMC because of the reduced role of status and leadership in a cue-free environment, because they may be de-individuated and because they are focused on the message rather than the social context. Furthermore, not only are the opinions expressed more extreme, but because participation is more equal, more of these extreme arguments are likely to be voiced. When these two factors (more extreme opinions and more people stating them) are added together, Kiesler *et al.* propose that social influence occurs based on the number and strength of the arguments made. As such, a lack of social context cues is closely linked to anonymity, and the role anonymity plays in encouraging uninhibited behaviour. This led Kiesler *et al.* (1984) to propose that CMC might encourage users into a state close to de-individuation.

De-individuation

The concept of de-individuation can be traced back to Gustav Le Bon (1890) and, more recently, Festinger in the 1950s and Zimbardo in the 1960s. According to Zimbardo (1969), de-individuation is a

> complex, hypothesized process in which a series of antecedent social conditions leads to changes in perception of self and others, and thereby to a lower threshold of normally restrained behavior. Under appropriate conditions, what results is the 'release' of behavior in violation of established norms of appropriateness. (p. 251)

These antecedent conditions include: anonymity, a reduced sense of responsibility, altered time outlook, sensory input overload, a novel or unstructured situation, and altered consciousness (see Table 2.3). When these antecedent conditions are in place, the person becomes more focused on the task in hand, and there is a concomitant reduction in self-regulation because of the reduction in self-awareness (Prentice-Dunn and Rogers, 1982). Although Zimbardo does not say which factors are either necessary or sufficient for de-individuation (Deiner, 1980), it is clear on first impression that behaviour on the Internet seems to fulfil many.

Table 2.3 Zimbardo's antecedent conditions and synchronous CMC	
Antecedent conditions	Applicability to Internet
Anonymity	Visual anonymity usual 'True' anonymity occasionally possible
Altered responsibility	Some evidence of lower feelings of accountability
Group size, activity	Much synchronous CMC in groups
Altered time outlook	Some limited evidence of time passing more quickly
Arousal	Little evidence that CMC is arousing
Sensory input overload	Possible in some asynchronous environments
Physical involvement in the act	Typing, especially in synchronous 'chat', is physically involving
Reliance on noncognitive interactions/feedback	Little time to stop and think in some Internet activities
Novel or unstructured environment	Possible, particularly for new users

A large proportion of Internet behaviour, including CMC, is engaged in *anonymously* (although there are different types of anonymity, as discussed earlier). Although the size of the group differs substantially depending on the type of CMC engaged in, again, in many cases users are members of a group.

According to Kiesler *et al.* (1984):

> Indeed, computer-mediated communication seems to comprise some of the same conditions that are important for de-individuation – anonymity, reduced self-regulation, and reduced self-awareness. (p. 1126)

More recently, McKenna and Bargh (2000) claim that 'It is not surprising then that de-individuation and the negative results that often accompany it ... readily occur on the Internet' (p. 60). McKenna and Bargh further argue that de-individuation on the Internet will also lead to greater self-disclosure: 'under the protective cloak of anonymity users can express the way they truly feel and think' (p. 62). In one of the few studies to examine de-individuation as an outcome of

CMC, rather than as an independent variable, Coleman, *et al.* (1999) found evidence that, compared with an FtF condition, CMC participants felt more submerged in a discussion and perceived that they were viewed less as an individual. However, they found no difference in participants' concern for being judged or evaluated, or their estimates for how long each discussion took.

Critiques of cues-filtered-out approaches

The argument that Internet behaviour is characterised by a loss of 'socialness', be it social presence, social context cues or individuality, has been critiqued on a number of counts.

Social information processing

Walther (1992) proposes that users of CMC have the same interpersonal needs as face-to-face communicators, and that CMC is quite capable of transferring social information between people, such as status, affiliation and liking and even attraction to the other person. However, because most CMC is type-based, the rate of message exchange is lower than face-to-face interaction (especially using asynchronous systems like e-mail). If this is the case, then the transmission of social information will be considerably slower during CMC than face to face. Thus,

> given sufficient time and message exchanges for interpersonal impression formation and relational development to accrue, and all other things being equal, relational [communication] in later periods of CMC and face-to-face communication will be the same. (Walther, 1992, p. 69)

In keeping with earlier reduced social cues (RSC) theories, Walther (1992) sees the loss of visual cues inherent in CMC as a disadvantage to be overcome over time, and through the development of 'various linguistic and typographic manipulations which may reveal social and relational information in CMC' (Walther, 1995, p. 190). Thus, the social information processing model offers a clear explanation of why early studies tend to find task focus in CMC – time constraints. Many CMC studies only have people discussing a topic for 15–30 minutes, not enough time, according to Walther, for social and relational information to be passed across the limited channel of CMC.

To test whether or not the time allocated to CMC experiments was crucial to understanding why it seemed to be task-focused, Walther *et al.* (1994) conducted a meta-analysis of 21 experiments of CMC. Meta-analysis is a method for summating findings from a large number of separate studies to test a specific hypothesis using the data reported in those experiments. In the case of Walther *et al.* (1994), the variable under consideration was whether CMC in the 21 experiments was time-limited or not. The dependent variable was the proportion of socially oriented, rather than task-oriented, communication (they were also interested in negative/uninhibited communication). Walther *et al.*, (1994) found higher levels of socio-emotional communication in time-unrestricted CMC groups compared to time-restricted groups. They also found that there was less of a difference in the level of socio-emotional communication between CMC and face-to-face groups when there was no time restriction compared with those studies with a time restriction.

The meta-analysis therefore confirmed one of the key predictions of the social information processing model, that over time the amount of social information communicated using CMC converges with the amount sent verbally face to face. The simple explanation for this finding is that typing is much slower than talking, so any social exchange will take place more slowly over CMC than face to face. Another key factor is that the communication of social information across a computer network requires the learning, and use, of linguistic and textual cues to convey relational information. Although there is plenty of evidence of users developing such 'paralanguage' (Walther, 1992), it may take time for CMC users to develop adequate skills in paralanguage to competently convey social information. The most obvious examples are the use of smileys or 'emoticons' and acronyms (see Table 2.4). The use of some

Table 2.4 Some common emoticons and social language acronyms			
Emoticon	Meaning	Acronym	Meaning
:-)	Smile	LOL	Laugh out loud
;-)	Wink	ROFL	Roll on floor laughing
:-P	Stick tongue out	LOL@	Laughs out loud at
:-(	Sad	a/s/l	age/sex/location?
:-0	Shocked	ty	thank you
		G (and BG)	Grin (Big grin)

Source: Joinson and Littleton (2002).

'emoticons' (meaning icons for emotions) is such an acceptable part of on-line communication that many e-mail programs now convert them to images. You will need to turn the page sideways to see the faces.

Often these paralanguage cues are used to convey social information and help build relationships (e.g. by conveying a joke, or laughter). If it takes users time to pick up these skills, then it is reasonable to assume that the communication of social information will be handicapped if time-restricted. Sonia Utz (2000) studied the impact of CMC experience (and so, time) on the development of relationships. She found that the longer people had spent using CMC on the Internet, so the more para-language they used, and the more relationships they formed.

One criticism of the social information processing model is that it is still firmly located in the 'loss' camp of CMC – Walther argued that, given time, CMC might be able to match face-to-face communication in its 'socialness'. For instance, Walther (1995) conducted a study in which he predicted, based on his social information processing model, that social behaviour would be greater in face-to-face than CMC groups, but that the difference would subside over a large amount of time. Walther had coders rate each person discussing face to face or by CMC. The coders then rated the complete discussions using a 'rela-tional communication' questionnaire (a way of organising their overall impressions of the 'socialness' of the discussions). The CMC and face-to-face groups discussed three separate issues on three different occasions, allowing a comparison of social communication across time.

Walther was surprised to find that the effect was the opposite of his prediction: CMC groups were rated higher in most relational commu-nication than the face-to-face groups, regardless of time-scale. For instance, the coders rated the CMC groups as higher than face-to-face groups in the level of affection seen in the group discussions, how simi-lar the group members seemed, and how composed and relaxed during the discussion the participants seemed. Most importantly, the CMC groups were rated as significantly *less* task-oriented, and *more* socially oriented, than the face-to-face groups during all the time slots. Thus, the key theoretical predictions of social information processing were refuted by Walther's 1995 study – CMC was significantly more social than face-to-face communication, and the developments over time were not in the predicted direction in most cases.

It is worth noting that Walther's conclusion that 'social information processing underestimates the positive effect of computer-mediation on relational communication' (Walther, 1995, p. 198) is equally applicable to all 'loss' theories of mediated communication. By focusing on the loss of social cues inherent in CMC (and the telephone), the potential increases in social behaviour, and plasticity of human behaviour when it comes to communicating social information, were ignored.

The social identity critique of cues-filtered-out

Perhaps the most damning criticism of all the cues-filtered-out approaches to Internet behaviour is the assumption that social information needs to be transmitted face to face through interpersonal interaction (Spears and Lea, 1992). In focusing on, for instance, non-verbal cues and their role in communication, it is hardly surprising that the CFO models predict that mediated communication will be less 'social' due to the attenuation of these cues. However, to belong to a group, or to identify with a group, we do not need to meet face to face. Indeed, not being able to see other members of our group might increase our identification with the group because the differences between group members go unnoticed.

The reduced social cues approach has also been criticised by Spears and Lea for combining a number of contradictory ideas. For instance, Kiesler *et al.* use both de-individuation and self-absorption to explain uninhibited behaviour, yet de-individuation depends upon a reduction in self-awareness, so the two should be mutually exclusive. Similarly, Kiesler *et al.* argue for anti-normative behaviour during CMC (via the lack of social cues and de-individuation), and also argue that one norm – the computing subculture (i.e. hacking) – could lead to uninhibited behaviour. However, they do not explain how this one norm can infiltrate their 'normless' environment. The alternative explanation of group polarisation during CMC from a social identity perspective is discussed in more detail later in this chapter.

Self-focus models

As we have seen, although the RSC model is based very much on the role of social context cues, the model also tends to invoke changes in self-focus via a de-individuation process. An alternative approach to understanding the effect of mediation on psychological processes comes from researchers who argue that the visual anonymity inherent in much CMC actually heightens people's self-focus, rather than diminishing it.

Dual self-awareness

According to early theorists Duval and Wicklund (1972), humans have two basic states of awareness – objective and subjective self-awareness. Objective self-awareness is when a person is focused inward on themselves, while subjective self-awareness is when the focus of attention is the environment. A further distinction has been drawn between the social and private aspects of the self (Carver and Scheier, 1987). The social aspects of the self involve those parts of the self (e.g. physical appearance) that are public. These parts of our selves are thus open for evaluation and judgement by others. Being focused on the social aspects of the self is termed 'public self-awareness'. Public self-awareness is evoked by situations that make us aware that we are being evaluated, judged or held accountable. Heightened public self-awareness tends to lead to increased attempts at managing the impression we make, and monitoring feedback from others.

On the other hand, the private aspects of the self are those that are available to us alone (unless we choose to share them), such as feelings, attitudes and values and so on. Heightened private self-awareness tends to invoke behaviour based on our internal motives, needs or standards. For instance, Carver and Scheier (1981) argue that private self-awareness instigates a self-regulation cycle where our behaviour is checked against our standards, and, in ideal circumstances, adjusted so that our behaviour and standards match.

In an important early study, Kimberly Matheson and Mark Zanna (1988) examined the impact of CMC on private and public self-awareness. As we have seen, both the RSC and de-individuation explanations suggest that self-awareness is reduced during CMC (hence the uninhibited behaviour). Matheson and Zanna re-examined the CMC literature and argued that the same results could be interpreted as being evidence of heightened private and reduced public self-awareness. For instance, high levels of self-disclosure and reduced levels of social desirability (Kiesler and Sproull, 1986) can be seen as more consistent with heightened rather than reduced private self-awareness (which increases self-disclosure) alongside a reduction in public self-awareness (hence reducing evaluation concerns).

To test the impact of CMC on self-awareness, Matheson and Zanna (1988) compared participants' levels of self-awareness (using a four-item questionnaire) after they had discussed using computers or face to face. They found that 'users of computer-mediated communication reported greater private self-awareness and marginally lower public self-awareness than subjects communicating face-to-face' (p. 228).

In line with this, Matheson (1992) reported that users find CMC a highly reflective experience. Weisband and Atwater (1999) found that CMC users overestimate their contribution to discussions compared to FtF, suggesting that they might experience heightened private self-focus.

In a series of three experiments (Joinson, 2001a), I examined the link between self-disclosure and self-awareness during CMC. The methodology was virtually identical for each experiment: pairs of participants arrived separately at the psychology laboratory, and were taken to a cubicle with a 'chat' program running on a computer. They were then given a dilemma to discuss (which five people should be saved in the event of a nuclear war?), and their conversations recorded. Self-disclosure was then measured by two raters who examined the transcribed discussions.

Experiment 1 In this experiment there were two conditions: the pairs discussed either face to face or anonymously using the computers. The results showed that the CMC participants disclosed four times as much information about themselves as the face-to-face participants.

Experiment 2 In this experiment, there were again two conditions: the pairs discussed using CMC while either visually anonymous or when they could see the other participant via a webcam. As predicted, very little was disclosed in the webcam condition, while the visually anonymous condition disclosed significantly more.

Experiment 3 In this experiment, participants' self-awareness was manipulated. Public self-awareness (concern about others' impressions) was increased using cameras and an expectation that the pairs would meet, and reduced using a darkened corridor and lack of cameras. Private self-awareness (focus on your own self) was increased by showing participants pictures of themselves, and reduced by showing them a cartoon. The results showed that the highest level of self-disclosure was when participants experienced increased private self-focus alongside reduced public self-awareness, implying that when people use CMC to disclose large amounts of information they might be experiencing these states interacting together. This interaction is shown in Figure 2.2.

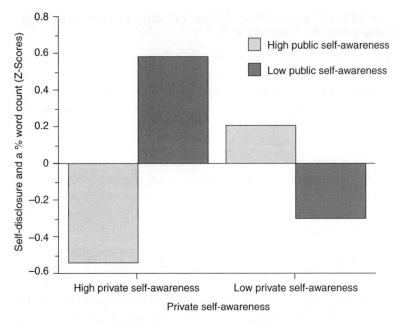

Figure 2.2 Self-awareness and self-disclosure during CMC

Source: Joinson (2001a, Study 3).

What is interesting about this final study is that an effective de-individuating condition was created at the same time. Prentice-Dunn and Rogers (1982) propose that de-individuation effects happen when people's private and public self-awareness is reduced.

However, the notion that private and public self-awareness can be separated has not been universally accepted (Wicklund and Gollwitzer, 1987), although Carver and Scheier (1987) provide a strong argument to support the distinction. Moreover, it is unclear in what conditions Internet use might encourage private self-awareness, and when it might be discouraged. For instance, private self-awareness is discouraged by external stimulation (Duval and Wicklund, 1972), for instance, physical activity (Webb *et al.*, 1989) or video games (Prentice-Dunn and Rogers, 1982). Presumably then, on-line gamers might not be privately self-aware, even though they can 'chat' during the game. As more immersive environments develop, including those that involve physical activity, the effect of Internet use in heightening private self-awareness may well be ameliorated.

Social identity explanation of de-individuation effects (SIDE) and CMC

The social identity explanation of de-individuation effects (SIDE) was developed by Reicher (1984) to provide an alternative, social identity-based explanation of de-individuation. According to the social identity theory (Tajfel and Turner, 1979), our identity is made up of both social and personal identities. Our social identities are the groups to which we belong – both real-life groups (e.g. as a student at college Y) and abstract groups (e.g. mothers, general political allegiance). When a social identity is salient, we engage in a process whereby we compare our attitudes and behaviour to other group members (and the imagined typical group member), and try to match our behaviour to that norm (called self-stereotyping).

According to Reicher, de-individuation research is premised on the faulty assumption that we are either focused on ourselves as individuals, or not focused on ourselves at all. He argues that one consequence of reducing personal identifiability is not to 'destroy identity but rather to increase the salience of social identity' (1984, p. 342). So, de-individuation as based on immersion in a group should increase the salience of the relevant social identity, and hence adherence to group norms. If people are also visually anonymous when immersed in a group, Reicher argues that this will strengthen the effect because intragroup differences are minimised, while intergroup differences are maximised. However, isolating group members and making them visually anonymous would remove group boundaries, and so reduce the salience of the social identity.

Reicher attempted to manipulate immersion in a group and visual anonymity independently, and found some limited support for his model. However, the strongest support for SIDE came from a study conducted by Spears et al. (1990). Spears et al. used a computer-mediated conferencing system again independently to manipulate group membership and visual anonymity. Groups of three students discussed a series of topics (e.g. 'All nuclear power stations should be phased out') using the CMC system. Group membership was manipulated by making salient throughout the experiment that participants were members of a group, or were individuals. Visual anonymity was manipulated either by seating the three participants together in a room, or in separate cubicles. Before the experiment, all participants completed initial measures of their attitudes to the discussion topics. Before the discussions, participants were also given a booklet

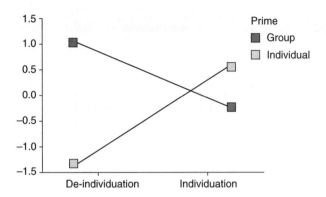

Figure 2.3   Polarisation of attitudes by condition

Source: Spears *et al.* (1990, p. 129).

that gave students the results of a survey of their peers in response to the topics. So, for the first issue they discussed ('Whether or not nationalised industries should be sold off'), the participants were informed that '32.2 per cent supported the sale of nationalised industries, and 67.8 per cent were against the sale'. Once participants had discussed the topics, they completed the same attitude measure, so that any shift in opinion could be measured.

The results of the experiments confirmed the predictions of Spears *et al.* and the SIDE model. In the visually anonymous condition, increasing the salience of the group led to a move towards the group norm, while increasing the salience of personal identity led to a shift away from the group norm (see Figure 2.3).

Spears and Lea (1992) argue that the visual anonymity inherent in most computer-mediated communication will, when a social identity is salient, strengthen the impact of social norms, and hence normative influence. The crucial element here is whether or not the social or normative context supports the salience of a personal or social identity. When a social identity is salient, visual anonymity will increase adherence to group norms. When a personal identity is salient, the same anonymity will reduce the impact of social norms, and increase the person's adherence to their own personal norms and standards. This model is illustrated in Figure 2.4.

The findings of Spears *et al.* (1990) are difficult for the reduced social cues approach to refute – in the visually anonymous condition, social context (in the form of group salience) had a marked effect on

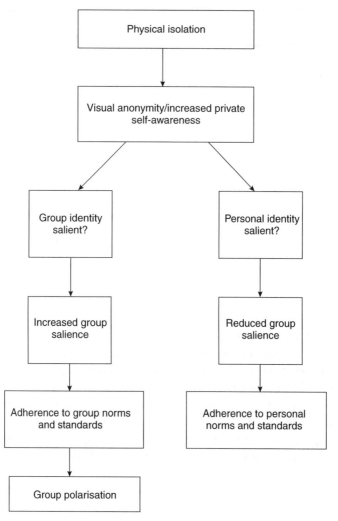

Figure 2.4   Social identity and group polarisation

Source: Spears and Lea (1992).

group polarisation. This is not what the reduced social cues approach would predict – for them, visual anonymity is all that should really matter, because their model of group polarisation relies on people making more extreme arguments only. What Spears *et al.* showed was that CMC does not occur in a social vacuum – instead, people's reliance on the norms of their group is heightened when a social identity is activated.

The finding reported by Spears *et al.* (1990) that group polarisation was reduced when participants' individuality was stressed is an interesting one. As we discussed earlier, there is considerable evidence that people become more self-focused when they are visually anonymous during CMC. In the Spears *et al.* experiment, when this was combined with a salient social identity, then conformity to the group norm increased. But when participants' individuality was stressed, conformity reduced. So, this suggests that whether or not people conform when interacting on the Internet depends on two factors: whether they are visually anonymous or not, and whether there is a shared social identity or personal identity salient at the time.

Identifying norms of behaviour

In the Spears *et al.* (1990) study, the norms for the group were made available and salient to the CMC users by providing a booklet showing them in easy-to-understand bar charts. Obviously, for most Internet users, norms of behaviour are likely to be less obvious. There are two distinct situations a new group member will face: the first is when they join an existing group and need to gain an understanding of the norms. The second is when a new group is formed, with few pre-existing norms for that specific group. Research on CMC provides clues about how users gain knowledge, and develop norms, in both situations.

Joining a pre-existing group

Netiquette (etiquette for the Internet) is a clear attempt to guide new users in the appropriate norms for behaviour on the Internet in general, and in many cases, in specific areas of the Internet like MUDs, IRC or Usenet. Like the etiquette for radio hams outlined in the previous chapter, most netiquette is focused on managing bandwidth use and misunderstanding. Group-specific norms can be found in the commonly used 'FAQs' (frequently asked questions) that usually provide information on what is, and is not, acceptable practice for a specific group, and provide background information on the history and culture of an on-line newsgroup or community. For a new member of the group, these guides, along with time spent lurking to observe how a group acts, provide as clear a statement of a group's norms as the bar charts in Spears *et al.*'s (1990) study. On-line groups also behave in ways to manage behaviour, for instance, by challenging inappropriate postings.

According to Smith *et al.* (1998), 'technological proficiency, demonstrated knowledge of the FAQ, and conformity to newsgroup practices are among the conditions for acceptance in many well-established newsgroups' (p. 97). However, they also note that it is common for these norms not to be adhered to, often due to ignorance or lack of technical proficiency with the newsgroup software by new or inexperienced users. McLaughlin *et al.* (1995) identified seven basic categories of norm violation in newsgroups:

1. *Incorrect/novice use of technology* Formatting problems, multiple signatures.
2. *Bandwidth piggery* Excessively long or pointless messages (e.g. too much quoting or long signatures).
3. *Violation of Usenet conventions* Lack of headers, posting or cross-posting to inappropriate groups.
4. *Violation of newsgroup conventions* Not using proper headers or abbreviations, going against the group norm for style, content and so on.
5. *Ethical violations* Posting private e-mail without permission, harassment.
6. *Inappropriate language* Flaming, linguistic affectations.
7. *Factual errors* Spelling and grammatical errors, errors of fact.

Smith *et al.* (1998) studied the pattern of offence and reproach amongst Usenet groups. They noted that a similar pattern seemed to emerge where the original offence would be reproached, an account would be provided by the offender, and then that account would be accepted or rejected. They give the example of the following post that was sent to the newsgroup soc.singles (that has a norm of not posting personal ads):

Hi, I'm a 23 year old graduate student and would like to
communicate with any females on this news net
- - - - - - - - (posted for a not-net friend)- - - - - - - -

One reprimand was:

Well, Howdy! Finally a request for a female that doesn't specify
species – you wouldn't believe how many people on this net want
a woman, which of course means a person
giggle

My name is Susa, and I'm a five-year-old Lemur in the Philly Zoo. My measurements are 12-12-12, which is considered quite sexy for a lemur *giggle* we all fail the pencil test *giggle*

My hobbies include running around, climbing trees, and picking lice; I hope you have a nice thick head of hair!

I only write to stupid people who post personals on soc.singles; the other ones are too smart for me – we lemurs may be very_cuddly *giggle* we tend to be on the low end of the smarts scale. I know that with that post, you'll be really_dumb for a human, and perfect for me! *giggle*

In accounting for the earlier posting, the original poster wrote:

In reference to my posting a few hours ago ... I have just discovered that this is the wrong newsgroup! Thanks to so many people, <postername> amongst others, so if you'll all quit sending me more messages, I move on. OK? But for those who seem to have nothing better to do <postername> feel free to do whatever you want!

However, in the small sample of reproaches studied by Smith *et al.* (1998), relatively few led to accounting behaviour. It is possible that this might be because it occurs out of sight in e-mail or, alternatively, new users are intimidated from replying to reproaches by the aggressive tone some take. Finally, an infrequent user might not even ever see or read the reproaches.

It is clear then, that for an established group on the Internet there are likely to be well-established, propagated norms of behaviour that new users are expected to adhere to. Newbies ignore these norms at their peril, for they risk often aggressive reproaches.

Developing norms for a new interaction

Of course, many interactions on the Internet are not within established groups with well-known norms for behaviour. To investigate the role of norms in new groups, Postmes *et al.* (2000) examined groups of students communicating using an electronic mail system. They argued that one of the oversights of social identity approaches to CMC is that the social identities and norms are assumed to pre-exist and are activated through associating oneself with a group label. The students in their study were taking part in a voluntary computerised statistics course called 'Dr. Stat'. The computer system also provided a 'mail' facility, something students soon discovered and began using. Postmes *et al.* hypothesised that, for the students using this 'mail' system, the norms they applied to their interactions will develop over time, and will only be applied within a group of students, and not to communication with members of staff at the university. When they analysed the messages sent by students, their hypotheses were supported. First, over time the typical type of communication (e.g. humorous or flaming) that characterised a group became more pronounced. So, if a group began by adopting a certain type of communication, this became more marked over time. This suggests that the norms within a CMC group are dynamically socially constructed during the interaction. Their second hypothesis, that these norms will be constrained to the participants' own group, was also supported. When they looked at communication between students and staff, there was no evidence that students applied the norms developed within their own group to their communication with staff members. This finding suggests that the use of normative communication styles within a group were based on social contexts and shared group identity, rather than learned responses.

Strategic social identities and SIDE

The SIDE explanation of de-individuation effects outlined above concentrates solely on what is called the cognitive dimension of SIDE (i.e. changes in the salience of social identities and so on). However, SIDE also contains what has been called a 'strategic' aspect. The strategic aspect of SIDE deals with the role of identifiability and power relations between groups (Reicher *et al.*, 1995). According to Reicher *et al.*, power between groups influences not the cognitive identity salience, but rather influences whether, and how, that identity is expressed. More specifically, they argue that if a group member is identifiable to the ingroup, but not to the outgroup, then ingroup congruent behaviour will ensue. However, if the group member is identifiable to a powerful outgroup, any behaviour that is likely to bring about sanction is likely to be repressed. An additional strategic dimension of SIDE was proposed by Douglas and McGarty (2001), who conducted a series of studies to test whether an ingroup or outgroup audience influenced CMC users' stereotyping of an outgroup. To test this experimentally, Douglas and McGarty had students writing critiques of a white-power e-mail. They manipulated a series of factors, including whether the participant and author of the white-power posting were identifiable or anonymous, and whether or not the participant's critique would be seen by an ingroup or outgroup. They found an interaction between the identifiability of the participant and the 'target' (i.e. the author of the white-power posting). That is, the participants used significantly more stereotypical language in describing the target when (a) the participant was identifiable to the ingroup and (b) the target was anonymous. In a third study, Douglas and McGarty found that identifiable participants felt more accountable for their message and less strongly about the issue of racism. They conclude that these feelings of accountability in those identifiable to the ingroup, alongside a lack of strength of feeling about the issue, led the participants to use more stereotypic language as a self-presentation device to the ingroup audience. That is, the participants felt obligated to go along with the ingroup.

In a series of follow-up studies testing both CMC and pen-and-paper responses (Douglas and McGarty, 2002), the researchers similarly found that being identifiable to an ingroup was associated with more stereotypic language. However, when they manipulated how committed the participants felt towards the issue, they found that it had no effect on stereotypic language. Instead, they found that the role of identifiability was mediated by whether or not participants felt that they had complied with the desires of the ingroup or not.

So, it would seem that the strategic aspect of SIDE is somewhat more complex than just whether or not a person is identifiable to the ingroup. Douglas and McGarty (2002) argue that identifiability to an ingroup influences communication both *implicitly* (i.e. without conscious awareness) and *explicitly* (i.e. by making people more sensitive to the reactions of the audience).

Anonymity, social identity and attraction to a group

Lea *et al.* (2001) conducted a study to examine the effect of visual anonymity on feelings of being a part of a group. In their study, 51 undergraduate female psychology students discussed three issues (vegetarianism, immigration and politeness) with two confederates using CMC who were believed to be German students (they were actually graduate students at the same university). Half the participants were visually anonymous, while half could see each other via a video link. Lea *et al.* then measured how much the participants categorised themselves as members of the small discussion group and as British (i.e. in comparison to the German group members), and the participants' attraction to the group. In line with the model outlined in Figure 2.4, Lea *et al.* predicted that visual anonymity would increase attraction to the group. They also predicted that this effect would not be direct, but rather would be via the participants categorising themselves as a group member. When they analysed the pattern of the data they found that visual anonymity was associated with categorising oneself as a member of the group, which in turn was associated with attraction to the group. They interpreted these findings as strong support for the social identity explanation of group behaviour during CMC. A second finding of note was that visual anonymity was associated with heightened evaluation concern – suggesting that when you can't see the other person you are more concerned about their evaluation of you than if you can see them. To an extent this finding might be an artefact of the design of the experiment – it is not clear how evaluation concern was measured. As Lea *et al.* note, as a finding, it does warrant further investigation. Another point worth noting is that the experiment conducted by Lea *et al.* does not discriminate between different types of anonymity, for instance, of you to others and of others to you. All of these different types of anonymity may have different effects during CMC (something Lea *et al.* recognise as a problem needing addressing).

Critiques of SIDE

The application of SIDE to CMC has received remarkably few critiques since the first paper in 1990. The most comprehensive critiques come from the SIDE research group itself (e.g. Spears *et al.*, 2001). They note that SIDE has focused singularly on anonymity as the defining feature of CMC, and effectively ignored other aspects of the medium (e.g. synchronicity). Although some SIDE research is beginning to address this gap, the reliance of SIDE on anonymity, and more specifically visual anonymity (i.e. anonymity of others to self) has restricted the application of SIDE outside specific contexts. Although much Internet behaviour is at least partially identifiable (e.g. e-mail address, ISP), and people are traceable in theory, it is unclear how low levels of perceived identifiability interact with visual anonymity. The strategic aspect of SIDE makes some predictions about identifiability and group behaviour, but the links between the cognitive and strategic aspects of SIDE are not well-developed.

Moreover, thus far the vast majority of SIDE research on CMC has focused on the cognitive aspects of SIDE, rather than the strategic aspects (but see Douglas and McGarty, 2001). Most SIDE research also tends first, to, equate visual anonymity with anonymity, and second, to, equate anonymity with de-individuation. Coleman *et al.* (1999) note that de-individuation is a psychological state that is the outcome of anonymity (amongst other factors), and should be treated as a dependent variable rather than as an independent variable.

More importantly, SIDE is vulnerable to instances of group polarisation occurring when individuals are identifiable or when no group is salient. Spears *et al.* (2001) note that such occurrences might indeed now be appearing. To an extent, the development of the strategic element of SIDE might account for some of these cases, but perhaps not all of them. Indeed, it would be a matter for some concern if SIDE provided an answer for every possible outcome of CMC. To a degree, this move towards circularity may have occurred. For instance, in the application of SIDE to flaming, Lea *et al.* (1992) claim that when there is evidence of flaming in a group, it is clearly normative, and when there is no flaming, it is clearly not normative. So, whatever the behaviour in the group may be, it is treated as confirmatory evidence. Without prior measurement of norms within the group, it is not possible to say whether a certain behaviour or set of attitudes is normative or not. Again, though, more recent work (and also the early work) is addressing this by priming norms and social identities (Spears *et al.*, 2001).

The link between self-awareness and SIDE is also open to some question. Isolation is commonly seen as an individuating experience, increasing a person's private self-awareness. Being privately self-aware is not necessarily compatible with the salience of a social identity, and the actual processes linking isolation from others with the salience of a social identity are not well-developed. However, that most of these problems of the application of SIDE to CMC have been raised by the SIDE researchers themselves suggests that at least some will be addressed by future research.

Rational actors and emergent properties: alternatives to technological determinism

The models of mediated communication outlined above share a number of key features. First, all (with the possible exception of SIDE) are broadly technologically determinist – the features of the technology have a psychological impact that determines the behaviour of the individual. A second similarity is the shared focus on mainly just one feature of CMC, visual anonymity, and more specifically its role in either attenuating self-focus, reducing accountability or increasing the salience of social identities. However, alternative conceptualisations of the relationship between technology and behaviour have come from researchers investigating information systems and media appropriateness (e.g. Daft and Lengel, 1984; Markus, 1994).

The rational actor approach (e.g. Kling, 1980; Markus, 1994) argues that the outcomes of technology use on behaviour come 'not from the technology itself, but from the choices individuals make about when and how to use it' (Markus, 1994, p. 122). The assumptions behind this approach are in keeping with the cues-filtered-out approaches. That is, computer-mediated communication has less interpersonal closeness, which can lead to negative effects like uninhibited communication and difficulties in decision-making. But, rather than the technology being necessarily bad, the rational actor approach would argue instead for good and bad uses of a neutral technology. Moreover, at times users might actually want 'bad' outcomes because they fulfil other personal goals. For example, if we have a colleague who is particularly verbose, we might choose to communicate almost exclusively by e-mail with him or her because we want brief, task-focused discussions rather than interpersonal closeness. Similarly, the lack of many social cues in e-mail or text messaging, while an apparent barrier to expressing socio-emotional content, could be chosen for specific communications precisely because of that lack of cues. For instance, teenagers using text messaging to ask for dates might deliberately choose that medium because it allows them to disguise their nervousness.

From this perspective then, negative outcomes of Internet communication occur because people have chosen the wrong medium for their task (Daft and Lengel, 1984).

A second alternative to technological determinism is the emergent process view (Markus, 1994; Pfeffer, 1982). According to the emergent process view, the interaction between a user's intentions and the medium via which they choose to communicate can have unforeseen, unintended consequences. This can happen despite the user's best efforts to avoid a negative outcome, and might even be because of their actions. In the following two chapters, some of the negative outcomes, both for the self and the process of interaction, are discussed.

Negative Aspects of Intra- and Interpersonal Internet Behaviour

3

The Internet has never lacked press coverage. Internet-based headlines have included 'Cyberporn!' (*Time* magazine front cover, 1995), 'Lonely sad world discovered in cyberspace' (*New York Times*, 1998), 'World-wide web of lies' (*Sunday Mirror*, 2001) and 'My Internet lover was a 20 stone pensioner with a dead body in the freezer' (*Sunday People*, 2000).

Is it just that the downside of the Internet makes good copy? Or is there something specific about the Internet that encourages deviance or antisocial behaviour? New technology tends to bring with it scare stories and utopian optimism in equal measure. As we saw, even the development of writing was linked with concerns about its social and psychological impact. A story in the *Electrical World* magazine in 1886 was titled 'The dangers of wired love' and recounted the tale of two telegraph operators who met over the wires (Standage, 1999). Maggie, the daughter of a news-stand owner, acted as the telegraph operator for her father's business. He soon found that she was 'keeping up flirtations' with a number of men, including the married Frank Frisbie. She invited Frisbie to visit her, something her father forbade. Her father moved his business, but she soon found work in the local telegraph office, and continued her relationship. Eventually, her father followed her to a meeting with Frisbie and threatened to 'blow her brains out', whereupon she had him arrested for threatening behaviour. Standage (1999), in recounting this story, does not say how the romance ended.

Similarly, the telephone was seen by many as both an unwelcome intrusion and a dangerous tool for carrying on affairs (Fischer, 1992). There was also considerable debate about the social impact of the telephone, as well as its role in generally lowering the tone of social discourse. A novel titled *A Call* by Ford Madox Ford, first published in 1910, details the problems and misunderstandings likely to be incurred when communication is separated from face to face interaction. Even the mobile telephone was associated in its early days with possible new crimes or the coordination of criminal activity. More recently, new technology (mobile phones, fax, e-mail) has been cited as crucial to the organisation of anti-globalisation demonstrations and, in the UK, protests and blockades around petrol prices. Following the terrorist attacks in America on 11 September 2001, there were many suggestions that new media technologies enabled the organisation of terrorist cells (despite evidence of a 'no-tech' rather than a 'high-tech' approach to communication). Writing in the *Daily Telegraph*, John Keegan (their Defence correspondent) even went so far as to propose the targeting of Internet Service Providers (ISPs) in the fight against terrorism:

> The World Trade Centre outrage was co-ordinated on the internet, without question. If Washington is serious in its determination to eliminate terrorism, it will have to forbid internet providers to allow the transmission of encrypted messages – now encoded by public key ciphers that are unbreakable even by the National Security Agency's computers – and close down any provider that refuses to comply. Uncompliant providers on foreign territory should expect their buildings to be destroyed by cruise missiles. Once the internet is implicated in the killing of Americans, its high-rolling days may be reckoned to be over. (*Daily Telegraph*, 14 September 2001)

We perhaps should not be surprised then that the Internet, like technologies before it, has similarly been associated with deviant behaviour, crime, and generally negative effects for people and society. The key question is whether or not the association between a new technology and its negative ramifications is simply a social representation developed by the mass media, or has some grounding in empirical evidence.

For the purposes of this chapter, the definition of 'negative outcome' is taken to signify any behaviour or psychological or social consequence of Internet use that is generally framed as negative by either the users themselves, academic research or more general discourse.

As we have seen, it is not unusual for new forms of mediated communication to be accompanied, at least in the early days, by varied
musings on the negative impact of the technology on both the person
and on society in general. The Internet is no exception. Indeed, if anything, the Internet has been associated with more negative outcomes
in its relatively short existence than any other new technology bar
perhaps the automobile.

Internet addiction

Internet addiction disorder (IAD) was first coined as a term (or alternatively, 'discovered') in 1991 by the psychiatrist Ivan Goldberg. Goldberg
originally published his definition as a satire on the pop psychological
'addiction' craze where it was claimed people could be addicted to, for
instance, shopping or sex (or both). However, Goldberg soon began to
receive e-mails from people claiming to suffer from IAD. Before long,
academic interest had generated two main domains of research into
IAD – the first, into the diagnostic criteria required to fit IAD, being
directly related to the second, the number of people 'suffering' from IAD.

One of the first empirical studies of Internet addiction was conducted
by Kimberly Young (1996). Young adapted the criteria for psychoactive
substance addiction used in the American Psychological Association's
Diagnostic and Statistical Manual (DSM-IV) and applied it to Internet
use (see Table 3.1).

To test the prevalence of Internet addiction, Young posted a message requesting 'avid Internet users' to Usenet sites, and in newspaper
and poster advertisements. She received 396 replies that she claimed
were Internet-dependent (of whom 60 per cent were female). Young
operationalised addiction as anyone who replied in the affirmative to
at least three of her items. She also reported that those classified as
addicts used the Internet for an average of 38.5 hours a week.

The number of studies examining Internet addiction has increased
substantially since Young's first work. Unfortunately, few use the
same criteria for addiction as Young, although most share similarly
low criteria for 'addiction'. For instance, Morahan-Martin and
Schumacher (2000) studied 277 students using a 13-item scale (see
Table 3.2).

They reported that 8.1 per cent of their sample were pathological
Internet users who reported four or more symptoms (12.2 per cent
male, 3.2 per cent female). A large proportion of the sample (64.7 per

THE PSYCHOLOGY OF INTERNET BEHAVIOUR

Table 3.1   Diagnostic criteria for Internet addiction

- Do you experience a tolerance in that you have a need for increased amounts of Internet use to achieve the desired effect OR do you find there is a diminished effect with continued use of the same time spent on the Internet?
- Do you spend longer periods of time on the Internet than you intended?
- Do you spend a great deal of time in activities to stay on-line longer?
- Have you given up any social, occupational, or recreational activities because of the Internet?
- Have you continued to use the Internet despite knowledge of having a persistent or recurrent problem that is likely to have been caused or exacerbated by the Internet (e.g. work-related problems, academic problems, financial problems or family problems)?
- Have you made unsuccessful attempts to cut down how much time you spend on-line OR do you have a lack of desire to cut down the amount of time you spend on-line?
- Do you experience withdrawal symptoms (e.g. depression, irritability, moodiness, anxiety) when you are off-line?

Source: Adapted from Young (1996).

cent) were defined as 'limited symptoms' with between one and three reported symptoms. The pathological group spent an average of 8.48 hours per week on-line, compared to the limited symptoms (3.18 hours) and no symptoms groups (2.47 hours). In keeping with other studies, males (12.2 per cent) were more likely to be 'pathological Internet users' than females (3.2 per cent). Pathological Internet users were more likely to use the following services on the Internet:

- Meeting new people
- Using adult-only resources
- Emotional support
- Talking to others with the same shared interests
- Playing games
- Recreation or relaxation
- Gambling
- Virtual reality
- Wasting time
- Staying abreast of new developments.

Table 3.2 Pathological Internet use questionnaire and % agreement of pathological Internet users (PIU) and limited symptom (LS) users

Item	% PIU	% LS
I have *never* gotten into arguments with a significant other over being online (Reverse scored)	68.2	68.2
I have been told I spend too much time online	63.6	6.3
If it has been a while since I last logged on, I find it hard to stop thinking about what will be waiting for me when I do	59.1	10.2
My work and/or school performance has not deteriorated since I started going online (Reverse scored)	54.6	44.0
I feel guilty about the amount of time I spend online	45.5	3.4
I have gone online to make myself feel better when I was down or anxious	40.9	6.9
I have attempted to spend less time online but have not been able to	40.9	1.7
I have routinely cut short on sleep to spend more time online	36.2	2.8
I have used online to talk to others at times when I was feeling isolated	31.8	11.5
I have missed classes or work because of my online activities	27.3	1.1
I have gotten into trouble with my employer or school because of being online	22.7	1.7
I have missed social engagements because of online activities	18.2	0.6
I have tried to hide from others how much time I am actually online	13.6	6.3

Source: Morahan-Martin and Schumacher (2000, p. 17).

Morahan-Martin and Schumacher also measured users' attitudes to the Internet. They found that pathological Internet users scored higher on their measure of 'social confidence' and 'social liberation'. The social confidence scale included measures like 'going online has made it easier for me to make friends', 'I have a network of friends made online' and 'I open up more online than I do in other forms of communication'. Meanwhile, the socially liberating scale included items like 'I am more myself online than in real life' and 'I have pre-tended to be someone of the opposite sex while online'. Pathological Internet users also scored higher on a measure of loneliness.

Scherer and Bost (1997) studied 531 students using a ten-item scale, and found that 49 (19 per cent) matched their criteria of addiction. These 'addicts' used the Internet for an average 8.1 hours a week and, in keeping with earlier studies, tended to use less mainstream Internet services (e.g. games, chat). Griffiths (1998) argues that, like the study by Young, 'the cut-off point for genuine addiction was perhaps too low' (p. 68).

Thus, the survey-based evidence for Internet addiction is remarkably thin, and questionable on a number of grounds (Griffiths, 1998). One problem is that the criteria for addiction are usually set too low – in the case of Young, it is possible to be classified as an addict by answering affirmatively to three questions only. So, to be an Internet addict in Young's study, one would only need to agree (1) that you had sometimes spent longer on the Internet than originally intended, (2) that you had given up one social, occupational or recreational activity because of the Internet and (3) that you do not want to reduce your Internet use. In the case of Morahan-Martin and Schumacher (2000), their diagnostic criteria allow them to claim that 'almost three-fourths of the under-graduate Internet users surveyed (73.8%) reported at least one symp-tom indicating Internet use is causing problems' (p. 21).

Using these criteria, presumably anyone could be an Internet addict. For instance, while I'm writing this book, I'm only checking my e-mail once or twice a week. This means that, whatever my best efforts, I spend longer doing on-line activity (replying to the backlog) than I intended. I've given up a number of activities because of the Internet: I tend to e-mail old friends rather than call them (it means we speak more), I do my weekly grocery shop on-line and I don't wander the library so much any more (I use the on-line catalogue and ordering service). Finally, I don't want to reduce my Internet use – perhaps not surprisingly.

Scherer and Bost (1997) similarly required their 'bona fide' addicts to answer in the affirmative to only three from ten of their items. Two of the items used by Scherer and Bost are based on amount of usage, and did relatively little to differentiate between true addicts and non-addicts. Indeed, it would be possible to answer 'yes' to the following two questions if you had a frustratingly slow modem or service provider:

- Used the Internet over longer periods of time than I had intended (98 per cent 'addicts', 45.2 per cent non-addicts)
- Spent a great deal of time accessing the Internet (87.8 per cent 'addicts' versus 20.6 per cent non-addicts).

Thus, in the Scherer and Bost study, the effective diagnostic criterion is one item from eight. It should come as little surprise that so many of the on-line population are thus confirmed as Internet addicts in the studies outlined above.

Diagnostic criteria revisited

Griffiths (1998) argues that addiction needs to fulfil six criteria:

1. *Salience*   Using the Internet dominates the person's life, feelings and behaviour.
2. *Mood modification*   The person experiences changes in mood (e.g. a 'buzz') when using the Internet.
3. *Tolerance*   Increasing amounts of Internet use are needed to achieve the same effects on mood.
4. *Withdrawal symptoms*   If the person stops using the Internet, they experience unpleasant feelings or physical effects.
5. *Conflict*   Using the Internet causes conflicts with those close to the person, or with their everyday life (e.g. their job, social life or hobbies).
6. *Relapse*   The addict tends to relapse into earlier patterns of behaviour, even after years of abstinence or control.

However, Griffiths notes that, with some exceptions, most survey-based studies of IAD do not address all these criteria. It would also seem that, in the majority of cases, it is possible to get within touching distance of fulfilling the criteria for addiction or pathological Internet use simply based on the amount of time you spend on-line. As such, the criteria used by Scherer and Bost could easily be turned into a 'socialising with friends while at university addiction scale', including the items:

- I have socialised with friends at college for longer periods of time than I had intended

- I have spent a great deal of time socialising with friends at college
- I have failed to fulfil major responsibilities at work, school or home due to my socialising with friends.

Griffiths (2000a) presents five case studies, two of whom he claims *might* be addicted to computers and/or the Internet.

From these two case studies, it is clear that excessive Internet or computer use might occur because of pre-existing social isolation or other problems. This does not mean that Internet addiction is not 'real' in any sense, or that it should not be treated. Rather, it means that any thoughts of treatment for excessive Internet use need to identify possible precursors, as well as the Internet use itself. The possibility that pathological Internet use is linked to pre-existing problems is discussed in more detail in Davis's (2001) cognitive-behavioural model of Internet addiction (outlined in the following section of this chapter).

Case study 1   Jamie

Jamie is a 16-year-old male, who lives at home with his mother (his parents divorced when he was a child). Jamie has no physical problems, although according to Griffiths he is 'very overweight' (p. 213). He spends around 70 hours per week on his computer, 40 hours of which is on-line, including two 12-hour sessions at the weekend. As a science fiction fan, Jamie spends much of his time discussing Star Trek on Usenet groups. In line with the diagnostic criteria outlined earlier, Jamie claims that the Internet is the most important thing in his life, and he thinks about it even when not using it. According to Griffiths, Jamie also claims that using the Internet can change his mood, and that he experiences withdrawal symptoms when denied access. He shows evidence of a relapse pattern of attempting to reduce his Internet usage, only to find the lure too strong. In keeping with survey evidence, Jamie uses the Internet to socialise using IRC, newsgroups and web-based chat services. He has no friends in his off-line life. Griffiths notes that 'It may be the case that Jamie feels comfortable in the text-based world of the Internet because of his obesity' (p. 214).

Case Study 2   Gary

Gary is a 15-year-old male. Gary spends around three to four hours a day during the week, and up to five or six hours during the weekend, on his computer. Gary suffers from neurofibromatosis, which can produce behavioural problems (sometime severe). Gary has always had problems socialising and making friends, and, according to Griffiths, he also 'suffers from an inferiority complex and lack of confidence when dealing with his peers. As a consequence, he gets very depressed' (p. 212). Gary's behaviour and mental health worsened when he got the computer. He spends time on-line to the detriment of time with family and friends, and has become increasingly challenging to his parents. Griffiths concludes that although Gary seems to fit many of the criteria for a computer addict, his excessive use of the computer as an 'electronic friend' may well be symptomatic of other underlying problems (i.e. his social isolation, illness and depression).

The search for adequate diagnostic criteria and verifiable case studies continues. In light of the various problems conceptualising and agreeing the criteria for Internet addiction, cyberpsychological research has begun to question what it is about the Internet that makes it potentially addictive. For all potential Internet addicts, the experience of the Internet can provide a potentially intoxicating experience. As was discussed in the previous chapter, mediated communication can lead people to behave in a less inhibited manner than they would face to face. The possibility of immersion in the on-line experience, along with the opportunities that that brings, can certainly be a giddying experience for novice users.

However, this initial experience does not equate to addiction. In many of the studies cited above, the people who came closest to the criteria for IAD also tended to be those who engaged in on-line gaming, Internet Relay Chat and cybersex (Griffiths, 1998). Of course, with a tendency to overdiagnose addiction in these same studies, it is possible that it was simply experienced or adventurous users who were categorised as IAD. This raises the question of what Internet addicts are actually addicted to. For instance, if someone was a compulsive gambler, and they were often on the telephone to their bookmakers, we would not categorise them as phone addicts. Similarly, if someone is using the Internet to fuel a primary addiction or dependence (e.g. gambling, shopping or whatever), it would be wrong to label them IAD.

That leaves the heavy users from these surveys who engaged in on-line activities like MUDs, chats and games. Looking at the studies of Internet addiction published to date, the regularity with which 'addicts' report using these three key Internet tools is strong (an exception, I would guess, would be downloading MP3s). These three on-line activities are also arguably the most immersive – the feedback you get is immediate, the focus on the task in hand needs to be high and the level of psychological involvement is likely to be similarly high. These psychological characteristics of certain on-line activities are similar in feature to another technology that has been subject to addiction claims – computer games.

What makes the Internet addictive?

While much effort has gone into developing diagnostic criteria to assess the prevalence of Internet addiction, models of what makes the Internet addictive are relatively sparse. In the main, these models identify aspects of the Internet that make it appealing and, presumably, also addictive. For instance, Kimberly Young (1997) argues that three aspects of the Internet make it potentially addictive: anonymity, convenience and escape (ACE). To turn this argument inside out, it could be argued that *some* aspects of the Internet are particularly appealing to *some* people. So, perhaps for someone looking for sexual kicks, to gamble or to play on-line games, the Internet is appealing because it is convenient, anonymous and might provide some degree of escape from everyday life and even changes in consciousness through the experience. Looking at the two case studies outlined above, it is clear that both Jamie and Gary use the Internet's anonymity to counter self-confidence or weight problems, and also to escape from the isolation of everyday life. A similar model, the triple A (Cooper, 1998), suggests that addiction to cybersex is due to the ease of access, the affordability and anonymity of the Internet.

However, both these models are too technologically determinist – by focusing on the attributes of the Internet, rather than the user, they provide little to explain exactly what the causes of Internet addiction are. For instance, my local off-licence sells one of the favoured drinks of alcoholics, Special Brew. It is convenient and easy to buy, high alcohol levels provide an escape at an affordable price, and it is sold in transportable cans to drink in the anonymity of your own home. However, no one would attempt to explain alcoholism by purely looking at the various benefits of, say, vodka over beer. So, it would seem to add little to our understanding to explain Internet addiction by describing what is appealing about the Internet.

An alternative approach that provides a more user-centred view of Internet addiction is proposed by Davis (2001). Davis argues that the behaviour- and symptom-led models of Internet addiction tend to ignore the cognitive symptoms of PIU that might precede them. Taking a lead from cognitive explanations of depression that argue that cognitions (e.g. depressive schema, rumination, low self-esteem) lead to the symptoms of depression, Davis argues for a similar approach to be adopted for PIU. He suggests first that pathological Internet use be divided into specific (i.e. cybersex or visiting porn sites) and generalised (i.e. wasting time on-line, taking part in on-line communities compulsively). He argues that specific PIU is likely to be due to a pre-existing psychopathology (e.g. gambling addiction), while generalised PIU is likely to follow experiences of social isolation. So, for specific PIU, a psychopathology would most likely exist without the Internet, while for generalised PIU, the Internet is the trigger that leads from perhaps a minor psychopathology (e.g. loneliness) to pathological Internet use.

Davis therefore adopts a diathesis–stress approach to Internet addiction, where an existing psychopathology is the necessary precursor to Internet addiction, but in itself is not sufficient for a person to show the symptoms of Internet addiction. The stress is the introduction of the Internet into the person's life. This experience might be immediately reinforcing (e.g. entering a chat room if lonely). Linked to this are 'maladaptive cognitions' of the Internet user. So, perhaps they will ruminate about their Internet use, they might hold negative self-views that can be escaped on-line, or they might generalise their on-line and off-line experiences (e.g. thinking that 'It's only on the Internet that people treat me well'). According to Davis, it is these maladaptive cognitions that lead to either specific or generalised PIU (2001, p. 192). This model is shown schematically in Figure 3.1.

Although Davis's model provides a valuable addition to the Internet addiction literature by introducing the user into the equation, it still grapples with the problems inherent in identifying the symptoms of pathological Internet use. So, for a person lacking social support, when are we to say whether the use is pathological or not? Davis

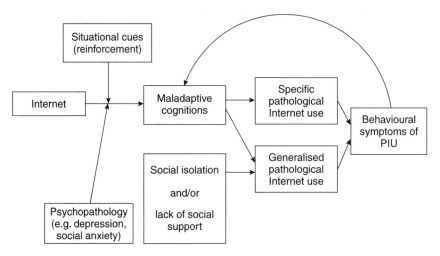

Figure 3.1   The cognitive-behavioural model of pathological Internet use

Source: Davis (2001, p. 190).

suggests that it might be when Internet use is a source of identity for the user rather than a 'helpful tool' (2001, p. 193). Obviously, this approach would be problematic for those gaining a positive sense of self from Internet use. In the end, Davis concludes that it is the individual that determines whether or not their Internet use is adaptive or maladaptive.

What all these models of Internet addiction suggest is that the Internet provides an escape from everyday problems, and that the anonymity on the Internet makes it particularly attractive (or addictive). The second 'negative' outcome of Internet use discussed here, flaming, has similarly been linked to anonymity.

Flaming and antisocial behaviour

In its original format, flaming referred to incessant talking or wittering. However, later it came to be generally seen as negative or antisocial behaviour on computer networks. When such antagonistic or aggressive messages are traded between people, it becomes a 'flame war'. Academic research into flaming has been hampered by a lack of clarity in the definitions used to measure it in laboratory research.

For instance, Kiesler *et al.* (1985) operationalised flaming as:

- impolite statements
- swearing/flirting
- exclamations
- expressions of personal feelings towards another
- the use of superlatives.

Other operationalisations of flaming include items such as profanity, 'typographic energy' (e.g. exclamation marks), name-calling, swearing, and general negative affect. When the focus of a research project moves from flaming to 'uninhibited' communication, the definition widens to include even non-task-based messages and conveying bad news.

A further problem with the definition and operationalisation of flaming is its *a priori* link to computer-mediated communication (Lea *et al.*, 1992). In many instances, flaming is, by definition, something that either only occurs on computer networks, or is more evident on computer networks than face to face. So, to a degree the definition of flaming ends up becoming any way in which FtF and CMC differ.

Empirical evidence for 'flaming'

According to Selfe and Meyer (1991), 'heated, emotional, sometimes anonymous, venting ... is a common, if not universal, feature of computer-based conferences' (p. 170).

In three early studies, Siegal *et al.* (1983) compared levels of uninhibited verbal behaviour in four conditions: face to face communication, anonymous computer conferencing (one-to-many), non-anonymous computer conferencing (one-to-many) and e-mail. In the experiments, groups of three people were asked to reach a consensus using a choice-dilemma task (a dilemma where groups weigh up two possible choices, often a risky and cautious option, and come to a joint decision). When Siegal and her colleagues looked at the level of uninhibited communication (defined in this instance as hostile comments such as swearing, name-calling and insults), they found higher levels of uninhibited verbal behaviour, in each experiment, when people used computers to communicate. The highest levels of uninhibited behaviour were recorded when people discussed anonymously using a real-time (synchronous) computer-conferencing system.

Castellá *et al.* (2000) compared levels of flaming between groups discussing a dilemma using e-mail, videoconferencing or face to face.

Table 3.3	Flaming by media		
	Face to face	*Videoconference*	*E-mail*
No. of remarks	3734	4074	1990
Informal speech	174	203	173
Flaming	8	16	94
Informal speech as a % of remarks	4.66	4.98	8.69
Flaming as a % of remarks	0.21	0.39	4.72

Source: Castellá *et al.* (2000, p. 150).

They categorised flaming into 'informal speech' (including 'ironic comments' and 'Expressions which try to endow the written speech with certain characteristics of oral speech' (p. 148), and outright flaming (aggressive and overtly hostile comments). The results for both categories are shown in Table 3.3.

So, although flaming was rare, it was significantly more likely to occur in the text-based discussions than face to face or videoconferencing. In further analyses of the data, Castellá *et al.* found no links between an individual's assertiveness or the familiarity of the group and flaming, although being more familiar with the other group members did predict levels of informal speech.

Aiken and Waller (2000) studied two groups of business students who discussed the impeachment of President Clinton and parking problems on campus (both judged as reasonably controversial issues). They found that flaming comments were written by a small but consistent group of people, who were all male. In one group, 20 per cent of the individuals wrote flaming messages for the parking discussion, and 50 per cent for the President discussion. All participants who wrote flaming messages in the first discussion also wrote them in the second. But they found no links between the controversy or perceived importance of the topic and flaming, suggesting that 'flames are probably due to the characteristics (such as gender, level of maturity, hostility, etc.) of the individual writing them' (p. 99). Indeed, Smolensky *et al.* (1990) found that uninhibited communication was related to an individual's level of extraversion, as well as the level of familiarity within the group.

Coleman *et al.* (1999) examined the discussions of 58 face to face and 59 CMC participants discussing a set topic in groups of 3–7 people. The subsequent discussions were rated on (amongst other things) negativity. Positive or neutral statements were scored as 1; statements containing overt disagreement or criticism scored 2; and profanity, hostility and name-calling were scored as 3. The level of negativity between the two groups did not differ: for the CMC groups it was 1.24, while for the FtF groups, it was 1.21. However, Coleman *et al.* do note that all cases of level 3 negativity, while rare, occurred in the CMC condition.

A second type of study into flaming involves asking Internet users to report *post hoc* the number of flames they see FtF and during CMC. One such study was conducted by Sproull and Kiesler (1986) when they studied the e-mail communications of 96 staff working for a large organisation in the USA. They also collected questionnaire responses. In accordance with their predictions, Sproull and Kiesler found that their participants reported seeing 33 flames on e-mail in a month, and just four in face to face interaction.

Niederhoffer and Pennebaker (2001) report a startling discovery for their experimenter in a study of linguistic synchrony using Internet chat as a methodology:

> The male experimenter who conducted the sessions debriefed the participants immediately after the interactions without reading the actual transcripts. He noted that the students were always low-keyed, unassuming, and moderately interested in the study. No participants appeared embarrassed, shocked, or, in the slightest way, upset or angry. At the conclusion of the project, when he was given the opportunity to read the transcripts, he was astounded – even overwhelmed – to learn what these polite students had been saying to one another. (Niederhoffer and Pennebaker, 2001, p. 14)

According to their analysis, nearly a fifth (18.8 per cent) of the chat sessions 'involved overt invitations for sex, explicit sexual language, or discussion of graphic sexual escapades' (p. 14). Thus, although flaming is usually seen as hostile argument, it may well be worth considering overly sexual chat as a similar, related behaviour.

Flame wars and the structure of argument

One of the problems with laboratory studies of flaming is that they tend to decontextualise flaming. Within a discussion, it is likely that flaming is most likely to occur via a developmental process of argumentation, rather than as single 'off the cuff' remarks. Most e-mail and bulletin board/Usenet software gives users the ability to quote earlier messages in their rejoinder. For instance, it would be common to see:

> person A said:
> If you're going to Cornwall, you must visit St. Ives

Yeah, right. Must if you're a typical tourist. St. Ives is packed with rowdy day trippers all summer. Like person A, I guess.

Mabry (1997) studied 3,000 messages for flaming and its association with the use of quotations. He noted that in face to face communication, quoting is called 'recounting', and involves restating or summarising an 'opponent's' argument with the aim of refuting and/or producing counter arguments (or agreeing). Mabry hypothesised that the easy availability of direct quoting in Internet software might support the use of recounting in CMC discussions. It might even encourage arguments because it is so readily available.

Of the 3,000 messages Mabry analysed, 125 (4.2 per cent) were disagreeing in tone, 65 (2.2 per cent) showed tension, 46 (1.5 per cent) antagonism and 20 (0.7 per cent) outright hostility. Mabry found a curvilinear relationship between the use of past messages and quoting and the emotional tone of the message. So, neutral or friendly messages used quotations significantly less than flaming messages. Interestingly, message dependency and the use of quotations seemed to reach a plateau as messages got more flaming, with hostile messages using less argumentative devices. Perhaps once a discussion reaches the level of outright hostility, what your opponent said earlier does not really matter.

So, in asynchronous discussions, the affordances of the tool used (i.e. quoting and cut and paste) certainly allow arguments to develop. Intriguingly, perhaps recounting on the Internet is relatively effortless compared to oral argumentation (where considerable effort needs to be used to remember and rephrase your opponent's arguments). Thus, the Internet provides the opportunity for people to develop their arguments like a skilled politician would – by attacking their opponent point by point. But it has the added bonus of allowing users to expend minimum cognitive energy on recounting, and focus on challenging the arguments of their opponent.

When does a disagreement become a flame?

Of course, not all disagreements are flames. Thompsen and Foulger (1996) wanted to see when a disagreement reached the level of flaming, and whether the use of quoting and emoticons moderated or encouraged the perception of a flame. To test this, they developed a fictitious argument between two skiing enthusiasts, Dr. Ski and Snow Pro. Thompsen and Foulger showed the argument to 164 participants who responded to a call for participants on the Internet. These participants were further divided into four groups: the first saw the message as laid out below. For the other three groups, the emoticons were removed for one, the quotes for a second, and both quotes and emoticons for a third. All groups rated each message on a seven-point 'perception of flaming' scale.

Message 1
Hi everybody. I need some suggestions. I want to learn how to ski, but I'm not sure where to start. Is there a good ski school or learn-to-ski package someone could recommend?
– A Total Novice

Message 2
A Total Novice asks:
> Is there a good ski school or learn-to-ski package someone could recommend?

Brighton is a good place to learn to ski. That's where I learned, and I think they offer a special deal for beginners.
– Snow Pro

Message 3
In response to A Total Novice who wrote ...
> I want to learn to ski

Alta is the ski area I would suggest. Alta has really great slopes, and a lot of them. I ski there almost every weekend.
– Dr. Ski

Message 4
Dr. Ski claims that
> Alta has really great slopes, and a lot of them

I disagree. I think Alta may be a good place for seasoned skiers, but not for those just starting out. Best to start on a reasonably priced, friendlier set of slopes, like Brighton.
– Snow Pro

Message 5
According to Snow Pro, it's
> Best to start on a reasonably priced, friendlier set of slopes, like Brighton.

I disagree. In my opinion, Brighton is fine for the occasional skier, but not for someone wanting to learn the real sport of skiing. Best to learn at Alta, a world-class ski area with a reputation for excellence.
– Dr. Ski

Message 6
If Alta has a reputation, it's for crowded slopes. Learning to ski at Alta is like learning to drive on the freeway! :-) For those just learning to ski, Brighton offers the best combination of great snow, comfortable surroundings, and relaxed pace.
– Snow Pro

Message 7
At least people move on a freeway. Learning to ski at Brighton is like learning to ski in a parking lot! :-) Alta is the best place to learn to ski, with superb snow, excellent trails, and genuine support for the skiing enthusiast.
– Dr. Ski

Message 8
Dr. Ski asserts that
> Learning to ski at Brighton is like learning to ski in a parking lot

Now hold on one second. Brighton is a great place to learn to ski, and is a fine place to go once you've learned. It may not be as expensive as other ski areas, but at least one doesn't have to put up with the ski snobs like Dr. Ski who go to Alta :-)
– Snow Pro

Message 9
Snow Pro made reference to
> the ski snobs like Dr. Ski who go to Alta

Snobs? What a joke! Real skiers like Alta because we take skiing seriously. Skiing is more than just snow, slopes and lifts, which is all Brighton offers, and barely that. Only nerds like Snow Pro would admit to liking a pit like Brighton :-)
– Dr. Ski

Message 10
It's obvious that Dr. Ski doesn't want to carry on a civil conversation. It's also obvious that Dr. Ski doesn't know a damn thing about skiing. Let me ask you, Dr. Ski, is your diploma from a cereal box? :-)
– Snow Pro

Message 11
The only thing Snow Pro is a pro at is snowing this discussion group. Snow Pro has taken this conversation to new lows. Snow Pro, you obviously don't know crap about skiing, so why not drop the act? :-)
– Dr. Ski

Thompsen and Foulger found that messages that showed disagreement (4 and 5 above) were not rated as flames (mean scores 1.71 and 2.23 respectively). But the 'flaming' score for messages increases substantially when tension (messages 6 and 7) is introduced (mean scores 3.6 and 4.12 respectively), although that these scores are around the midpoint of the scale suggests that they are probably not true 'flames'. Once antagonism is introduced (messages 8 and 9, mean flame scores 5.52 and 6.09 respectively), the raters clearly perceived these to be flames. The profanity used in the final message further increased the perception of a flame. The researchers conclude that messages showing tension, but not antagonism, are most probably precursors to a fully blown 'flame war' (these have been called 'flame bait').

The inclusion of emoticons (smiley faces) in the discussions did influence whether or not a message was perceived as a flame. When the messages showing tension were accompanied with a 'smile', the perception of a flame was reduced by almost three-quarters of a point on the scale. However, when the messages became antagonistic and included personal attacks, the inclusion of a smile actually increased the perception of a flame (by 0.38 on the scale). Perhaps once a discussion reaches that level of antagonism, ending your attack with a smile is not perceived as credible friendliness, and may fan the flames, rather than douse them.

The results on the effect of quoting were more difficult to interpret. Overall, quoting did not have a significant effect on the perception of flaming. However, when examined individually, quoting reduced the impression of flaming in messages showing merely disagreement, and heightened the impression when the messages showed antagonism. This suggests that the use of quotes in flame wars is a somewhat more complex matter than simply that they encourage flame wars. Only when they are used as part of an antagonistic cycle do they contribute to the impression of flaming.

Stereotyping outgroups and flaming

That software enables and perhaps even encourages flaming on the Internet does not explain why flaming seems to get out of hand. In a well-publicised case in the UK, a senior member of the Welsh Nationalist Party Plaid Cymru, Gwilym ad Ioan, was forced to resign following his postings to various Welsh newsgroups. For instance, according to news service The Register (9 August 2001) comments included that Wales had become a 'dumping ground for England's oddballs and misfits' and that 'our language and culture is wilting at an alarming rate because of the over powerful and unbalanced effect and influence the alien culture has within our nation'. The Register also reports ad Ioan stating that 'In my experience the vast majority of people who settle in Wales are either: 1. Past their working age ... 2. Are unemployed and/or suffering from long term illness ... 3. Are social dropouts from the cities of England'.

Although the 'flaming' described above would seem reasonably clear-cut, we need to consider exactly what form of 'real life' activity would be a comparable behaviour. If ad Ioan had published his views in print form (e.g. in a newspaper letter), I imagine the reaction (and his downfall) would be similar. However, if the comments had not been archived (e.g. a Friday night discussion in a bar), one would imagine the reaction would be quite different.

To understand the comments posted by ad Ioan, it is also important to understand the context in which they were posted. First, they were not posted anonymously. Second, they were part of an ongoing discussion. Third, the audience was the ingroup (all posts were to Welsh newsgroups), while the target was an outgroup (the English).

The case of ad Ioan is interesting because it seems to directly relate to the strategic dimension of SIDE (Reicher et al., 1995). According to Reicher et al., when someone is identifiable to a powerful outgroup, the threat of sanction will usually suppress the expression of ingroup norms. However, there is some evidence that having the co-presence of ingroup members provides the support to express an ingroup identity despite possible sanction (Reicher and Levine, 1994). Although co-presence normally means 'physically present', unpublished work by Lea and Corneliussen (see Spears et al., 2001) suggests that CMC can provide social support for the expression of ingroup norms despite possible punishment by an outgroup. The results of the Lea and Corneliussen study suggested that (1) visual anonymity led to higher levels of endorsement of normative non-punishable behaviours like missing lectures (in line with the predictions of cognitive SIDE), and that (2) social support, in the form of CMC as compared to non-verbal co-presence (sitting in the same room but silently), led to higher levels of endorsement of punishable attitudes (like copying essays).

So, it may be that CMC, as well as increasing the salience of social identities, also encourages the expression of those identities through the provision of social support.

In the case of ad Ioan, co-presence needs to be interpreted as belonging to a Welsh newsgroup, but assuming that, then it would seem that the Internet encourages the expression of negative stereotypes of an outgroup by both activating a relevant social identity, and providing group support for the expression of ingroup congruent attitudes. Alas, as the case of ad Ioan shows, just because the group gives you the strength to express what may be a normative attitude for your ingroup, this does not guarantee any avoidance of punishment, especially now that newsgroup postings are archived and searchable.

How prevalent is flaming?

Spears and Lea (1992) remark that in their earlier studies of group decision-making using CMC, levels of flaming were too rare to be statistically analysed. Lea *et al.* (1992) also argue that occurrences of flaming are relatively rare. They conclude that, like many negative events, flaming tends to be remembered more often than more benign CMC, which has contributed to 'the illusion of universality' (p. 108). Walther *et al.* (1994) similarly argue that much of the acceptance of flaming as a widespread phenomenon during CMC is based on 'erroneous analysis and reporting practices' (p. 463). However, reports of flaming continue to appear (e.g. Niederhoffer and Pennebaker, 2001), suggesting that, while rare, it is still worth investigation.

Explanations of flaming

That flaming is a rare occurrence during CMC does not preclude the need for an explanation on those occasions that flaming does happen. A number of approaches have attempted to explain flaming in terms of the psychological impact of on-line communication.

Cues-filtered-out approaches

The reduced social cues explanation of flaming follows the rationale outlined in the previous chapter, although it also incorporates other features of CMC like rapid transfer of text and a 'hacker' subculture. Kiesler *et al.* (1984) begin by outlining six key social–psychological features of computer-mediated communication that might influence social behaviour:

1. *Time and information-processing pressures* The ability to send messages and replies instantaneously.
2. *Absence of regulating feedback* CMC may be inefficient in regulating, modifying and controlling exchanges due to the lack of non-verbal cues.
3. *Dramaturgical weakness* CMC users cannot use the normal techniques for adding emphasis to a message.
4. *Few status and position cues* 'Once people have electronic access, their status, power and prestige are communicated neither contextually ... nor dynamically' (Kiesler *et al.*, 1984, p. 1125).
5. *Social anonymity* CMC might be depersonalising, with the 'other' in the communication often forgotten about.
6. *Computing norms and immature etiquette* There is not a well-developed etiquette for using CMC, apart from a computer sub-culture.

Kiesler *et al.* identify two characteristics of CMC of particular interest: the lack of social context information and few widely shared norms. According to Kiesler *et al.*, it is the combination of reduced social context cues with a lack of established norms that leads to flaming both directly (through lowered regulation of communication) and indirectly (through de-individuation-type conditions).

A social identity explanation of flaming

In contrast to the explanation of flaming developed by the RSC researchers, Lea *et al.* (1992) argue that flaming is both normative and context-dependent. Lea *et al.* argue that if flaming was due to reduced social cues, then one would expect the effect to be felt evenly across on-line groups. However, they note that flaming does not seem to be evenly distributed across newsgroups. Rather, the relatively rare occurrences of flaming they noted tended to be restricted to certain groups. They go on to argue that perhaps in these specific groups flaming is actually the norm (especially newsgroups with 'flame' in the title), rather than evidence of anti-normative or uninhibited behaviour.

What they mean is that in some cases, flaming within a virtual group is an established or developing norm (hence the various FAQs about the acceptability or otherwise of flaming), and so occurrences of flaming in these groups could be counted as normative. When flaming breaks out in a group where it is not the norm, they suggest that it might be an attempt to establish a competing norm for the group.

However, the social identity model of flaming as outlined by Lea *et al.* (1992) is somewhat disingenuous. According to Lea *et al.*, SIDE 'predicts that uninhibited behaviour is more likely when a social group becomes salient that includes uninhibited behaviour among its norms' (p. 107). This argument is circular – frequent occurrences of flaming suggest that flaming would be normative for that group. Outbursts of flaming in groups where it does not usually occur indicate perhaps an emerging or competing norm. Finally, a group with little or no flaming suggests that flaming is not the norm for that group. Thus, as applied to flaming, SIDE becomes purely descriptive – it is not possible to assert that a behaviour is due to adherence (or otherwise) to norms because the norms are derived from the observed behaviour in the first place.

It could also be argued that the SIDE view of uninhibited computer-mediated communication as normative somewhat overplays the role of social identity. For instance, there is ample evidence that experimental participants are less inhibited when writing notes or completing questionnaires, particularly by computer, compared to face to face interview (Weisband and Kiesler, 1996). While there are a number of possible explanations for these effects (e.g. anonymity, increased self-focus when writing, desire to please experimenter), it would not be tenable to argue that the reason we find less inhibited answers to psychological measures answered on paper than in an interview is because of the activation of a social identity that happens to be linked to uninhibited behaviour.

A self-awareness explanation of flaming

The dual self-awareness (DSA) explanation of flaming rests on the proposed differential impact of CMC on private and public self-awareness. A reduction in public self-awareness should lead to a reduced concern for evaluation. Conversely, a heightening of private self-focus should lead to an increased focus on one's own attitudes, feelings and standards.

The DSA approach thus predicts that CMC would be likely to heighten people's focus on their own attitudes, goals and feelings, with a concomitant decrease in how concerned they were with the likelihood of being evaluated. Uninhibited communication, then, would be seen as representing a person's true feelings without the brake of evaluation concerns. For flaming, this explanation might also suggest how 'flame wars' might develop. Being privately self-aware also increases the likelihood of attributing events as being directed at oneself. It would seem possible, then, that a flame war between two people is in part due to their perceiving a slight as being directly addressed to them.

However, the DSA approach to flaming runs counter to the usual outcome of private self-awareness. According to Carver and Scheier (1981), private self-awareness triggers a self-regulatory process, where a person's behaviour is compared to certain standards and adjusted if possible. While it is possible that 'being pedantic' or 'arguing with strangers' is a guide for ideal behaviour for some people, it is not likely to be for many. However, in this respect the close links between dual self-awareness models and SIDE suggests that perhaps in group inter-actions, private self-awareness leads to behaviour in accordance with an established or developing norm.

A more likely explanation for flaming on-line is that occurrences of flaming are due to a combination of the users' own goals, motives, needs and so on, the designed elements of the interaction (e.g. automatic quot-ing) and the more universal aspects of the Internet and their impact on self-awareness and accountability. Importantly, it is likely to be only through the process of interaction that these factors lead to flaming. That is, when a user sits at his or her computer, while some of the vari-ables needed to encourage disinhibited, negative communication are in place, it is only through interaction that these factors find a 'voice'.

Person × situation and flaming

Although most explanations of flaming suggest that aspects of the media cause flaming, Smolensky et al. (1990) found that uninhibited communication was more prevalent in groups who were familiar with each other (i.e. pre-acquainted) compared to unacquainted groups. Smolensky et al. also found that extraversion was correlated with the amount of uninhibited speech. Similarly, Aiken and Waller (2000) found that the same people engaged in flaming across two different discussions. Sherry Turkle quotes one MUD user saying:

I was always happy when I got into a fight in the MUD. I remem-ber doing that before tests. I would go to the MUD, pick a fight, yell at people, blow a couple of things up, take the test and then go out for a drink. (Turkle, 1995, p. 189)

So, although aspects of the media might enable or even encourage flaming, a complete explanation needs to include the characteristics of the flamer, as well as the technology they use to flame.

Internet relationships: too close too soon?

The use of the Internet to form romantic relationships is a hot topic. Recent self-help books on the topic include titles such as *The Joy of Cybersex* (Levine, 1998). While many accounts of on-line relationship formation and cybersex paint an essentially rosy picture, the downside of cyberrelationships can be equally compelling. For instance, there are many reported cases of outright deception within cyberrelationships, and the prevalence of cyber-affairs threatens, according to some commentators, to force up the divorce rate in the USA.

Deception and misrepresentation in on-line relationships

When 27-year-old Briton Trevor Tasker met American Wynema Shumate on the Internet he was smitten by the seemingly attractive young woman. He left his job in the UK and flew the 3,000 miles to be with her. When they met at the airport, he was surprised to be greeted by a 'twenty stone pensioner', who admitted to sending him pictures from 30 years ago. Rather than turn around and return home, Tasker went on to spend a week in Shumate's home. It was only when he discovered the dead body of her former employer amongst the frozen food in the freezer that he notified the local police and left.

Although the case of Tasker is an extreme example of Internet deception, it does illustrate the potential for deception within a developing cyberrelationship. Of course, such deceptions are just as possible in real life as on-line: for instance, a study conducted by Metts (1989) found that 92 per cent of people report lying to their romantic partner at least once. However, the Internet does provide the opportunity for greater levels of misrepresentation, particularly in the early stages of a relationship when commitment is low, and self-presentation and enhancement agendas are paramount (Tice *et al.*, 1995). In an empirical study of commitment and misrepresentation on the Internet, Cornwell and Lundgren (2001) surveyed 80 chat-room users, half about their 'realspace' relationships, and half about their cyberspace relationships. They found that 'realspace' relationships were considered to be more serious, with greater feelings of commitment, than the cyberrelationship participants. Both groups, however, reported similar levels of satisfaction and potential for 'emotional growth' with regard to romantic relationships. Cornwell and Lundgren went on to ask about whether the participants had misrepresented themselves to their partner in a number of areas: their interests (e.g. hobbies, musical tastes); their age; their background; their appearance and 'misrepresentation of yourself in any other way' (p. 203). Participants responded using either yes or no to each question, and their score was summed into a misrepresentation measure. The results of the misrepresentation questions are shown in Table 3.4.

So, the level of misrepresentation was remarkably low in both cyberspace and realspace relationships. The only significant differences in misrepresentation were for age and physical characteristics, which may represent degrees of freedom as much as anything else (it is difficult to misrepresent your appearance to someone sitting opposite you). The overall level of misrepresentation did not differ between Internet and 'realspace' relationships.

It would seem then that deception on the Internet in the development of romantic relationships is relatively rare, and that when it does occur it tends to be about either age or physical appearance (which may be one reason for using the Internet to form a relationship in the first place). Moreover, misrepresentation in these cases might be best thought of as creative self-presentation rather than outright deception.

For instance, imagine your on-line sweetheart asks for a picture. While outright deception would be sending a picture of someone else,

Table 3.4   Misrepresentation in cyberspace and realspace relationships

Misrepresentation of...	Cyberspace relationship	Realspace relationship
Interests	15%	20%
Age	23%	5%
Background	18%	10%
Physical characteristics	28%	13%
Other	15%	5%

Source: Cornwell and Lundgren (2001, p. 207).

you are also likely to spend some time thinking about what picture to send. If you chose a picture from a couple of years back, or perhaps one that made you look particularly handsome or pretty, would this be deception? Perhaps it is more analogous to the use of a favourite outfit for a first date. In support of this proposal, there is some evidence from McKenna *et al.* (2002) that it is people who are best able to present their 'true' self on-line who form relationships. McKenna *et al.* (Study 1) surveyed posters to 20 Usenet newsgroups about their levels of social anxiety and loneliness, as well as whether or not the person felt more able to reveal their 'real' self on-line than in 'real life'. They found that those with potential problems expressing their real self in real life (for instance, because of social anxiety) were more likely to say that they were able to express their real self on-line than face to face. And, the more people were able to express aspects of the 'real me' on the Internet that are normally inhibited in real life, the more likely they were to have formed strong attachments to people they met on-line, extending to phone calls and meeting face to face. In a second study, McKenna *et al.* recontacted the sample from the first study two years later. Fully 71 per cent of the romantic relationships reported two years earlier were still intact, a rate comparable with most studies of 'real life' relationships.

So, deception in close relationships is not an all-or-nothing. The Internet (and other mediated courtships) provide space not only for deception and creative self-presentation, but also for the expression of a more authentic, *truer* self that is normally inhibited from expression in face to face interaction.

Idealisation in on-line relationships

It is also possible that this process of communication leads to the idealisation of one's romantic partner. For instance, Stafford and Reske (1990) studied 71 undergraduate couples, 34 of whom were geographically close, and 37 who had long-distance relationships. The long-distance couples lived, on average, 422 miles apart. They found that long-distance couples, compared to those geographically close, scored higher on measures of relationship satisfaction, quality of communication, romantic love and idealisation of their partner. The percentage of the couples' interaction spent face to face was negatively correlated with these measures (except for love), while the percentage spent via letters was positively correlated with all measures, including romantic love for the partner. The couples were followed up six months and one year after the study. After six months, 24 of the 34 geographically close couples were still together, while all 25 of the contactable long-distance couples were still dating. At one year, 12 of the 16 geographically close couples contactable were still together, compared to 23 of the 25 long-distance couples contacted. It would seem, then, that long-distance couples are happier with their relationships, more in love, and the prognosis for the relationship is more positive. Although not significant, the 'still togethers' spent more of their early interaction by letter and telephone than the 'not together' couples, and less of their interaction face to face.

A second process heightening the sense of intimacy between people on the Internet is self-disclosure. Self-disclosure is used to develop a relationship from its early stages to later stages that rely on trust

---

Case study: Deception online

June '98 – I wish to God I would have come to your site 9 months ago! I started chatting in a chat room for my favorite musical group. I became a 'regular' and subsequently met a man there. I wasn't looking for a relationship but we really hit it off. To make a long story short, I ended up spending a small fortune to fly to Australia to meet him. (I live in the eastern US).

I sent him packages because he claimed he was too poor to buy things for himself. It turns out everything this man had me believing was a total lie. He was at least 10 years older than his pictures, horribly overweight and the personality was totally opposite of his online presence. He was rude, selfish, inconsiderate and had the manners of a rattlesnake. I knew that he had two previous online romances, but didn't listen to my intuition. I was so much in love with this man and I'm still hurting over the whole thing. After I arrived in Australia I found out that he had been having an affair with his best friend's wife! I've come to realize that an affair or online relationship is the only type of relationship he is capable of having. He is too selfish to invest the time and money on anything 'real'. That way he is able to come and go as he pleases and has no one to answer to. I've recently learned that he has yet another victim cornered.

(From www.saferdating/lies.htm)

---

and the sharing of intimate details and vulnerabilities (Archer, 1980; Laurenceau *et al.*, 1998). If the Internet encourages self-disclosure (see Joinson, 2001a, and Chapter 5 of this book), then the sense of trust between two people may well be higher than is truly warranted.

The critical issue is whether idealisation and a heightened sense of intimacy of romantic attachments on the Internet are negative or positive. Although the study of Stafford and Reske (1990) suggests that restricted communication leads to higher levels of satisfaction in a relationship, it is unclear how this might translate when the couple move geographically closer to be together. The reason many of the geographically close relationships in the Stafford and Reske study failed was because the couples were not suited. Thus, courtship is a selection process for a long-term partner, and the longer a couple date before marriage, the greater the likelihood of the marriage succeeding (Lewis and Spanier, 1979), presumably because the selection process has been more rigorous. If Internet relationships do involve idealisation of partners, then it is possible that a couple who commit while still holding idealised notions of one another are likely to come down with a bumpy landing once the idealisation (via limited communication channels) has gone. The story above provides one example of the potential impact of idealisation via the Internet, and the rude awakening that can occur once the couple meet face to face.

In the above case, there is evidence of both the intensity of love that can arise through on-line interaction (and presumably idealisation) and creative self-presentation, and the problems associated with both. Although many an Internet romance ends happily, the dangers of creative self-presentation and idealisation mean that, for many people, the transfer from on-line to off-line relationships will not be successful. Bargh *et al.* (2002, Study 3) studied idealisation within pairs of students chatting using a CMC programme for 40 minutes. Before they interacted, the participants completed measures designed to assess the attributes they would like in an *ideal friend* and an *ideal romantic partner*. They then chatted either face to face or using an Internet chat system, and then rated how much they liked their interaction partner and wrote ten attributes to describe them. Bargh *et al.* found, first, that those who talked on the Internet liked the other partner more than those who met face to face. Second, in the Internet condition, but not the face to face condition, if the participant liked their interaction partner, then they tended to project the attributes of an ideal close friend onto the partner. Bargh *et al.* conclude that the idealisation of partners on the Internet

> is a double-edged sword. Even for people who are not presently looking for friends or romantic partners, these features of Internet communication are likely to be seductive. Before one realizes it, one can find oneself in a friendship or intimate relationship one wasn't looking for and which in fact causes complications and difficulty within an established social circle and home life. (Bargh *et al.*, 2002, pp. 18–19)

On-line infidelity

The web site Saferdating (http://www.saferdating.com) has a large number of moving stories of husbands and wives cast aside by their current partner following an Internet affair. The case study outlined below is typical.

Case study: Online cheating

In November 1999, I noticed a change in my husband, he was being nasty toward me and always started arguments. I knew something wasn't right. I asked him if there was another woman, he said no. I told him something is not right. One day I seen him come out of the post office opening mail, our mail is always delivered at our home. I confronted him several days later about him having a post office box. He denied it several times until I told him I was in my car and seen him coming out of the post office opening mail. He said he wanted his privacy, I told him it's a sudden change after 23 yrs. of marriage. Well, he got me fired up. I asked him where the phone bill was for the past two months, he said that I never look at the phone bill why now? Through the phone company I had them to send me copies. He had been making phone calls to New Zealand. The phone bill was outrageous. He said he made a bad mistake doing the phone calls and apologised. He thought that was the end of it. Wrong! that even got me more agitated. He was telling me that he talked to this woman that was married and a school teacher and they were only friends. Friends don't run up phone bills and sneak around and get P.O. boxes. That just made it worst, I knew he was lying. I hurt inside so bad I thought my chest was going to explode. If I begged him to tell me what was going on and he would say nothing. If I did something right or wrong I had to know, I wasn't about to let almost 24 yrs of marriage go down the tube. I took his hard drive out of his computer and put it in mine.

Boy! did I find out. He was telling this woman how much he loved her and she was doing the same. She was sending him sexual fantasies in the email and anyone could tell this was not her imagination she had copied this from some book or got this off the internet, they had been sending each other gifts and I found out that she had called my house and he sent her money for her phone bill. I was a topic of their discussion it goes on and on. I called him at work and told him what I had done and what I found out he came home and told me I had no right taking his hard drive out and I told him he had no right hurting me, and acting like it was nothing. I was so upset and hurt I felt like taking a gun and blowing my brains out, I knew better I just wanted the hurting to stop. He told me that she was the most intelligent woman he's ever talked too. He was adding insult to injury and they were only friends. Lord it just got worse, I told him friends my #@$%. He said he liked talking to her. That he loved me and that he would never leave me. I asked him if he would talk to her in front of me and tell her he didn't love her, he wouldn't do it. He said no one is going to try and make him do anything. I asked him. That even hurt worse. I don't trust him anymore. What can I do? I hurt so bad and my life is pure hell at the moment. Why can't he understand what he has done? This isn't over yet I'm not saying anything else to him about it, I'm just letting him think everything is okay.

(From http://www.saferdating.com/adultery.htm)

On-line adultery, according to the president of the American Academy of Matrimonial Lawyers (Quittner, 1997) has led to an increasing number of divorce cases. According to Young *et al.* (1999):

It is hard to image ... a wife who would never pick up the telephone to dial a 900-number could engage in erotic chat or phone sex with men she met online. It is equally difficulty to understand how stable marriages of 15, 20, or 25 years end because of a three or four month old cyberaffair. Yet, these are typical scenarios plaguing many couples today. (p. 1)

Young *et al.* apply the ACE (anonymity, convenience and escape) model to explain Internet adultery (see the Internet addiction section at the start of this chapter). They also propose a number of warning signs for spotting an Internet affair, including:

- *Changes in sleeping patterns* e.g. The use of chat rooms late at night.
- *A demand for privacy* e.g. Increasing secrecy or privacy concern about their Internet use.
- *Evidence of lying* e.g. Hiding phone or credit card bills.
- *Personality changes* e.g. Becoming cold and withdrawn.
- *Loss of interest in sex* e.g. An Internet affair might provide sexual satisfaction via mutual masturbation, so it is likely the partner will be less interested in love-making.
- *Declining investment in relationship* e.g. Internet adulterers might not be so interested in spending quality time together as a couple.

Aligned with the ability to present as single, and the relative anonymity, safety and convenience of the Internet for conducting affairs, on-line adultery may well be subject to the same effects of creative self-presentation and idealisation described earlier. This pattern of interaction may well also enter a self-fulfilling cycle on the Internet (Walther, 1996). We tend to like people who like us, so idealisation is likely to lead to higher levels of affiliation as an interaction progresses. For the on-line adulterer, this represents a potent combination that might even lead to the break-up of a previously happy marriage.

Depression, Deception and Pornography: The Dark Side of Life On-line

Although the Internet was originally conceived as a network linking computers, it was not long before the early users developed and used e-mail to forge virtual communities.

Stone (1991) argues that virtual communities are 'incontrovertibly social spaces in which people still meet face to face, but under new definitions of both "meet" and "face to face"' (p. 85). An early question posed by researchers was whether or not these communities were 'real' or were 'pseudocommunities' – a pattern of relating that, while looking like highly interpersonal interaction, is essentially impersonal (Beniger, 1987). The essence of a pseudo-community is a lack of sincerity, or genuineness (Jones, 1995). It is perhaps not surprising then that Rheingold asks:

> Is telecommunication culture capable of becoming something more than what Scott Peck calls a 'pseudo-community' where people lack the genuine personal commitments to one another that form the bedrock of genuine community? ... Is the human need for community going to be the next technology commodity? (Rheingold, 1993, pp. 60–1)

As Haythornwaite *et al.* (1998) note, the existence of virtual community is not usually questioned by those who have experienced it.

Jones (1995) reports that traditionally community has been categorised into three distinct types:

- Community as solidarity institutions
- Community as primary interaction
- Community as institutionally distinct groups.

Jones notes that virtual communities do not seem to fit any of these categories particularly neatly, although they might best be seen as institutionally distinct groups. Although the argument that virtual communities can be best characterised as groups with a shared interest (e.g. Licklider and Taylor, 1968) has some validity, groups based on shared interests are usually seen are relatively 'weak' because of the limited breadth of conversational topics. Thus, in this case, while on-line communities might be 'real', they are only relatively weak versions of 'real life' communities or networks.

The debate about the exact nature of virtual community has left a legacy of doubt as to whether or not on-line community membership provides the same support or benefits of membership as membership of a real-life community. Indeed, some research even suggested that there might be a quantifiable cost in terms of mental health and social isolation due to Internet use.

Internet use and psychological well-being

In 1998, a group of researchers led by Robert Kraut and Sara Kiesler published the preliminary findings from the HomeNet project at Carnegie Mellon University (Kraut, *et al.*, 1998). The HomeNet project gave computers with an Internet connection to 256 people in 93 households in Pittsburgh, Pennsylvania (following withdrawals, the sample was 169 people in 73 households). They tracked their Internet use and mental well-being over two years. Their conclusion? 'Greater use of the Internet was associated with small, but statistically significant declines in social involvement ... and with increases in loneliness ... Greater use of the Internet was also associated with increases in depression' (p. 1028).

This finding not only drew an enormous amount of media coverage (e.g. 'Sad, lonely world discovered in cyberspace' was a front-page headline in the *New York Times*; Harmon, 1998), but also a large amount of scrutiny and criticism from psychologists involved in

Internet research. It seemed paradoxical that a medium used mainly for social ends seemed to be de-socialising. One possibility is that the Internet is another technology that tends to 'privatise' leisure time (like other essentially private entertainment like watching television or reading a book), and so people have less time for social activities and involvement. However, Kraut *et al.* rejected this argument because the 'major use of the Internet is social' (1998, p. 1029).

Kraut and his colleagues go on to suggest that the ties created between people on the Internet might be generally weak, whereas ties built in real life tend to be strong. A strong tie is characterised by 'frequent contact, deep feelings of affection and obligation ... that generally buffer people from life's stresses and that lead to better social and psychological outcomes' (Kraut *et al.*, 1998, p. 1019). Conversely, weak network ties are characterised by 'superficial and easily broken bonds, infrequent contact and narrow focus' (p. 1019). Thus, although the main use of the Internet in their sample was for interpersonal communication, the ties that bound these people communicating were weak, and so did not offer the same psychologial support as a strong (i.e. face to face) tie. For instance, the HomeNet researchers point out that few of their sample made new friends on-line (although they only seem to count people who met FtF at some point in this respect). They also argue that because on-line friends are not physically close at hand, they are unable to offer tangible support, nor are they likely to understand the 'context' for conversation, 'making discussion more difficult' (p. 1030). They continue with two case studies from their sample which imply that the Internet is not suitable for more delicate or emotional subjects, with participants reverting to the telephone in these situations. In the first case, one participant noticed how although she liked e-mail contact with her daughter at college, if she needed to support her when homesick or depressed the mother tended to revert to the telephone. In the second case, a clergyman used the Internet to swap sermon ideas, but used the telephone for advice about negotiating his contract.

Critiques of the Internet paradox study

However, the picture is not quite so clear-cut. First, it has been argued that Kraut *et al.* use correlation to infer causality (Shapiro, 1999). It is just as reasonable that people who were feeling depressed turned to the Internet rather than that the Internet caused depression. For instance, lonely people tend to watch television more than the average non-lonely person (Canary and Spitzberg, 1993), although again which is cause and which is effect is difficult to disentangle. Without a control condition in the HomeNet project, the experimenters could not tell whether increased Internet use was a cause or an effect (Shapiro, 1999).

A second problem was that the HomeNet study involved families with children who were due to enter college. It would be expected that if your child went to college, there would be both reduced social contact in the home (they have, after all, moved away), while the family might communicate by e-mail more to keep in touch.

A similar problem occurs with the selection of their sample: parents involved in the running of a local school. People who are at an extreme end of a continuum (in this case, community involvement) tend to reduce their involvement over time (a methodological phenomenon called regression to the mean). So, the HomeNet participants would be expected to reduce their involvement whether they had computers or not. Again, there was no control condition, so it is impossible to say (Shapiro, 1999).

Rierdan (1999) argues that the measures used by Kraut *et al.* did not really measure depression. Kraut *et al.* used a shortened form of the 'Centre for Epidemiological Studies Depression Scale' (CES-D) to measure depression. According to Rierdan, the interpretation of low scores on this measure is particularly problematic. Items on the CES-D are scored on a four-point scale, with zero indicating the absence of symptoms. The average score for the HomeNet sample before Internet use on this scale was 0.73, afterwards it was 0.62 (so, for the overall sample, depression dropped during the study). Rierdan suggests that the sample thus showed very few signs of mental distress, questioning the headlines that resulted from the press release. A second point Rierdan makes is that the size of the effects linking Internet use to CES-D scores are low, and that for some of the analyses the significance level of $p < 0.07$ is adopted rather than the more usual $p < 0.05$. Using the rule of thumb proposed by Cohen (1977), Rierdan notes that a large effect size is in the region of 0.50, a medium 0.30 and a small 0.10. She also notes that the effect sizes linking hours of Internet use to CES-D scores are 0.15 and 0.19, which qualify as 'small'. She concludes that such small effect sizes should not be used to draw implications for public policy.

Wastlund *et al.* (2001) surveyed 329 undergraduate students on their Internet use and mental health (using measures of optimism, personality, loneliness, daily hassles and depression). They found no correlation between the measures of mental health and Internet use (surfing and number of e-mails sent). However, in their sample young people tended to use the Internet more, and also to experience greater psychological distress. However, Internet use and psychological distress were not related. Wastlund et al. suggest that age may have been a confounding variable in the HomeNet study.

Moody (2001) argues that loneliness should be divided into emotional and social loneliness. Emotional loneliness comes from the lack of an intimate relationship, while social loneliness comes from a feeling of being marginalised, of not belonging. Moody hypothesised that Internet users might suffer increases in emotional loneliness, but would feel less socially lonely because of the time spent on-line in communities. He sampled 166 undergraduate students on Internet use and social and emotional loneliness. He found a significant *negative* correlation between the frequency of Internet activity and social loneliness, but no correlation between the frequency of Internet activity and emotional loneliness. However, the size of the participants' Internet network of friends was significantly positively correlated with emotional loneliness, while the size of the participants' social network of face to face friends was negatively correlated with emotional loneliness. So, according to the results of Moody's study, Internet use seems to decrease feelings of social loneliness, but might be associated with increased feelings of emotional loneliness. Of course, both the studies by Moody and Wastlund et al. are 'one-shot' correlation studies that cannot make causal claims.

Similar criticisms of the HomeNet research were proposed by Katelyn McKenna and John Bargh (2000). They began by noting that new technology is often associated with fear stories – there was even a movie called *Murder by Television*. They also note that an earlier Carnegie Mellon study (Rimm, 1995) that claimed that the Internet was 'awash with pornography' was not only based on false premises and quickly discredited, but that the ramifications of the initial press coverage of these faulty results were still being felt (e.g. the doomed Computer Decency Act in the USA).

McKenna and Bargh point out that any critique of the strength of the results (e.g. that the change in depression scores due to Internet use was less than 1 per cent) is meaningless because 'for the entire group of participants, the average reported level of depression after 2 years of being on the Internet was less than it had been before being on the Internet' (2000, p. 59). They also note that although Kraut et al. (1998) are correct in noting that their participants' local social circle decreased (from 24 to 23 people), their wider social network increased from 25 to 32. So, overall, Internet use seems to be associated with a widening in the number of friends and acquaintances. It is also worth questioning whether a small change (e.g. from 24 to 23) is meaningful as well as being statistically significant.

Support for the Internet paradox

Kiesler and Kraut (1999) accept Rierdan's critique of the size of the effect they report, but reply that 'The importance of our results is not in the size of the effects, which were admittedly small, but in their direction. Even small negative changes experienced by tens of millions of people can be socially significant' (p. 783).

Kiesler and Kraut also reply to the critique of Shapiro by noting that although regression to the mean might explain changes in the group as a whole, it does not explain why only those using the Internet a lot experienced heightened mental distress. They further note that although the causal chain Shapiro proposes (that increased loneliness leads to more Internet use) is plausible, it is not supported by their time-series data. They found that measures of loneliness did not predict subsequent Internet use either a month or two after the measures, or during the whole study.

The Internet paradox effect reported by Kraut et al. (1998) has also received some limited support through replications and some reformulation. For instance, LaRose et al. (2001) reformulated the link between Internet use and depression to include users' experience and self-efficacy. The hypothesis of LaRose et al. proposes that novice Internet users experience a number of problems (e.g. computer crashes) that can cause stress and perhaps depression. According to a self-efficacy approach, depression is caused by an inability to control those stressors that can influence the quality of your life (Bandura, 1977).

So, the impact of the Internet on depression might be mediated by users' sense of self-efficacy. To test this, LaRose et al. surveyed 171 undergraduate students on their Internet usage, Internet self-efficacy (e.g. 'I feel confident using the Internet to collect data') and depression (using CES-D). Using path-analytic techniques, they found no direct link between Internet use and depression. However, they did find a positive link between Internet usage and self-efficacy, which was negatively correlated to Internet stress, which was linked to the users' reporting of daily hassles, which finally was linked to depression. A second path linked Internet use (in the form of e-mail) to social support, and then to reduced daily hassles and depression. They conclude that Internet use to seek support can alleviate depression and the experience of daily hassles, while stressful interactions with the Internet, and low Internet self-efficacy to face these stresses, rather than Internet use *per se*, led to depression.

The Stanford Institute for the Quantitative Study of Society

The key findings of the HomeNet study received limited support from a study of Internet use conducted by the Stanford Institute for the Quantitative Study of Society (Nie and Erbring, 2000). In this study, Nie and Erbring surveyed 4,113 people in 2,689 households with access to WebTV. In keeping with the work of the HomeNet research group, SIQSS found that e-mail was the most common Internet use. Of particular interest is the finding that Internet use was associated with reduced social activity – for users of the Internet for more than five hours a week, 8 per cent report attending fewer social events, 13 per cent report spending less time with friends or family, and 26 per cent report talking less to friends or family on the telephone. Even for Internet users clocking less than an hour per week, 9 per cent report talking less on the telephone to family and friends. This trend is illustrated in Figure 4.1.

The SIQSS study also showed that Internet use seems to be to the detriment of traditional forms of mass media. Increased Internet use was linked to both decreased watching of television and reading newspapers (see Figure 4.2).

However, the SIQSS study is difficult to interpret for a number of reasons. First, its not clear how much of a reduction there was in either social activity or use of traditional media – users were simply asked whether, since the Internet, each activity has decreased, increased or remained unchanged. Also, the method of dividing the sample by hours of Internet use tends to make any effect look larger than it actually is. For instance, those using the Internet more than five hours a week made up only 35.2 per cent of the sample, so from the population as a whole, only 8.6 per cent reported spending *less* time with family and friends, and 6 per cent report spending *more* time with family and friends. So, from a sample of 1,690 responses, just 145 participants reported less social interaction due to the Internet, compared to 101 who reported more social interaction. So, although the figures initially look impressive, they actually represent a small proportion of the sample, and overall there would be no

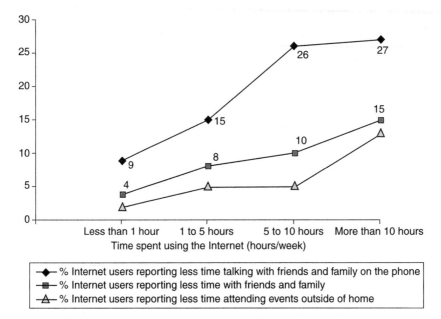

Figure 4.1 Internet use and social isolation

Source: Nie and Erbring (2000).

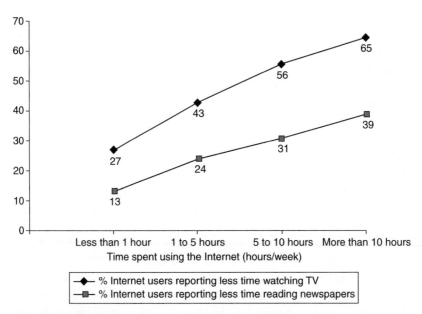

Figure 4.2 Internet use and traditional media

Source: Nie and Erbring (2000).

significant difference between those reporting decreased and those reporting increased social interaction.

Second, it is unclear whether or not, for instance, telephoning family and friends has been replaced by e-mailing, or is due to the household phone line being tied up with Internet access. Data from the Pew Internet and American Life Project (discussed below) suggest that e-mail might be used to communicate with distant family. Finally, the report is based on self-reporting of social activity and use of mass media, which is unreliable unless tied to a very specific time frame (e.g. who did you speak to yesterday?).

The Pew Internet and American Life Project

Another attempt to map the impact of the Internet on everyday life comes from the Pew Internet and American Life Project funded by the charitable Pew Foundation. The Pew Internet Project (www.pewinternet. org) surveys Internet users daily by telephone, enabling them to ask what activities they engaged in 'yesterday'. The findings of the Pew Project (e.g. Howard *et al.*, 2001) suggest that Internet use enhances social contact, rather that diminishes it. From their survey of 6,413 Internet users questioned about their Internet use, Howard *et al.* report that 59 per cent of those who e-mail relatives say that it has increased the amount of contact they have with their main family contact. Similarly, 60 per cent of those who use e-mail to contact friends say that it has increased communication with their 'primary' friend contact. Nearly a third (31 per cent) of e-mail users report that they have begun communicating with a member of their family with whom they had no previous contact.

The analysis of Howard *et al.* of the Pew data set also yields some startling statistics about the impact of the Internet on social activity and social support. They found that, controlling for all other variables (like education and so on), those who have *ever* used the Internet were 24 per cent more likely to be able to turn to 'many people' for support than someone who had never used the Internet. An even stronger pattern emerges for telephone use: Internet users were 46 per cent more likely to have called a relative or friend to chat the previous day than non-Internet users.

The HomeNet sample revisited

Kraut *et al.* (2002) conducted two follow-up studies that also seem to cast serious doubt over the initial findings of the original HomeNet research. In Study 1, Kraut *et al.* (2002) followed up 208 of the original HomeNet participants. Unlike in the original study, Internet use was not associated with any changes in loneliness, depression or social involvement. An analysis at different time frames found that Internet use had a negative impact early on in the time cycle (when they were studying new users), but that this pattern reversed at later time points. So, once their users became more experienced (or the Internet developed or expanded), increased Internet use was associated with decreases in depression, and exerted no effect on loneliness.

In a second study, Kraut *et al.* compared computer purchasers (to half of whom they gave Internet access) with people who had recently bought a new television. Because so many of the computer buyers in the control condition independently got Internet access (85 per cent), the computer conditions were collapsed into one. As in the original HomeNet study, Kraut *et al.* (2002) asked participants to complete a battery of personality and well-being measures, as well as tests of their community involvement, trust in people and intentions to stay in the local area. Internet use was self-reported, although self-reports correlated moderately well with the log records of those provided with Internet access.

The results of Kraut *et al.* (2002) directly contradict those of the original HomeNet study (Kraut *et al.*, 1998). Specifically, *increased* Internet use was associated with

- Increases in the size of their local social circle ($p < 0.01$)
- Increases in the size of their distant social circle ($p < 0.01$)
- Increases in face to face interaction with family and friends ($p < 0.05$)
- More involvement with community activities ($p < 0.10$)
- Greater levels of trust in other people ($p < 0.05$)
- Increases in self-reported computer skill ($p < 0.001$).

Kraut *et al.* (2002) propose a 'rich get richer' hypothesis that states that the impact of the Internet on social involvement and well-being will be to amplify pre-existing differences between people (they also provide an alternative, that those worse off gain the most, a 'social compensation' hypothesis). They found moderate support for the 'rich get richer' hypothesis. For instance, for extraverts, increased Internet use was associated with decreases in reported levels of loneliness, negative affect and increased self-esteem and community involvement. For introverts, increased Internet use was associated with higher levels of reported loneliness and decreased levels of community involvement.

So, the follow-up work by Kraut *et al.* (2002) seems to provide both a refutation and refinement of the original Internet paradox findings. The general contention that Internet use inevitably leads to decreases in mental well-being was refuted, and, in many cases, the opposite found to be the case. However, the Internet paradox may still hold true for some people. Specifically, for introverts, increased Internet use seems to amplify any social isolation or loneliness, while for extraverts, Internet use amplifies their existing levels of social involvement. To a degree this may be linked to the different uses of the Internet exhibited by introverts and extraverts. Kraut *et al.* (2002) found that higher scores on their measure of extraversion were linked to an increased use of the Internet for social purposes like keeping up with family and friends ($r = 0.10$, $p < 0.05$), and to meet new people on-line and use chat rooms ($r = 0.11$, $p < 0.05$). But, as Kraut *et al.* note, these associations are weak, and they do not seem to predict overall Internet use. However, the possibility of Internet use interacting with pre-existing psychological states certainly warrants further attention.

Kraut *et al.* (2002) propose a number of possible reasons for the discrepancy between the original Internet paradox findings and their later work. One proposal is that their Internet users became more experienced, meaning that the novelty of some 'unrewarding' Internet activities has worn off, leaving them free to concentrate on psychologically rewarding activities. While this might account for the changes found in Study 1, most of the participants in the second study were new Internet users, suggesting that it might not be a complete explanation. Alternatively, the nature of the Internet may well have changed since the original Internet paradox study. As access has increased, the potential of the Internet to maintain social relations with friends and family has increased. Also, more tools (e.g. instant messaging, digital cameras, HTML editors) were either developed or became accessible that enable families to communicate and share news, pictures and so on.

Concluding thoughts

What are we to make of all this? First, I doubt we'll be reading the front page of the *New York Times* exclaiming 'Happy, friendly world discovered in cyberspace' anytime soon. Second, it also illustrates the problems associated with study of the social and psychological impact of the Internet. Although earlier technologies, as we have seen, were associated with various utopian and dystopian outcomes, their true impact was not well-understood until much later. For those academics working on psychology and the Internet, it is easy to forget that we are still dealing with a new, developing technology. Third, the assumption that relationships forged or maintained on-line are somehow less satisfying, fulfilling or meaningful that those forged face to face (e.g. Putnam, 2000) needs careful examination. Research investigating educational uses of CMC has tended to produce sceptical results (e.g. Tolmie and Boyle, 2000) because more attention is paid to the efficacy of on-line as opposed to face to face teaching. While participation rates might be low in education CMC, this is rarely compared to levels of participation in equivalent face to face tutorials or lectures. For any student who has sat in a lecture hall with hundreds of fellow students, or a single person who has experienced the quality of discourse in a noisy night club, the notion that face to face interaction is inherently more satisfying than a virtual equivalent would no doubt ring hollow.

The HomeNet programme of research also highlights the methodological problems of conceptualising the nature of a 'strong' tie on the Internet. If a romance develops on the Internet, a strong tie will quite likely lead to a meeting face to face. For instance, America Online (AOL) estimates that 10,000 marriages have come to be through its on-line dating service. Once a relationship leads to marriage or cohabitation, it is extremely likely that Internet contact ceases between the two parties, apart from maybe 'for old time's sake'. So, in that sense, the Internet is an enabling technology rather than a replacing one.

In a non-romantic setting, the prevalence of 'weak' ties is likely to be relatively high because most groupings on the Internet are based on shared interest, so the focus of any interpersonal communication is likely to be limited to that specific area (part of the definition of a 'weak tie'). But, as we saw earlier, the combination of shared group membership and visual anonymity can create highly socially motivated behaviours (Spears and Lea, 1992). Perhaps the social network ties are weak in a traditional sense, but the ties that bind a group together in a shared sense of identity are high.

Social support on-line: the dangers of bad advice, victimisation and demarginalised deviance

As we have seen, the ability to seek social support on the Internet can provide an invaluable buffer to the stresses we face in everyday life.

However, the 'support' received, and advice given on such lists is not always positive. For instance, Worotynec (2000) studied two child-care e-mail lists for four years. Alongside more positive interactions, she reports numerous occasions of 'venting', when children are called 'brats', and subject headers refer to a child as 'devil's spawn', 'screamer', 'the wild thing' and 'hateful child' (pp. 800–1). Many of the day care providers are scathing of the parents of the children they care for. In one e-mail exchange (the 'devil's spawn'), one child care provider asks about a 7-month-old boy who, since joining her care three days ago, has cried constantly. Worotynec notes than none of the replies focused on either the term 'devil's spawn' for a 7-month-old baby, or the reasonableness of his behaviour given the situation. All posts gave unconditional support to the care giver, with one even proposing that the parents might be on drugs. The common consensus on the list was to lock the child away in another room. When the child is removed to different day care by his mother, the original author shows, according to Worotynec, some evidence of self-reflection that is quickly quashed by the other group members. Worotynec concludes that the endless venting with little or no self-reflection by day care providers is a 'wasteful exercise and ultimate contributor to poor quality child-care for children' (p. 808). It is also possible that the nature of the e-mail list (e.g. venting, name-calling of parents and children, unconditional support of other care givers) led to the acceptance of practices that, at the least, were not child-centred, and, at worst, potentially damaging to the child. In this sense, the community fostered on-line led to the legitimisation of negative attitudes and approaches (and might have led to them becoming more extreme or at least grounded in social reality), and so may well have led to the continuation of these behaviours.

The legitimisation of behaviour is conceptually similar to the notion of the demarginalisation of identities on-line (McKenna and Bargh, 1998). McKenna and Bargh found that participation in on-line communities led to users feeling less estranged from society. If the identity in question is potentially dangerous (e.g. anorexia, pro-suicide, paedophilia), then the experience of support on-line may well lead to the demarginalisation and legitimisation of negative, harmful behaviours.

Finn and Banach (2000) further argue that women can be subject to victimisation when seeking 'human services' on-line. They give the example of one 'counselling' service that seems to provide 'racist, sexist and homophobic' advice (p. 245). While sites like this are essentially a regulatory issue, Finn and Banach also argue that social support sites, because of the 'disinhibitory' effect of the Internet, may also leave users open to abuse in the form of profanity, personal attacks or seduction. However, these issues are not restricted to on-line counselling, and presumably anyone seeking professional help should look for the same accreditation of professionals as they would expect off-line. In addition, cases of flaming in on-line social support are remarkably hard to find.

Deception and gender-bending in on-line communities

The issue of deception in Internet interaction is not restricted to romantic relationships. Indeed, it would seem that the majority of on-line deception occurs not in one-to-one relationships, but rather in on-line communities in the form of MUDs and bulletin boards (Donath, 1999). At times this deception might be warranted and should be encouraged in some instances (e.g. seeking social support anonymously). In these cases, the Internet is simply providing a high-tech version of the old 'my friend has a problem' level of deception in search of support. Another type of arguably acceptable deception in MUDs is gender-bending, that is, males presenting themselves as females and vice versa.

For instance, Bruckman (1993) notes that 'without makeup, special clothing or risk of social stigma, gender becomes malleable in MUDs'. However, there has been little research into either the prevalence or impact of identity manipulation on-line. A number of 'educated guesses' have posited that most IRC usernames are gender-neutral, thus at least allowing for gender-bending (Danet, 1998). Similarly, it is also estimated that more men gender-bend than women – Stone (1993) reports that the ratio of males to females on a Japanese site is 4:1, but that on the actual site, the number of male presenters to female presenters is 3:1.

Gender and communication style

According to Standage (1999), most telegraph operators claimed to be able to spot not only individual operators by their Morse coding style, but also to be able to identify a female operator easily. Standage quotes an article from the *Western Electrician* in 1891 stating that: 'Ordinarily an operator can tell a woman the moment he hears her working the wire. He tells by her touch on the key. Women, as a rule, telegraphers say, do not touch the key of their instrument as firmly as men do' (p. 127). If it were possible to spot gender by the style of Morse code tapping, it is reasonable to assume that experienced Internet users should be able to spot males and females on-line as easily. The work of Herring (e.g. Herring, 1993) suggests that many of the face to face differences between men and women transfer to CMC. Herring (1993) reports that men tend to use more self-promotion, sarcasm, insults and strong assertions, and to post issue- or information-related messages. Meanwhile, women are more likely to hedge, suggest ideas, express doubt and to post personal topics and questions.

Savicki *et al.* (1996) analysed 2,692 messages posted on 27 discussion groups for language content and gender. They found that groups involving higher proportions of men tended to use more fact-oriented language, while groups with higher proportions of females tended to show more self-disclosure and attempts at tension prevention and reduction. Thomson and Murachver (2001, Study One) asked 35 participants (19 females and 16 males) to send at least six messages to a 'net pal' of the same gender. The messages were then coded on linguistic style and content. The results indicated that females tended to post more references to emotion, more personal information about themselves, more modals or hedges (e.g. I *sort of* agree with you) and more intensive adverbs (e.g. the game was *really* good). In a follow-up study, Thomson and Murachver (2001, Study Two) showed 78 participants a selection of messages from Study One, and asked them to rate the gender of the author using a six-point scale (1 = definitely written by a female, 6 = definitely written by a male). Of the 16 messages shown, the gender of the author was correctly identified by a majority of participants for 14 (the percentage of correct answers ranged from 62 per cent to 95 per cent). It would seem, then, that the differences in language used by males and females does make identification of gender possible during CMC. Thomson and Murachver (2001, Study Three) also developed their own messages based on the criteria identified in Study One. They found that gender predictions followed the use of language as predicted. The 'female' message (which included an apology, an intensive adverb and emotion) was judged as more likely to be written by a female, while the 'male' message (which included an insult and longer sentences) was judged as more likely to be written by a male.

A common heuristic on the Internet is to assume that overly sexualised females are likely to be males in real life. Curtis (1997) notes

that 'one is advised by the common wisdom to assume that any flirta-
tious female-presenting players are, in real life, males' (p.127). This
heuristic would seem to support evidence on gender differences in
CMC use, in that there is little evidence to suggest that females can
be spotted on-line through the use of more sexually aggressive language. It also draws attention to one possible motive for gender-
swapping on the Internet: the desire for attention.

The motives for gender-swapping or the taking of gender-neutral
names seem reasonably straightforward for women: according to Deuel
(1996), 'a female wishing to avoid eager suitors will present as a relatively non-descript male' (p. 134). For males, meanwhile, the motives
seem more complicated. In the few confessions available (see the case
study of Nowheremom below), one self-reported justification is to provide a role model for 'real life' (RL) women on the Internet. Alternatively, in many environments (chat, MUDs, bulletin boards), women
tend to receive a large amount of attention (Curtis, 1997), so any male
presenting as a female will undoubtedly garner more attention than if
he presented as a male. The upshot of this is that many female presenting Internet users are asked to 'prove' their gender status.

Deception in on-line communities

The issue of gender deception on-line is closely linked to trust, and
violations of trust, in on-line communities. While most on-line communities seem to be characterised by relatively high levels of trust
and honesty (Rheingold, 1993), there are a number of well-publicised
cases, and surrounding mythology, to suggest that deception and
serious violations of trust can occur in on-line communities.

For instance, one of the earliest cases was of the disabled 'Joan' and
'Alex', two popular figures in an on-line community in the early 1980s
(Van Gelder, 1991). Joan was reluctant to meet people face to face
because of her physical disability, but she did forge many friendships
with other women in the community, and was a confidante to several
who had real-life affairs with Alex. As it turned out, Joan was a
persona developed by Alex, leading to a sense of shock, outrage and
betrayal within the community (O'Brien, 1999).

Feldman (2000) reports four cases of 'Munchausen by Internet',
where people in on-line support groups claim illnesses that they do
not have. In one case, a woman called Barbara posted to a cystic
fibrosis support group. Barbara claimed that she was waiting at home
to die, and was being cared for by an elder sister (Amy). The group

sent many supportive messages to Barbara, and were distressed to learn from Amy that she died a few days later. It was only when the group noticed that Amy shared Barbara's spelling errors that they questioned the story. Amy admitted to the hoax, and taunted the group for their gullibility. Feldman warns that a common reaction to such cases is for the on-line group to split into believers and doubters of the claims, or for people to leave the group in disgust.

During 2001, the case of Kaycee was the first large-scale deception to hit the weblog community. Weblogging is the posting on web sites of daily links to articles or events of interest on other web sites. It is also the terminology for on-line diarists, who often use the same soft-ware to post their daily diary. Like many similar stories, the decep-tion seemingly began quite innocently when a group of schoolgirls developed an imaginary friend (Kaycee), and developed some simple hoax web pages sometime around 1997 or 1998. However, it would seem that when one of the girls' mothers (Debbie) found this out, she developed the imaginary teenager to be diagnosed with leukaemia, and at around the same time, Kaycee joined an on-line community called CollegeClub. When the author of a weblog suggested that Kaycee and her mother begin a weblog on his own site, the tales of Kaycee's battles against cancer, and her seeming recovery, became popular amongst the weblog community, with many members sending Kaycee cards and gifts. After a couple of years, when it looked like Kaycee might be recovering fully, Debbie posted in early 2001 that she had died of an aneurysm. According to the Kaycee FAQ (http://rootnode.org/article. php?sid=26), 'The community outpouring of support was remarkable and those who knew Kaycee well suffered serious bouts of grief'. However, suspicions began when Debbie would provide no details about the funeral, or address for condolence cards. Investigations by Internet users revealed no trace of Kaycee at any high schools or hos-pitals, or of an obituary. This and other evidence led to an admission by Debbie, who claimed that she had created Kaycee from a composite of three cancer sufferers she had personally known, and that the pic-ture of 'Kaycee' was of one of these sufferers (as it turned out, this was not true either). According to the Kaycee FAQ, Debbie felt that she had done nothing wrong.

On-line punishment

There have been a number of studies of on-line punishment following misdemeanours in a virtual environment. For instance, Reid (1998) outlines the punishment meted out to a virtual offender on Jenny-MUSH, a virtual community for abused women. On one occasion, when the community's controllers were off-line, a user changed their persona to 'Daddy' and began verbally abusing the other members. When the 'Wizards' logged on they found all the members of the community collected together in one 'room'. The Wizard 'toaded' the member called 'Daddy' (effectively removing his or her ability to speak), whereupon the remaining members of the community turned to a vitriolic assault on their tormentor. Reid points out the similarity of this treatment with medieval notions of justice, and concludes by stating that the community never really recovered after this breaking of trust.

In a similar case, Dibbel (1993) details the case of 'virtual rape' in the LambdaMOO. One user, called Mr Bungle, created a 'voodoo doll' (allowing them to control other users' characters) and forced them to perform sexually violent acts upon him, themselves and each other. Following a discussion of community members (that had not reached any resolution), Mr Bungle was 'executed' in private.

MacKinnon (1995) argues that forced removal of a persona from an on-line community is the virtual equivalent of RL execution. Because without visible presence (i.e. the written word in most cases) there is no virtual self, the removal of the presence is effectively the same as execution. MacKinnon (1997) also notes that in the Mr Bungle case it was the persona, not the embodied person, who was punished. However, McKinnon argues that: 'I appreciate the seriousness of Mr. Bungle's crimes, but the virtual death penalty is the ultimate or most severe punishment available to cybersociety. To assign it to anything other than the most serious crime, such as murder, confuses the social priorities' (MacKinnon, 1997, p. 225).

Case study of on-line deception and punishment: the death of Nowheremom

An interesting case study of on-line deception on the Anandtech forums is reported by Joinson and Dietz-Uhler (2002). The Anandtech forums are asynchronous bulletin boards used primarily by information technology professionals. There are twelve main forums, covering issues such as hardware, CPUs, memory and so on. The forum of interest in this case study is the 'Off Topic' bulletin board. In the Off Topic board members of the forums can discuss issues not covered by the main forums. When people join the Anandtech forums they are able to select a username and icon to visually represent themselves.

They can also use sigs and have profiles hosted of, for instance, their 'rig' (the specification of their computer). The Anandtech forums also have a hierarchy of members, based on activity, longevity and, for promotion to the top level 'elite member', some form of judgement from the community 'enforcers'. Membership ranges from junior member through diamond and platinum to elite.

During October 1999, a new member, using the username 'Nowheremom' (NWM), began posting to the Off Topic forum. Her postings were characterised by terrible spelling mistakes, something the community members seemed to find endearing. During the course of 1999, NWM was attracting the attention of a number of men on the forum, and a flirtation with fellow member DF began. Many other members of the community were seemingly enthralled by this developing relationship, some even describing it as a 'soap opera'.

However, on 5 January 2000 DF posted the following message under the subject heading: 'NOWHEREMOM's dead ...' .

AUGGGGGGGGGGGGGGGGGG!!! I just got a phone call from Mr. Anderson (her father). He said he tried to reach me all afternoon. I was at the university and just got back 15 minutes ago. He said that both Lili Marlene and Agnetha are dead ... that they got killed just after noon Newfie time. He said that it was very windy and there was some freezing rain along the coast and that they were walking back from Agnetha's school and that they were at the bottom of a hill in a curve walking on the roadside and that a car went too fast downhill and missed the curve and hit them. He said that Agnetha was killed instantly but that Lili Marlene survived for a little while and that she died on the way to the hospital. Too many internal injuries, she hemmoraged internally. He was called to identify them. The guy who killed them lives only 2 houses away and is in his focking late seventies. What the hell was he doing on the road driving in adverse conditions. Geriatric motherf. I'd strangle him with my bare hands ...

I am so focking sad ... What will I do? She was the light of my life ... She was so young so sweet so full of life and hope. Were gonna mend our lives together Now she's been taken away from me ... She shone like a beacon and now theres only darkness. All we had was 9 days together ... I wanted a lifetime, not just 9 focking

(contd.)

days. I never got a chance to meet Agnetha. I am so depressed ... I can't cry because I know when I start i will wail, but my eyes hurt so much. I can't keep all the tears in and it's dripping down my chin. I'm so angry I could kill a million people and even then she wouldn't come back. Why does life suck so much. Why us why us why us? We were so happy for crying out loud ... We had projects. We were so similar. We liked the same things knew many same things laughed at the same stuff We thought so alike that we could end each others sentence on the phone. We talked just last night I never got a chance to say goodbye.

Why o why o why o why is life so damn unfair???

Many members of the community expressed shock and grief, a reaction that continued for many months. The username and icon used by NWM were retired by the moderators of the community. During the next year, the loss of NWM was often referred to in discussions – and DF was given the role of protector of her memory. Some members of the community also set up a memorial web page to NWM (real name Lili Marlene Maltese).

However, a small number of members of the community began to investigate NWM's death further. They found no records of her death in local papers, and began to question her actual identity.

On 16 May 2001 DF posted the following confession to the Off Topic forum:

I, DF, come here today to reveal that I have deceived this community and deceived myself into believing that I was doing the right thing.

I am revealing this now because some people came to my defense without knowing that they were defending a lie.

I am revealing this now because the people who uncovered the truth will not let the matter die and this forces people to take sides, threatening to uncover the fabric of our community.

I am revealing this now because it was never my intention to harm anyone or have anyone harmed in my name. In October 1999, I created a cyberpersona called NOWHEREMOM partly out of elements from real people I had encountered, partly out of my imagination. I started this simply as a joke and to see what it would be like for a woman to post on the forums. Women were really scarce on the forums at that time and, as time went by, I deluded myself into thinking that this portrayal of a strong woman would help female lurkers be less afraid of overwhelming male presence and what I perceived as strong misogyny on the boards. NOWHEREMOM was hit on instantly by a couple of male posters in emails, so I decided to make her flirt with me to prevent this by having us be a declared couple. These male posters need not be afraid. They were just making innocent first contact and I was not about to pull a Thunderbooty on them. Their identity is and will remain secret.

Throughout November and December 1999, I engaged in a banter with this persona. At that time, I wanted mainly to bring some humour and entertainment to the forums. People were indeed entertained during those two months and some called it a soap opera. As time went by, NOWHEREMOM started to take an air of reality even to me. Once again, it never was my intention to hurt anyone. I simply had not realized how much people and even myself had become attached to her.

In early January 2000, after Ornery mentioned the word 'marriage', one day I simply panicked and in that instant, my mind was clouded enough that, instead of simply revealing that it was a hoax, I killed her.

I had never expected the grief that overcame this community. It even overcame me and I sobbed for three days as if she had been real. I even mourned for 6 months before I let myself court WombatWoman. On April 29th, Yucky posted a thread entitled 'Has everyone forgotten about dennilfloss' tragic loss?' and the reaction of many who posted in that thread convinced me that they did not want to be reminded of her demise. That thread was placed into my Favorites list and I read it several times during the next months. I came to the conclusion that to reveal the hoax would hurt too many innocent people and I was hoping that the whole thing would simply fade away. It was not meant to be.

In July 2000, a member named vapor uncovered evidence of the hoax and revealed it to a few people. Instead of coming clean, still believing that the hurt to our community would be too great, I denied the whole thing. vapor was vilified and ostracized for this. To him, I can only offer my sincere apology for I am truly sorry for the way he was treated on this matter. I lied to some people closest and dearest to me because I thought that, in doing so, I was protecting them from becoming accomplices in my cover-up. Unfortunately, many came to

(contd.)

my defense in a spirited fashion and ended up unknowingly defending a lie. I thought that I could carry the guilt and the reproach on my lone shoulders but these friends ended up unwittingly carrying some because of my misjudgement. To all those who fought on my behalf, please accept my sincere apologies for having deceived you. There was no malice on my part and I truly thought that I was somehow protecting you by leaving you in the dark. I and only I am to blame.

The matter never rested and many of my friends and acquaintances ended up being divided into two clans. Some people who had other grudges against me never let the matter rest. So now we arrive at this point in time and I am not willing to see the community of Anandtech members divided into two clans, one of which would be defending a lie on my behalf. In particular, I know some outside individuals who would be pleased to no end watching the fabric of this community unravel over this. The well-being of this community is paramount in my book for I do consider you my Internet family.

To all the people close to me who defended me: please believe me when I say that I wanted to somehow protect you from this knowledge. I hope that you will find it in your heart to forgive me.

To all the members of Anandtech: please believe me when I say that I never wanted to hurt anyone and that I am truly sorry. I hope that you too will find it in your heart to forgive me.

It was simply a hoax which I thought was harmless and which got out of hand when I panicked 16 months ago.

I sincerely apologize to everybody involved or hurt by this matter.

I and only I am to blame. I and only I must bear the shame.

Before the thread was locked by the moderators of the conference, 458 messages had been posted in reply to the confession between the first posting (6.29 a.m. on 17 May) until the last post (2.03 a.m. on 18 May).

Early on in the discussion in reaction to the confession, many of the messages were broadly supportive of DF, expressing sentiments along the lines of either 'what can you expect on the Internet?' or 'that was a brave confession'. However, as the discussion developed, the reactions became increasingly negative – in part as evidence of DF's deception was introduced to the discussion, and in part as long-term members posted their reaction (many of the newer members had not been around at the time of NWM's 'death'). Discussion of the appropriate punishment began in the middle of the discussion, and ranged from suggestions that DF have his status removed to that he should be 'run out of town on a rail'. The discussion ended with the moderator posting that DF had been banned from the forums.

Quite apart from the condemnation and discussion of punishment, a number of other interesting themes emerged from the discussion. One was that the community debated the nature of the Internet. This began when some (newer) members posted broadly supportive messages noting that this is, after all, just the Internet. In response, members posted their own take on the nature of the community they had developed:

> But internet forums are NOTHING if we can't have a degree of trust. What he did cannot be tolerated, not because any of us are perfect, but because it undermines EVERYTHING that an internet community is supposed to be. We can't walk around saying 'Anandtech is the best community on the net – we have over 50,000 members! But some of them are fake ...'
>
> I happen to take these forums very seriously. I'm not one to deceive people, & I anticipate the same in return. I'm not a critical person, I take people at their word until I have reason not to. While some people may view this as 'only' the internet, it's a community of real people.

Associated with this, community members also discussed a number of conspiracy theories, including questioning the 'real' identity of other members, and DF's possible role as a moderator (and earlier banning from the community of those who questioned the 'death' of NWM). Some members decided to leave the forums altogether, although this was a relatively rare event. Once the thread was locked, no further discussion of the NWM episode was allowed on the forums, and after a while the thread was deleted from public viewing. Joinson and Dietz-Uhler (2002) suggest that the reaction of the community to the revealed deception may be a reflection of the 'Black Sheep effect' in an on-line environment. The Black Sheep effect is when a deviant member of one's own group is treated more harshly than if they were a member of an outgroup. According to Joinson and Dietz-Uhler, the 'deviant' behaviour of DF in this case, and subsequent punishment and discussion, bears many of the hallmarks of an attempt to reassert the group's (positive) social identity.

Disinhibition and the WWW

Throughout this discussion, the focus of attention has been communication. However, there is also considerable evidence that behaviour on the World Wide Web, while not necessary 'deviant', can be seen (at least at times) as disinhibited. Psychological studies of the WWW tend to focus on three main areas: the use of the WWW for conducting psychological research (e.g. Birnbaum, 2000; Buchanan and Smith, 1999); interaction with WWW interfaces and usability; and psychological processes involved in WWW behaviour.

To take the first, there have been a considerable number of empirical studies that examine the 'best practice' for conducting experiments on the WWW, including the nature of the sample, response rates, drop-out, incentives, equivalence between WWW and paper measures and experimentation on-line (see Birnbaum, 2000; or Reips and Bosnjak, 2001). Generally, the results of these studies confirm that WWW and paper measures are driven by the same psychological processes. For instance, factor-analytic studies of personality measures confirm the equivalence of the two media for research, in most cases (Buchanan, 2001). On the other hand, there is some evidence that responses on the WWW might be more candid than on paper (Joinson, 1999), and that responses might be more varied, as evidenced by greater standard deviations of measure using the WWW compared to pen and paper. However, this second finding might simply be because an Internet sample is likely to be less homogeneous than the typical pen-and-paper sample of psychology undergraduates. While there is limited space to discuss the use of the Internet to collect psychological data (and books by Birnbaum (2000) and Reips and Bosnjak (2001) provide an excellent coverage of this area), the implications of cyberpsychological research for the use of the Internet as a psychology lab are potentially far-reaching for the equivalence of web and paper surveys, and for designing studies to maximise self-disclosure without violating privacy (Joinson, 2001b).

However, despite its importance in popularising the Internet outside academic and military circles, the psychological processes associated with information seeking (or 'browsing') on the World Wide Web have received scant attention from psychological researchers. Of the few studies published that do not deal exclusively with its use as a research tool, the majority deal with the evaluation of WWW sites, or in rare cases the use of search engines and/or navigation strategies, from a human–computer interaction perspective. This pattern is repeated in medical research, with the majority of work that deals with the WWW focusing almost exclusively on the content of the web sites rather than users' behaviour in accessing information.

This omission of the WWW from the body of developing knowledge of social behaviour on the Internet is problematic because the WWW drove much of the development on the Internet in terms of usage and application/innovation. While the almost limitless amount of information available on the WWW is often touted as one of the main reasons to access the Internet, little is known about the psychological processes that underpin the seeking of that information.

Researching web behaviour

Behaviour on the World Wide Web (WWW) has been effectively ignored by cyberpsychology researchers for a number of reasons. First, social interaction, rather than web surfing, is the primary use of the Internet in the home. Second, methods for analysing web behaviour are limited, and usually require the researcher to have access to the web server to produce meaningful data. As much of the most interesting web behaviour occurs on sites not suitable for hosting on the networks of a university, this is not generally possible. Finally, the tendency has been to see the WWW as a publication device (e.g. home pages), which removes attention away from those seeking that information.

The obvious starting place for understanding WWW behaviour is the *log files* kept by web servers. All web servers keep a record of what files (HTML and image files) were sent to users, along with the domain or IP (Internet Protocol) address of the user, the time and the date. It is also possible to track the referral site (the user's last site), their browser and the operating system they are running. The number of accesses to a web site, or specific pages, are called 'hits'. So, if ten different users access a specific web page on any one day, the log file will record ten 'hits'. However, there is one contraindication to the mass measurement of hits – particularly popular web sites are cached locally (on the user's hard drive) and at network caches (Goldberg, 1995). This technique was designed to speed up access to the Internet by storing copies of popular pages to avoid overloading bandwidth. Users are only served the page from the web server if the page has changed since they last visited. However, any dynamic content on a page (even a counter) subverts caching, so it is not such a problem as it seems.

A second method for understanding user behaviour is through the use of *cookies*. Cookies are files that are saved on the user's own hard drive by a web server. The next time the person visits the web site, the server can read (and alter) the cookie. So, a cookie can record how often someone visits a web site, what they look at and the route they take through the site. Techniques like cookies are ideal for studying an individual's use of a web site, while log files are best suited for studying patterns of behaviour amongst larger numbers of people.

Other research methods are also available, although again they have been little used. One experimental method employed by this researcher (Joinson and Banyard, 1998) was to use scripting and buttons/selections to measure information seeking. In one study, participants chose web pages to read by clicking a radio button next to the description of the content. When they had made their selection, they clicked 'OK'. This sent a record of their selection to a file on the server, and served them their chosen articles. While something of a roundabout method for measuring information seeking on the web, this technique did allow for comparison with a paper condition, and also for the generation of data comparing the two essentially 'like for like'.

Other alternatives include recording the screen activity of web users in the laboratory, eye tracking and audio recording pairs of participants as they browse the web. All these methodologies are potentially useful for understanding how people interact with specific web pages and the mechanisms by which they decide on links to follow.

Internet pornography

As Young *et al.* (1999) note, pornography is considerably more accessible on the Internet than on paper. This increase in accessibility not only circumvents any locally held laws on obscenity (effectively reducing what is acceptable to the lowest common denominator because that is where web sites will be hosted), but it also removes many of the psychological inhibitions associated with, say, purchasing pornography in one's local shop.

It is commonly alleged that pornography has been at the forefront of technological developments on the WWW. To be sure, pornographers have been quick to use new technologies – the invention of photography, the telephone, cine and 8 mm film and VHS video has quickly been followed by the use of each new technology for the production and consumption of pornography. Moreover, as different technologies have been adopted, so the consumption of pornography has become increasingly a private affair. The cost of producing and distributing cine film meant that, until the advent of video, most pornography was viewed by groups. The development of peep shows (where individuals watch pornography in a small booth relatively anonymously) served to privatise pornography (and was a massive success before the advent and widespread adoption of video in the mid- to late 1970s). Indeed, back in the 1980s, it was similarly argued that pornography and horror movies were the 'killer app' of video, and video 'nasties' were implicated in negative social outcomes in the same way the Internet is today.

However, the content and quantity of pornography on the Internet have been under-researched by cyberpsychologists. In part this is due to the controversy that followed the publication and ensuing publicity of a study by Rimm in 1995. Rimm, a researcher at Carnegie Mellon University, surveyed sexually explicit images available on Usenet and pay-to-view subscription services. The report was picked up by *Time* magazine, which ran a cover story on 'Cyberporn!' Based in part on the study by Rimm, the *Time* magazine story claimed that 83.5 per cent of images on Usenet are pornographic in nature, and that trading in pornography is one of the most popular, if not the most popular, activity on the Internet. However, the data collected by Rimm did not support this at all. Of the 900,000 occurrences of sexually explicit material collected, less than 1 per cent came from Usenet – the rest was from the subscription servers (that generally require credit card details). Following the ensuing outcry from Internet users who felt tarred by this allegation, independent investigations were conducted by both Carnegie Mellon University and Georgetown University (who had originally published the study in their *Law Review*). *Time* magazine posted a partial retraction of their story. But the idea that the Internet is awash with pornography still persists.

What's out there, how popular is it?

The contribution of Internet pornography to the finances of mainstream pornography companies is relatively small. One estimate is that combined revenues from legal CD-ROMs, DVDs and Internet sites earn around 1.5 billion US dollars per year in America (Morais, 1999). This compares to revenue of $20 billion from videos, $11.5 billion from escort services, $7.5 billion from magazines, $5 billion from sex clubs and $4.5 billion from phone sex. The provider of soft-core pornography *Playboy* earns over $300 million per year from its various services, but only a small proportion of this income ($7 million) comes from Internet services (La Fanco, 1999). And although traffic to pornography sites is large (up to 30 million unique hits a month for some sites), the number of pages containing pornographic material is estimated to be around 1.5 per cent of the whole web (Lawrence and Giles, 1999). In one of the few academic studies of the Internet porn industry, Cronin and Davenport (2001) note that the industry shows some of the signs (e.g. a few sites dominating consumer access) that occur in mainstream e-commerce. They also note that e-pornography is attempting to become legitimate, for instance, by seeking stock market flotation and courting couples rather than the traditional consumer of on-line pornography (youngish males).

Formats of pornography on the Internet

Rimm's (1995) study of pornographic images attempted to analyse them for content by automatically collecting the descriptions of the images. As the description of the images is likely to be more linked to advertising than to the actual content, it is likely that this method inflated the level of obscenity.

To counter this inflation of obscenity, Mehta and Plaza (1997) analysed 150 sexually explicit images taken from 17 newsgroups on a single day in 1994. A majority of the images posted were by anonymous non-commercial Usenet users (65 per cent). The main themes that emerged from the analysis were close-ups of human genitalia (43 per cent), erect penises (35 per cent), fetishes (33 per cent) and masturbation (21 per cent). The amount of material most likely to be deemed illegal in most countries was also high: 15 per cent of the images either contained children or adolescents, or signified youth in the image or text. Other paraphilias were noted, including bondage and discipline (10 per cent), the insertion of foreign objects (17 per cent), bestiality (10 per cent), incest (1 per cent) and urination (3 per cent). Mehta and Plaza note that the distribution of types of images is similar to that found by Rimm in his study of bulletin boards.

Mehta and Plaza also note that the content of Internet pornography seems to differ from that of magazines and videos. For instance, fellatio, homosexuality and group sex were more often found on Internet sites (15 per cent, 18 per cent and 11 per cent respectively) than in comparable studies of traditional media (8.1 per cent, 2–4 per cent and 1–3 per cent respectively: Garcia and Milano, 1990). Compared to the anonymous, non-commercial users, commercial users (i.e. those effectively posting adverts) were significantly more likely to post explicit material (use of a foreign object, fellatio and children/ adolescents).

Mehta and Plaza conclude that the amount of explicit/illegal mate-rial posted by commercial users reflects an unregulated, fiercely com-petitive market where pay-to-view bulletin boards and web sites need to offer something different (i.e. increasingly explicit or unusual images). They also note that many of the images of children or adolescents gave the illusion of youth, but may well have been a model aged over 18. None of the images involving children or adolescents were sexu-ally explicit – 'the vast majority of the small number of images depict-ing children and adolescents probably come from nudist magazines ... We never came across an image depicting a sexual act between an adult and a child/adolescent, or acts between children' (Mehta and Plaza, 1997, p. 64). They further note that most of the images uploaded by users seemed to be scanned directly from magazines.

Psychological aspects of Internet pornography consumption

Manning et al. (1997) presented some early evidence from the Home-Net study that suggests that although many Internet users might have once looked at sexually explicit material on the Internet, few return to do so again. Curiosity then, rather than any other variable, would seem to drive many initial visits to Internet pornography sites. Recent work on pro-anorexia web sites (Moore, 2001) has suggested that increases in activity are associated with negative press coverage, suggesting that the curiosity value of 'deviant' sites might drive a considerable volume of traffic.

However, the perception of anonymity of web browsing may well make the accessing of pornographic images socially and psychologically safer on-line than off-line. Of course, it is also considerably more convenient, as well as providing, at least for home users, privacy of consumption (something pornography distributors aim for much of the time).

Explaining disinhibited and deviant behaviour on the WWW

Anonymity, or at least the perception of anonymity, is the usual explanation for disinhibited web behaviour (e.g. Joinson, 1998). However, to understand fully the impact of anonymity on web behaviour, we need to take into account the various different types of anonymity and differential impact on behaviour. So, perhaps a home user with an anonymous ISP account or direct dial in to a bulletin board will feel anonymous when seeking on-line pornography. But, for the vast majority of users, anonymity is also associated with a recognition that their privacy is an illusion when on-line. For a user willing to enter their credit card details to access a subscription web site, when we talk about anonymity, we need to think of to whom the user is anonymous. Not the web site, to be sure, who have not only his or her credit card details, but also details of their IP address or at least their ISP. In this case, the user may well be seeking information or images away from the gaze of friends, family or local community, and willingly accepts (or ignores) other privacy concerns. The perception of anonymity is something to be designed into systems, rather than something that the Internet provides as a birthright. Sites that design in a clear lack of anonymity (e.g. compulsory registration procedures) are effectively entering a negotiation with users that may well limit the potential benefits of anonymity on the Internet. When we think about anonymity and web behaviour, we also need to factor in the actual content sought, and as such the users' concern about how willing they are to suspend privacy concerns in seeking information. For someone browsing health information sites, perhaps the balance between relative anonymity (compared to, say, picking up leaflets in a local medical centre) and privacy concerns wins out. For someone seeking potentially illegal or vulnerable material, privacy and anonymity concerns need to be addressed through the design of systems or protocols before we see a disinhibitory effect.

Positive Intra- and Interpersonal Aspects of Internet Behaviour

5

In late 1998 I attended a medical conference which was focused on a developing area called 'medical infomatics' (including the Internet and medicine). Many of the papers dealt with evaluations of the qualities of medical web sites, and attempts by medics to provide some form of quality assurance (or perhaps control) for the information provided. However, of all the no doubt worthy efforts to protect lay people from incorrect information, just one comment stayed with me. A speaker was relating how patients used to arrive at his surgery and pull a small piece of paper from their pocket. This piece of paper would contain their own diagnosis based on whatever (generally) informal networks of information they could get hold of. The doctor called this 'small paperitis' (cue laughter). In a grim tone, the doctor then went on to relate how this 'illness' had now developed in his practice to 'large printoutitis' as patients arrive at his surgery armed with huge printouts from Internet sites (cue more laughs). Quite apart from the implications of labelling patient empowerment attempts (however jokingly) in the same terms an ailment, the story above also demonstrates how, even relatively early in its development, the Internet was being used positively by patients.

The case of a doctor–patient interaction well illustrates the validity of the phrase 'information is power'. The power of an expert over a lay person is based on their specialised knowledge and, to a degree, their command over resources that we want or need. If an expert decides upon a course of action, for instance, a type of treatment, the patient is unlikely to be fully aware of the implications of that choice, possible alternatives and contraindications. Later in this chapter, we look in more detail at beneficial applications of the Internet for seeking health information and social support.

Utopianism and new technology

When a new technology develops, there inevitably follow forecasts envisaging a variety of positive outcomes. The telegraph offered the promise of an end to war through the creation of a 'global community' (Standage, 1999), while the telephone promised business benefits (Fischer, 1992), as well as an end to isolation for rural families. The Internet, meanwhile, has been forecast as a great democratising force, bringing the world into the embrace of a global community. In the spirit of these forecasts, this chapter and the next look at positive aspects of Internet use.

Internet addiction revisited

It may seem difficult to find an upside to Internet addiction or, indeed, excessive Internet use, unless we ask number of pertinent questions. For instance, are specific types of people attracted to use the Internet excessively? What are they using the Internet to do? And what activities is Internet use replacing?

So, if perhaps there is evidence that chronically shy people are using the Internet excessively, that they are using it to engage in social interaction, and that the Internet use has replaced TV-watching, then perhaps we should be encouraged by excessive Internet use, rather than discouraged by it.

Who is using the Internet excessively, and to what end?

In amongst the various demographics on Internet users, there is some evidence that a fair proportion of those 'diagnosed' as addicts or excessive users might be either chronically shy, socially anxious or in some other way impeded from engaging in satisfying face-to-face interaction (Griffiths, 2000a; Sheperd and Edelman, 2001). For others, their

Internet experience might be a proxy therapy, a journey of self-discovery (Biggs, 2000).

Virtually all studies of pathological and everyday Internet use confirm that social interaction is by far the most popular use of the Internet (e.g. Kraut *et al.*, 1998; Morahan-Martin and Schumacher, 2000). So, the main concern is whether or not social interaction on the Internet replaces 'real life' social interaction. This issue is discussed in more detail in the next chapter, but the balance of evidence seems to suggest that, at least with experienced users, Internet use is linked to increased levels of social involvement (Howard *et al.*, 2001), and that amongst Internet users, a higher level of use is positively correlated with community involvement (Kraut *et al.*, 2002).

Although it could be claimed that socially anxious or disabled people using the Internet for social interaction is in some way 'avoiding the problem', this paints a somewhat rosier picture of societal acceptance of, say, stammering, than is generally the case. As we shall see throughout this chapter, there is every reason to believe that on-line social interaction, from groups of hobbyists to cybersex, can be as emotionally rewarding and 'positive' as face-to-face encounters. For instance, Grohol (1999) argues that

> Researchers seem to have not considered that perhaps people who spend a lot of time on-line are simply engaging in normal, healthy social relationships with other human beings ... In fact, because of the unique psychological components of on-line social interactions, on-line friendships and relationships may be of higher quality or value to some. (p. 399)

We should also not forget that social interaction is important to the health of people. For someone denied quality social interaction because of, say, disability or chronic social anxiety, it would seem churlish to term their affiliation-seeking behaviour an addiction. Indeed, it is arguable that we should applaud and encourage their seeking of social contact, rather than pathologising it. For some people, their interactions on the Internet might be the only area of their life in which they can exercise control, or indeed escape from the judgements or discrimination they experience in everyday life.

Perhaps, then, we should rather be concerned that people are not using the Internet enough. For the vast majority of the world's population without access to a telephone, never mind the Internet, the issue is perhaps how to widen access to the Internet, rather than ways to limit Internet use.

As one of the few studies that actually measured Internet use, rather than relying on self-report measures, the HomeNet study (Kraut *et al.*, 1998) found that the Internet was used for an average of three hours a week in their households. This weekly average is below the time spent viewing television programmes *per day* in American households. While the scope of this book does not allow for a complete discussion of the relative merits of leisure time spent watching TV versus using the Internet, it certainly does suggest that we should consider the proposed nefarious outcomes or uses of the Internet for everyday living with some due scepticism.

For those typical users of the Internet in the home where use is dominated by social interaction rather than, say, gambling or cybersex, the concept of addiction can be seen to be based solely on the notion that interaction over the Internet is in some form a poor relative (or indeed, is in itself a dysfunction) compared to 'quality' face-to-face interaction. Of course, this is nonsense – just as the telephone did not destroy the art of polite conversation, so the Internet is not going to make us a nation of lonely, shy individuals. It is arguable that UK and US society has been moving to weaker social networks over the last fifty years (Putnam, 2000). While this might be due to any number of factors (increased mobility of workforces, later ages for marriage, interstate highways or motorways and indeed the automobile), it is certainly not because of the Internet. But the Internet might be a technology ideally suited to the maintenance of long-distance relations with family and friends. Later in this chapter, I discuss the benefits of belonging. I would argue that one of the best and most popular uses of the Internet is to create this sense of belonging. In this sense, an 'addict' to the Internet might well be benefiting socially and psychologically from their alleged 'addiction'.

Positive aspects of the Internet and identity

RL [real life] is just one more window, and it's not usually my best one. (Doug, talking about MUDs in Turkle's *Life on the Screen*, 1995, p. 13)

As we saw in the previous chapter, the construction of new and multiple identities on the Internet is relatively commonplace. Creating an on-line persona usually only leads to negative reactions when doing so violates the norms of the particular environment – on MUDs and

MOOs it is expected, while on places like the Anandtech forum (where Nowheremom 'lived' and 'died'), it violated a general assumption that each on-line persona was associated with a single embodied person in real life.

However, this is not to say that identities on-line, even when there is an implicit or explicit norm against multiple personae, do not represent something other than a reflection of identity in real life. On-line one's identity is constructed through text – what you choose to say and reveal about yourself, and how you say it. This brings with it the opportunity for people essentially to craft an identity that exists quite apart from the usual pressures of RL identity and impression management. Turkle (1995) argues that the Internet (and in particular, MUDs) makes concrete the postmodern condition of multiple, fragmented identities. In many of the examples Turkle cites, the participants in MUDs see a very real connection between their on-line persona and their real-life identity. For instance, in discussing MUD devotee 'Gordon', Turkle notes that

> On MUDs, Gordon has experimented with many different characters, but they all have something in common. Each has qualities that Gordon is trying to develop in himself. (1995, p. 190)

The theme of self-development in persona-building seems to be a common thread of many people's experiences of MUDs:

> In real life, Stewart felt constrained by his health problems, his shyness and social isolation, and his narrow economic straits. In the Gargoyle MUD, he was able to bypass these obstacles, at least temporarily. Faced with the notion that 'you are what you pretend to be,' Stewart can only hope it is true, for he is playing his ideal self. (Turkle, 1995, p. 196)

Thus, for some Internet users, on-line activity affords them the opportunity to be themselves, freed from the constraints of face-to-face interaction. One female MUD user sums up this argument well while discussing an on-line relationship with a fellow MUDder:

> I didn't exactly lie to him about anything specific, but I feel very different on-line. I am a lot more outgoing, less inhibited. I would say that I feel more like myself. (quoted in Turkle, 1995, p. 179)

Perhaps then the use of on-line personae can serve a useful purpose for expressing and understanding our 'core' selves unfettered by shyness, social anxiety and physical states. Bargh et al. (2002) argue that the Internet may allow people the freedom to express what Carl Rogers called the 'true self'. According to Rogers (1951), a goal of therapy is to discover the 'true self' in order to allow its more full expression in everyday life. In comparison, the self we express in everyday interaction is the 'actual self', the social persona we adopt that might not be what we truly are, but is used to protect the self from vulnerability.

Bargh *et al.* (2002) note that the Internet seems to be akin to the 'strangers on the train' phenomenon, where people seem willing to disclose details about their lives to a stranger. This happens both because of the anonymity, and because the potential cost of disclosing is reduced because the stranger is not part of one's close social circle (so there are not likely to be any repercussions). Bargh *et al.* hypothesised that the Internet might allow people to more freely express their 'true' self, because of the anonymity and reduced social cost of disclosure. Bargh *et al.* directly tested this in two experiments:

- *Experiment One*   In this study, participants' reaction times for a 'true' and 'actual' self, were measured following CMC or FtF interaction. Participants completed measures of their true and actual selves, then interacted either face to face or using a CMC system, and then answered 'yes' or 'no' to a series of attributes and their reaction time was measured. The results showed that following FtF interaction, the actual self was more accessible, while after CMC interaction, the true self was more accessible.
- *Experiment Two*   To counter the possibility that the effect found in the first experiment was due to anticipated interaction, rather than actual interaction, the second experiment replicated the first, but removed the actual interaction (but kept the expectation of interaction). The results showed no difference between those who expected to interact FtF and those who expected to interact using the Internet. So, it would seem that it is the process of interaction that is important, not the expectation of interaction.

Bargh *et al.* (2002) conclude that the relative anonymity of Internet interaction allows people to express their true selves. By anonymity, Bargh *et al.* include both reductions in accountability through lack of identifiability, and visual anonymity, although they do not tend to distinguish between the two in their experiments. Research on social identity during CMC and self-awareness (e.g. Joinson, 2001a; Matheson and Zanna, 1988; Spears and Lea, 1994) suggests that isolation and visual anonymity have a quite separate effect from lack of identifiability.

Visual anonymity and isolation increase self-awareness, which may well explain the increased accessibility of the 'true' self in Bargh *et al.* (Experiment One). Meanwhile, lack of identifiability or reduced accountability increases the ability to express the 'true' self without fear of the consequences. Joinson (2001a) found that it was the interaction of visual anonymity and reduced accountability that led to increased self-disclosure (and presumably also the activation of a true self). This work suggests that the Internet may well facilitate the expression of a true self, but only under certain circumstances.

On-line identity and real life

If we see on-line identity as a tool for either developing desired characteristics of ourselves or expressing a true self, this obviously raises the question: what are the implications of on-line identities for real life? While Turkle presents case studies that suggest both therapeutic and counterproductive outcomes of on-line identities, the social psychological literature on ideal selves suggests that working through desired identities might be beneficial.

Internet activity and marginalised identities

A number of commentators have discussed the idea that the Internet, and role-playing games in particular, might provide suitable identity 'workshops' (Bruckman, 1993) for people to work through 'identity projects'. For instance, McKenna and Bargh (1998) studied newsgroup participation by people with marginalised but non-obvious identities (as opposed to conspicuous identities like stuttering or being overweight). They predicted that participation (but not lurking) in newsgroups would lead to an increased importance of the marginalised identity to the person, and thence to greater self-acceptance, and decreased estrangement from society and loneliness (see Figure 5.1).

In their first study (McKenna and Bargh, 1998, Study 1), McKenna and Bargh found that users of newsgroups dedicated to those with marginalised–concealable identities showed greater commitment to the groups (by posting and responding more) than members of mainstream and marginalised–visible groups. They interpreted this finding as suggesting that groups with concealable–marginalised identities (in their studies, homosexuality, drugs and spanking/bondage) mattered more to their members because opportunities to 'demarginalise' their identities were rare in 'real life'.

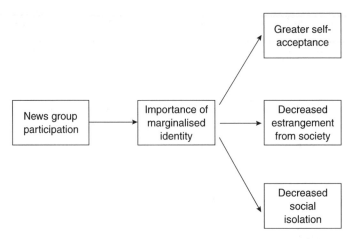

Figure 5.1   A process model of identity demarginalisation

Source: McKenna and Bargh (1998, p. 683).

In a follow-up second study, McKenna and Bargh (1998, Study 2) sent a questionnaire to members of alt.homosexual, alt.sex.bondage and alt.sex.spanking. The questionnaire asked a series of questions to assess a person's involvement in the group, the importance of the group to their identity, their level of self-acceptance and their feelings of social isolation (i.e. the crucial elements in Figure 5.1 above). The results of the second study showed that participation in the newsgroup as a poster (as compared to a lurker) was associated with increases in the importance of the group to the person's identity. And the importance of the group to the person's identity was linked to increased self-acceptance, coming out to family and friends and to reduced feelings of estrangement from society (see Figure 5.1). Although these effects were mediated by changes in the importance of the identity, there was one direct effect of newsgroup participation. Increased levels of participation were linked with lower feelings of social isolation. In Study 3, McKenna and Bargh sent the same questionnaire to marginalised ideological identities (skinheads and white power). They found the same pattern of increased participation leading to higher importance of the identity, and thence to greater self-acceptance and 'coming out', and reduced estrangement (but no direct link to social isolation).

McKenna and Bargh conclude that, although virtual groups seem to operate in the same way as real-life groups, the benefits of the Internet lie in the encouragement of participation via anonymity.

They also note that the percentage of their respondents who came out in real life following their Internet activity (37 per cent in Study 2 and 63 per cent in Study 3) suggests that for these participants, the virtual is very real.

Eichhorn (2001) recounts the use of the Internet by gay and lesbian students at a US university to campaign for a gateway to a computer conference, alleged to contain homophobic postings, to be severed. Eichhorn argues that the virtual environment set up to support the students provided not only a voice, but also supported resistance, in direct contrast with the relative silence of the same students about 'real life' issues (e.g. the teaching of lesbian, gay and bisexual issues in the curriculum). So, as well as providing an environment for the demarginalisation of identities, the Internet also provides a support for resistance and the organisation of resistance, even for groups based within the same university department. And, as in the case outlined by Eichhorn, there is no reason to doubt that resistance or campaigning on the Internet is any less effective than, say, writing a letter or signing a petition. Certainly, a study of green campaigners in the Netherlands by Postmes and Brunsting (2002) suggested that Internet-mediated collective action is seen as equal to more traditional modes of protest by activists and non-activists alike.

Possible selves and Internet identity

The concept of possible selves (Markus and Nurius, 1986) is also useful for understanding the potential role of the Internet in self-development. Possible selves are the way people think about their potential and future (Markus and Nurius, 1986). They are the selves we would like to become, we could become, and we fear becoming. These future self-conceptions form part of the core of a person's self-concept.

Possible selves are effectively personalised versions of higher-level motivations – so, for instance, a need for affiliation might be translated into a possible self as married or in a long-term relationship. But they are also particularly vulnerable to changes in the social environment – according to Markus and Nurius 'as representations of potential, possible selves [they] will thus be particularly sensitive to those situations that communicated new or inconsistent information about the self' (1986, p. 956).

For the various array of possible selves we hold, only a portion will be salient, and then only part of the time. Cues in the environment (e.g. looking in a mirror) might activate a possible self (e.g. feared possible self as overweight). For someone on the Internet, it is possible that positive experiences (e.g. being accepted into a virtual community or making friends on-line) will activate a hoped-for possible self (as a popular, socially capable person). Not only will this possible self provide a context for the person's real-life experiences (e.g. I might be shy now, but will be socially able in the future), but it might also encourage the transference of on-line experiences into the interpretation of events off-line. So, for someone with a hoped-for possible self that receives some validation on-line, it is possible that this bolsters their attempts to achieve the possible self off-line too.

Deception and possible selves

Curtis (1997) noted that a large number of personal descriptions in MUDs were of 'mysterious but unmistakably powerful' figures (p. 129), suggesting that the development of personae in virtual worlds may well be an exercise in wish fulfilment. But, at least for some users, the Internet also allows them to elaborate and practise their hoped-for possible selves, or even to express a 'true' self normally suppressed (McKenna *et al.*, 2002). In another sense, the Internet may provide an incentive for people to change in their 'real life' existence – if one can act (and be perceived) as a certain type of person on-line, this may well serve as an incentive to achieve a similar state off-line (McKenna and Bargh, 1998).

Media choice, impression management and metaperception

In the discussion of identity thus far, we have assumed that the pursuit of identity *per se* is an activity in itself. However, if we consider Internet users as also strategic choosers of a specific medium, then the Internet, and indeed any mediated communication, provides a further opportunity to manage the impression they make. While so-called lean media like the Internet limit certain modes of communication, they also provide unique opportunities to create new identities, and to manage the self we present to others.

Patrick O'Sullivan (2000) developed an impression management model to outline the functional and strategic role of communication choice in social relationships. O'Sullivan, like the rational actor approaches discussed in Chapter 2, asks not what is the impact of technology on users, but rather, what are people using the technology for, and why. He argues that one thing people are motivated to do is to manage their self-presentation (Schlenker, 1980), such that they are able to achieve desirable outcomes. This does not imply deception – most self-presentation is aimed at allowing the person to see the 'true' you – but it does suggest some selectiveness in how we present ourselves. As such, the choice and use of a medium to communicate depends on the setting of a goal for a communication episode, choosing a strategy for the communication episode, and evaluating the outcome. When it comes to choosing a strategy, the communicator needs to take into account two key things: the symbolic meanings or norms attached to a medium (e.g. thank you notes should be handwritten), and the content of the message.

This strategic approach to mediated communication based on self-presentation suggests that people might choose to communicate by, say, letter or e-mail because it confers a number of advantages. For instance, letter-writing or e-mail allows communicants to control the timing, duration and content of an interaction, as well as perhaps avoiding the chance of becoming tongue-tied when trying to express one's emotions. O'Sullivan (2000) also found evidence that people will prefer a mediated communication channel if their self-presentation is threatened.

Impression formation on the Internet

Although Internet communication does not seem to be instantly amenable to impression formation, even before an interaction begins, cues are available that allow other users to form an early initial impression. E-mail addresses usually convey information about the person's country of origin, possibly their occupation or employers and even their name. A private user's choice of Internet Service Provider (ISP) is also used to form an impression – particularly if the ISP, like AOL or Freeserve, is seen as catering to 'newbies' (new users). Hancock and Dunham (2001) examined the breadth and intensity of first impressions made via CMC and FtF. They found that, after a relatively short interaction, participants had made less wide-ranging, comprehensive impressions of their interaction partners if they met using CMC compared to FtF. But participants in the CMC condition made more extreme evaluations of their discussion partner compared to the FtF condition, suggesting that the limited impression made was more intense than the more comprehensive impressions formed face to face. They conclude that although many of the attributes normally used to form an impression (e.g. if someone laughs a lot, or stares at the floor) are missing, the use of paralanguage, descriptive devices and communication style all provide information useful for forming an impression. That the impressions tend to be more intense on-line is congruent with research suggesting that CMC is associated with heightened affiliation (e.g. Walther, 1996) and idealisation of communication partners (McKenna *et al.*, 2002).

When there is free choice available, then, we would expect that the user's choice of nickname would be carefully chosen, jealously guarded and, in turn, used to form an impression by others on the Internet.

Bechar-Israeli (1998) argues that the nicknames adopted by Internet users (in this case IRC) are critical in how that person is perceived. The most common type of 'nick' is one related to the self (e.g. shy-dude, sexylady: 35 per cent), followed by those linked to various flora and fauna (tulip, tiger: 10 per cent), technology (e.g. pentium, aixy: 9 per cent), plays on language/typology (e.g. BeaMeUp: 8 per cent) and those that make some reference to either their identity or lack of identity (e.g. me, unknown: 6 per cent). Bechar-Israeli argues that nicks serve specific functions in IRC – they allow people to enter into identity play, while at the same time providing continuity as people tend to use the same nick over time.

Interpersonal interaction

As we have seen, having a choice of media for social interaction, including the Internet, provides people with the opportunity to choose strategically, based on the goals of their self-presentation. However, this is not to say that the media might have an independent impact on interpersonal interaction as well.

Benefits of mediated communication

Using the Internet to communicate provides a number of benefits for the user. The most obvious are those shared by many other forms of communication technology: for instance, being able to communicate across time and/or distance. Mediated communication also may allow people the time to compose messages and replies, enhancing self-presentation and reducing the cognitive load of real-time impression management.

A range of media, as we have seen, also gives people the chance to act strategically in their choice of communication technology. Shifting an interaction from, say, e-mail to the telephone not only changes the 'richness' of the communication channel, but also conveys a symbolic meaning in that voice communication is generally considered more 'personal' than text-based communication. So, when an interaction shifts from one form of mediation to another, the effects are as much grounded in the strategic goals adopted by the participants as in the symbolic meaning and specific affordances of each technology. From a strategic viewpoint, then, the Internet and its variety of communication formats provides a valuable addition.

However, while the strategic approach to on-line interaction provides a valuable insight into people's choice of media to maximise benefits, there is considerable evidence from laboratory studies that mediated communication also impacts directly on people's communicative behaviour.

Early studies of mediated communication were grounded in theories that argued that a loss of visual cues led to a reduction in the socialness of an encounter. As such, one of the early predictions of work on CMC was that it would tend to be 'task-oriented', in that the medium is well-suited to conveying plain information, but unsuitable for carrying socio-emotional information. For instance, Hiltz and Turoff (1978) reported that only 14 per cent of CMC groups' communication was socio-emotional in content, compared to 33 per cent in face-to-face groups. Rice and Love (1987) studied 2,347 sentences exchanged using CMC: 28 per cent were positive socio-emotional messages, 4 per cent negative socio-emotional messages and 71 per cent were task-oriented messages. So, for early CMC theorists, the existence of moderately high levels of socio-emotional content during CMC was a paradox given the 'desocialised' nature of the media.

Hyperpersonal interaction and social information processing

One attempt to integrate task-oriented laboratory findings and the existence of social information exchanged on-line was Walther's social information processing model (discussed in Chapter 2, this book). Although there was some evidence to support the contention that CMC retarded the transfer of socio-emotional information, a criticism of the social information processing model is that it is still firmly rooted in the 'loss' camp of CMC – Walther argued that given time CMC might be able to match face-to-face communication in its 'socialness'. For instance, Walther (1995) conducted a study in which he predicted, based on his social information processing model, that social behaviour would be greater in face-to-face than CMC groups, but that the difference would subside over a large amount of time. Walther had coders rate each person discussing face-to-face or by CMC. The coders then rated the complete discussions using a 'relational communication' questionnaire (a way of organising their overall impressions of the 'socialness' of the discussions). The CMC and face-to-face groups discussed three separate issues on three different occasions, allowing a comparison of social communication across time. The CMC groups were rated as significantly *less* task-oriented, and *more* socially oriented, than the face-to-face groups during all the time slots. So, it would seem that even when virtual groups have only just met, they can often be more social than in a comparable face-to-face condition.

Overly social behaviour on the Internet

As outlined above, Walther (1995) found that CMC groups were consistently rated as more affectionate than FtF groups. Indeed, there are numerous examples of relationships and romances occurring in many different areas of the Internet, including chat groups (Reid, 1991), Usenet groups (Parks and Floyd, 1996), multi-user text-based virtual reality systems (e.g. MUDs and MOOs: Utz, 2000) and within on-line communities (Rheingold, 1993). Some of these relationships are serious enough to culminate in cohabitation or marriage (Parks and Floyd, 1996). Helen Petrie (1999) reports that even the love letter is making a renaissance on-line, for instance: 'knowing you are there and remembering the ecstasy of being with you, places light in the darkest of times for me' (male author, sent to female).

In fact, for a communication medium that, according to early theorists, should discourage it, social interaction is the main use of both e-mail (Petrie, 1999) and the computer in the home (Kraut *et al.*, 1998). An overwhelming body of anecdotal and experimental evidence has shown that people use computers to form social relationships: a more pertinent question is whether (or in what contexts) CMC is highly social, and how this can be reconciled with early findings that CMC is task-oriented.

To address the first point, Walther's 1995 finding that visually anonymous CMC groups are more socially orientated than FtF groups has been replicated a number of times. For instance, Chilcoat and DeWine (1985) found that participants who could not see each other rated each other more highly on attitude similarity, and on social and physical attractiveness (see also Walther *et al.*, 1999).

Walther (1994) argues that one possible explanation for this is that longitudinal CMC groups anticipate future interaction, and so have higher levels of social communication compared to one-off groups who do not expect to meet again in the future. When groups do not expect to meet again, the level of social communication is low compared to when they expect to meet in the future (Walther, 1994). This may explain why early studies using 'one-shot' experimental groups tended to find low levels of social communication. Moreover, the time limits imposed on most early studies would not have allowed the time for social information to be communicated due to the reduced rate of socio-emotional communication in CMC (Walther *et al.*, 1994).

So, according to Walther's explanation, for CMC groups to exhibit high levels of affiliation, they need to anticipate future interaction (if they seem to be social from the word go), or meet over a length of time (if they are task-oriented at the beginning). Walther distinguishes between CMC environments that seem to encourage impersonal interaction (e.g. time-limited, no anticipation of future interaction) with those that encourage interpersonal interaction (e.g. time unlimited, anticipation of future interaction). Indeed, Walther argues that: 'There are several instances in which CMC has surpassed the level of affection and emotion of parallel FtF interaction' (Walther, 1996, p. 17). He termed this phenomenon 'hyperpersonal communication': that is, communication which is 'more socially desirable than we tend to experience in parallel FtF interaction' (p. 17).

According to Walther (1996), hyperpersonal interaction is created by four main factors. First, because many on-line communicants share a social categorisation, they will also tend to perceive greater similarity between themselves and their conversational partner. As we tend to like those whom we see as similar, people communicating on-line will be predisposed towards liking their communication partners.

Second, the sender of a message can optimise their self-presentation – that is, they can present themselves in a more positive light than they might be able to face to face because they do not have to worry about their non-verbal behaviour. Walther recalls the phrase 'the waist is a terrible thing to mind' to argue that being freed from having to allocate scarce mental resources to controlling our visual cues and appearance means that we can allocate more to message construction, again leading to a more positive impression being conveyed to the receiver. Walther also suggests that being freed from concerns about our appearance might be linked to a heightening of focus on our own inner self. This would mean that messages sent during CMC would include more content on personal feelings and thoughts, and that the senders might be more in touch with their self-ideals (again, helping with their self-presentation).

A third factor in hyperpersonal communication is the format of the CMC. Walther argues that asynchronous CMC (e.g. e-mail) is more likely to lead to hyperpersonal interaction because (1) the communicants can devote a special time to CMC, rather than being distracted by other goings on, (2) they can spend more time composing/editing the message, (3) they can mix social and task messages and (4) they do not need to use up the cognitive resources answering immediately, so can pay more attention to the message.

The final factor Walther invokes is a feedback loop that causes these effects to be magnified through social interaction. In line with work on self-fulfilling prophecies and behavioural confirmation, as the interaction progresses, so the inflated positive impressions will be magnified as the communicators seek to confirm their initial impressions, and in turn respond to the positive impressions conveyed by their partners (Walther, 1996).

Walther's theory of hyperpersonal communication relies on visual anonymity and asynchronous communication. Indeed, Walther (1999a) warns against the trend to plug video cameras into PCs, arguing that visual cues *detract* from social impressions during CMC. For instance, Walther *et al.* (1999) report that long-term CMC groups show lower attraction and affinity if they have seen a still picture of their fellow participants. One factor that might be involved in hyperpersonal CMC is self-disclosure – the tendency to tell someone intimate facts about yourself.

Self-disclosure and CMC

A rapidly increasing body of experimental and anecdotal evidence suggests that CMC and general Internet-based behaviour can be characterised as containing high levels of self-disclosure. Rheingold (1993) claims that new, meaningful relationships can be formed in cyberspace because of, not despite, its limitations. He further argues that 'the medium will, by its nature ... be a place where people often end up revealing themselves far more intimately than they would be inclined to do without the intermediation of screens and pseudonyms'.

Similarly, Wallace (1999) argues that 'The tendency to disclose more to a computer ... is an important ingredient of what seems to be happening on the Internet' (p. 151). Self-disclosure has been studied in a number of different settings using computers. For instance, in the medical field, increased levels of candid disclosure to a computer as compared with face-to-face consultations have been reported in psychiatric interviews and pre-interviews (Ferriter, 1993; Greist et al., 1973). Robinson and West report that clients at a sexually transmitted disease clinic admit to more sexual partners, more previous visits and more symptoms to a computer than to a doctor (Robinson and West, 1992).

When non-medical Internet behaviour is studied, similar findings also emerge. Parks and Floyd (1996) studied the relationships formed by Internet users. They also asked their participants to report the level of self-disclosure in their Internet relationships (e.g. 'I usually tell this person exactly how I feel' and 'I would never tell this person anything intimate or personal about myself'). They found that people report disclosing significantly more in their Internet relationships compared to their real-life relationships. McKenna et al. (2002) and Bargh et al. (2002) found evidence that people are more able to express their 'true' selves on the Internet, which may involve disclosing information about the self that would normally be socially unacceptable. Similarly, in their study of 'coming out on the Internet', McKenna and Bargh (1998) argue that participation in on-line newsgroups gives people the benefit of 'disclosing a long secret part of one's self' (p. 682).

On the WWW, self-disclosure might be similarly prevalent. For instance, Rosson (1999) analysed 133 stories posted by Internet users on a resource called 'Web Storybase'. Overall, 81 of the stories contained personal information of some sort. Rosson concludes that 'users seem to be quite comfortable revealing personal – even quite intimate – details about their lives in this very public forum' (p. 8). Finally, compared to a pencil-and-paper survey, answers to an electronic survey are less socially desirable and lead to the disclosure of more information about the self (Joinson, 1999; Kiesler and Sproull, 1986; Weisband and Kiesler, 1996). In a meta-analysis of self-disclosure on computer forms, Weisband and Kiesler found that the effect of using a computer on self-disclosure is highest when collecting sensitive information.

In the series of studies reported by Joinson (2001a), the level of self-disclosure was measured using content analysis of transcripts of face-to-face and synchronous CMC discussions (Study 1), and in conditions of visual anonymity and video links during CMC (Study 2).

In keeping with the predicted effect, self-disclosure was significantly higher when participants discussed using a CMC system as opposed to face to face.

In the second study, incorporating a video link while the participants discussed using the CMC programme led to levels of self-disclosure similar to the face-to-face levels, while the comparison condition (no video link) led to significantly higher levels of self-disclosure.

These two studies together provide empirical confirmation that visually anonymous CMC tends to lead to higher levels of self-disclosure. The results of these studies also suggest that high levels of self-disclosure can effectively be designed out of an Internet interaction (e.g. through the use of a video link or accountability cues (Joinson, 2001a, Study 3)), as well as encouraged. It should also be noted that the findings of these studies, that 'hyperpersonal' communication can occur during short-term, synchronous discussions when the participants do not expect to meet, also cast doubt on the explanatory value of the various processes in Walther's hyperpersonal model, or at least that further models are needed to explain hyperpersonal interaction in situations that do not fit Walther's model.

Within e-commerce, the potential of the Internet to encourage disclosure by consumers (for marketing purposes), and the possible links between disclosure, trust and brand loyalty, certainly require further investigation. A consistent finding seems to be that the design of the system, and the context and cues it provides, may have a large impact on consumers' willingness to divulge information about themselves. For instance, Moon (2000) has argued that people treat computers as social agents, and apply the same rules of social interaction to human–computer interaction. To examine this, Moon tested the self-disclosure reciprocity rule in the collection of data via stand-alone computers. She found that when the computer essentially disclosed information about itself (e.g. 'Sometimes this computer is used by people who don't know how to operate it. It ends up crashing. What are some of the things that make you furious?'), the participants reciprocated in kind, leading to a greater breadth and depth of disclosure. In a pilot study testing the applicability of this effect to Internet surveys, Joinson (2001b) assigned participants to either an experimenter disclosing or non-disclosing condition. In the experimenter disclosing condition, participants were directed to a web page with information about the experimenter, while in the non-disclosing condition, participants did not receive information about the experimenter until after the experimental procedure. All participants answered six personal questions using free text. Participants' answers were analysed for the breadth (word count) and depth (opening self up to vulnerability) of self-disclosure. Although in the pilot study there was no effect of reciprocal self-disclosure on the depth of self-disclosure, there was an effect on the breadth of disclosure. That is, participants who answered the questions following self-disclosure by the experimenter went on to disclose more about themselves than those who went straight to the questions.

Olivero and Lunt (2001) studied the willingness to disclose information about the self to a commercial organisation, and manipulated the level of trustworthiness of the organisation, whether a financial reward was offered for disclosure and the level of intrusiveness of the questions. She found that the level of trust was associated with participants' willingness to disclosure in answer to highly intrusive questions, but that an awareness of data-mining/privacy concerns moderated this effect of trust.

In a similar vein, Buchanan *et al.* (2001) argue that while the 'disinhibiting' effect of the Internet on self-disclosure can enable researchers to gather data on sensitive issues (in this case, drug use), privacy concerns remain high. While it may seem paradoxical that the Internet seems to encourage self-disclosure, while at the same time highlighting privacy concerns, these effects are undoubtedly both context-dependent and designed. What is meant by this is that the Internet does not exert a universal impact on self-disclosure or accountability/privacy concerns. Rather, self-disclosure on the Internet can be heightened (and ameliorated) by the nature of the interaction, the recipient, the process and dynamics of the interaction and the designing in of accountability cues (or a reduction in accountability cues). Although the 'natural state' of the Internet may well encourage self-disclosure through a reduction in accountability concerns and an increase in private self-awareness, these effects are neither universal, nor should they be taken for granted.

Self-disclosure is important not only because of its role in collecting data for psychological studies, but also because it is closely associated with the development of trust and intimacy within relationships (Archer, 1980; Derlega *et al.*, 1993).

Romantic relationships on the Internet

As we have seen, then, the Internet, and more specifically CMC, is not only capable of carrying social and relational information, but might actually encourage it. Moreover, a combination of the affordances of the technology and the self-presentation agendas of the users might lead to 'hyperpersonal' interaction and increased self-disclosure.

These ideas obviously have important implications for the development of romantic relationships on the Internet, and for their prognosis if they migrate to real life.

Using the Internet to form and develop romances

The use of the Internet in romantic attachments can take a number of formats.

Types of Internet-enabled relationships

1. *Courters* In these cases, people meet on the Internet by accident or design, and develop their relationship through chat, e-mail, the telephone and, eventually (in a proportion of cases), face-to-face meetings. There is likely to be a continuum as the relationship develops, moving from public to private spaces (e.g. chat sites to e-mail), through phone contact, with an eventual end point of a face-to-face meeting (Parks and Floyd, 1996).
2. *Maintainers* For many long-distance relationships the Internet provides a medium for maintaining a relationship that began with a face-to-face setting. The aim of Internet use in these cases is to maintain an existing relationship, that is likely to also include face-to-face meetings, letters and telephone calls alongside, rather than developing from, Internet use. Also within this category are couples who live close by, or even cohabit, but who also use the Internet (mainly e-mail and instant messaging) to talk during the day.
3. *Cyberflirts* Cyberflirts, while also developing relationships on the Internet, never (at least to begin with) intend to meet face to face the people they meet on-line. They may be attached in 'real life' to an existing partner, and use the Internet as a escape or outlet, or they may accidentally develop relationships following on-line interaction. In some cases, there may be little in the way of relationship development, with cybersex the primary goal of the interaction.

Estimates of the number of romantic relationships that develop over the Internet are difficult to establish. Some evidence comes from MUD and Usenet participants. Parks and Floyd (1996) found that over 60 per cent of their sample reported forming a relationship using the Internet. Utz (2000), in a study of 103 MUD users, found that 73.6 per cent reported forming relationships with fellow MUD users, of whom 24.5 per cent reported forming a romantic relationship with a fellow user, and 76.7 per cent reported an on-line friendship developing into an off-line friendship. McKenna *et al.* (2002), although not directly measuring the prevalence of relationship formation on-line, report that from their sample of 568 Usenet participants, an initial meeting on the Internet had led to a telephone conversation for 63 per cent of all participants, 56 per cent had swapped photographs, 54 per cent had sent a letter, and 54 per cent had met face to face (on average eight times). America OnLine (AOL) estimates that 10,000 marriages have culminated from responses to personal adverts on its web sites. But how much of the courtship is conducted using the Internet and how much by other media/face to face is not known.

The Internet and attraction on-line

Whenever or wherever a romantic relationship develops, it is reasonable to guess that attraction plays a major part in bringing people together in the first place. Although the role of physical attractiveness might well become less important as people move towards a long-term relationship (Buss, 1988), it is likely to be a key factor in determining whether two people will get together in the first place.

It is perhaps not surprising, then, that the idea that you can be attracted to someone you have never met, or indeed, seen a picture of, should be greeted with such incredulity in a visually dominated Western world. However, at the same time, familiar sayings suggest that you 'can't judge a book by its cover', and that 'appearances can be deceptive'. Evolutionary psychologist David Buss (1988) identified ten behaviours by men and women that were judged as attractive by the opposite sex. Although physical attractiveness featured, more than half of the attributes (sense of humour, sympathy, being well-mannered, offering help and making an effort to spend time together) are easily conveyed by text.

There are other social–psychological reasons why attraction on the Internet might occur relatively easily:

- *Similarity* People who are similar to each other tend to form relationships, and those relationships tend to be longer-lasting. Because many meeting places on the Internet are based around shared interests, users who meet are likely to share similar interests. Even if they do not share a love of bonsai trees, being an Internet user in itself provides a shared identity. Moreover, a shared social identity tends to lead to increased liking for ingroup members.

- *Self-presentation*   As we have seen, the Internet allows people to be strategic in their self-presentation, maximising their plus points and minimising their weaknesses (Walther, 1996). As a relationship develops, people are more motivated to present an accurate presentation of themselves (Swann, 1983). If people are more likely to present their 'true' self on-line (McKenna *et al.*, 2002), then this may well lead to the seamless development of a relationship.
- *Self-disclosure and reciprocity*   Self-disclosure is important during the development of a relationship for establishing trust, as well as moving a relationship forward (Derlega *et al.*, 1993; Laurenceau *et al.*, 1998). If using the Internet does increase self-disclosure (see earlier section), then it is possible that on-line relationships develop at a faster pace than RL ones (McKenna *et al.*, 2002). Increased self-disclosure on-line might lead to a reciprocal cycle of disclosure, leading to heightened intimacy and trust.
- *Idealisation*   There is a tendency to idealise people we talk to on-line, leading to higher levels of liking (McKenna *et al.*, 2002). There is little evidence to suggest that this leads to lower levels of stability (McKenna *et al.*, 2002, Study 2).

Developing relationships using the Internet

Internet relationships tend to follow a similar pattern of initial contact in a public arena, then to a private domain (e.g. e-mail or AOL messenger), then to the telephone and then to face-to-face meetings (Parks and Floyd, 1996). Obviously, not all relationships follow that route, and many drop out at each stage. The movement through media may be associated with establishing trust, legitimacy and commitment, at least in part due to the symbolic meanings conveyed by different media.

Baker (2000) outlined two case studies of on-line relationships – one which culminated in marriage, the other which failed. In many respects, the development of the relationships was remarkably similar:

Couple A
Blake and Neva were both based in the States. They met on an on-line forum. Following their meetings on the public site, they progressed to e-mail, then to telephone calls, then to an exchange of photographs, and

finally to a face-to-face meeting. Once they began communicating by telephone, their conversations became increasingly intimate. They met at a hotel and became intimate within a few hours of meeting. This was to be their last meeting – although the relationship continued for a while, it did not succeed.

Couple B

Mark met Claire when he sent her an e-mail because her profile matched his interests. Both were currently married when they began communicating. They communicated regularly by e-mail (at least daily), and then by Instant Messaging. Claire visited Mark after a short while, although the relationship remained platonic. On her return to the States, their communication became more intimate, including the exchanging of sexual fantasies, telephone sex and cybersex. They met again some months after the first FtF meeting, and this time 'cemented their bond' (Baker, 2000, p. 240). After a third visit, Claire moved to the UK on a trial basis. Mark and Claire are now married.

Baker (2000) discusses the similarities and differences between the two couples. She notes that although both couples share a number of similarities (all were previously married (or currently married), all were well-educated, aged in their forties and geographically distant), the developmental pattern for the two couples were distinct. She suggests that there might be two important reasons for the success or failure of on-line relationships. The first is *shared values* and the *relative importance of physical attractiveness*. Couple A held dichotomously opposed political philosophies (one liberal, the other conservative), while couple B seemed to share a value structure (something they discussed in their e-mails). Baker (2000, p. 242) suggests that: 'Early in-depth sharing of important dimensions of each person's values and lifestyles and the resolution of identified conflicts may offset minor problems encountered later in real life.'

The second key factor Baker identifies is *commitment, risk and resources*. While neither couple could afford to travel regularly for FtF meetings, Claire did have some flexibility following her divorce. Blake was unemployed for much of the courtship, and despite his efforts, could not find a job near Neva.

From chat to consent: psychology and cybersex

According to Doring (2000), cybersex is 'computer-mediated interpersonal interaction in which the participants are sexually motivated, meaning they are seeking sexual arousal and satisfaction' (p. 864). Although the term has been used for a wide variety of Internet behaviours, like, for instance, accessing pornography, an interpersonal-based definition is more appropriate to differentiate it from 'solo sex' which is basically human–machine interaction. Cybersex requires the participants to negotiate and adapt their behaviour as a cybersexual encounter develops. Doring (2000) identifies three main forms of cybersex:

1. *Virtual reality-based cybersex* A sexual encounter in a three-dimensional virtual reality. This would require substantial developments in current technology (e.g. a full body suit and data helmet) which, while possible, are some way off being commercially available. An alternative is 'teledildonics' – a remote-controlled (by the other participant) sex toy.
2. *Video-based cybersex* A sexual encounter in an Internet videoconference using webcams, and sometimes text or audio. Participants will typically strip, expose their bodies and sometimes masturbate in view of the camera.
3. *Text-based cybersex* A sexual encounter based on the rapid exchange of real-time ('chat') messages. Doring differentiates between two main types of text-based cybersex: TinySex and HotChat.

    TinySex is cybersex in MUDs. MUDs allow for both actions and spoken words, as well as props, descriptions of people and specific locations. For instance, Doring (2000, pp. 865–7) gives the following example of the beginning of a TinySex encounter in LambdaMOO:

Logging you in as 'Blue_Guest'
   [@go Lady's Orgy Room]

Lady's Orgy Room: The first thing you notice are several restraints in the room and chains hanging from the ceiling. You smell the soft scent of sex from what went on here not long ago. In fact, you can almost hear the screams of pleasure bouncing off the walls. You notice a four-post bed with silky sheets. A sign on the south wall notes: NO MEN ALLOWED!!!! Type 'help here' for features and commands on this room. Exits lead west to Sensual Respites and northwest to the Sex Room.
Faustine, Autumn and hippie_girl are here.
Blue_Guest arrives
Autumn says, 'Hi Blue!'
   [say oh, hi]

You say, 'oh, hi'
Autumn smiles at you
   [:smiles at Autumn]
Blue_Guest smiles at Autumn
   [look Autumn]
Autumn
   About five and a half feet tall with straight hair the colour of
   Autumn leaves hanging just past her shoulders. She is dressed
   in a black and brown patterned skirt with a black sweater that
   is a bit too big. It constantly falls off one shoulder. She is bare-
   foot, and you notice that she has a tattoo of a Celtic design on
   her left ankle. There is always a slight smile hovering around
   the corners of her mouth.
   [say Autumn: hey, nice Tattoo :-)]
hippie_girl hugs Faustine warmly and offers her a joint.
you say, "Autumn: hey, nice Tattoo :-)
Autumn grins, stretches her left leg gracefully and kicks you in
   the butt.
   [laugh]
You fall down laughing
hippie_girl giggles.
   [:removes her blue dress and her shoes]
Blue_Guest removes her blue dress and her shoes
   [:sit on bed]
You pull back the top silk sheet of the bed and slip under it, feeling
   the fabric caress your skin.
Autumn follows you to the bed.

Hot Chat is cybersex in chat environments. Unlike MUDs, chat
environments provide little by way of accessories for cybersex
(like props), and people are known only by their 'nicks' (although
some services like Yahoo allow users to access others' profiles). As
such, cybersex in chat can be based on any kind of shared fantasy
('we're on a desert island') or based on the reality of the encounter
('I've locked myself in the office. I'm getting so horny chatting to
you'). Doring thus notes that 'All in all, however, virtual self-
presentation in chatting tends to be much more realistic than in
mudding' (p. 866). For instance, in the except below from Doring
(pp. 866–7), the virtual and real overlap.

Ulrike turns the light off
Julien takes off his tee-shirt

Julien: that's better
Julien: (kiss)
Ulrike: giggles
Ulrike: snuggles against your warm body
Julien: snuggles up against you and caresses your breasts
Ulrike asks herself what she should do
Ulrike decides to do nothing for now and let herself be caressed
Julien: very gently, only with his fingertips
Ulrike feels her nipples hardening
Ulrike squeezes Julien's thigh
Julien kisses your breasts and nuzzles your nipples with his
  mouth
Ulrike's heart beats faster
Julien: ... a hand is caressing your pussy
Ulrike: it is already wet
Julien wonders whether he should type with only one hand
Ulrike: I don't mind
Ulrike: (in case you need my permission)
Julien lays you on your side
Julien: and lays your leg over his hip
Ulrike lays her upper leg over his hip
Julien moves one hand downward

It was argued in the previous chapter that there may well be down-sides, in the form of addiction and victimisation, to cybersex. However, an alternative approach to cybersex from feminist researchers is that cybersex liberates women from the norms of sexual expression (or lack of) imposed upon them by a patriarchal society (Doring, 2000; Levine, 1998). For instance, it has been argued that cybersex, for women, can mean *more sex* (something discouraged in RL), *better sex* (due to the removal of penetration as the goal of a sexual encounter) and *different sex* (freedom to experiment without shame or guilt).

The prognosis for on-line relationships

Drees (2001), in an analysis of an ongoing research project, reports that one in twenty Internet romances in her sample culminated in cohabitation or marriage. McKenna *et al.* (2002) report similar levels of stability in Internet relationships as in real-life relationships. As well as increased initial liking for a partner, Internet interaction might lead to heightened attraction that persists after a meeting face to face. For instance, Dietz-Uhler and Bishop-Clark (2001) tested the quality of later face-to-face discussions following computer conferencing. They found that participants who had discussed a target article first on-line, and then met face-to-face, compared to those who met only face-to-face, rated the subsequent face-to-face discussion as more enjoyable. So, perhaps meeting on the Internet first leads to enhanced face-to-face interaction later.

Enhancing existing relationships using the Internet

On-line infidelity

There is an argument that infidelity is usually only seen as beneficial by the cheater, rather than the cheated. In keeping with the idea that personae can help real-life identities, there is some evidence that cyber-sex might be used by some people to improve their current RL relationships. Maheu (2001) has been collecting survey data on Internet infidelity via the web site selfhelpmagazine.com since 1997. By November 2001 there were 2,838 responses. Of these responses, just under half (1370) say that a cyber-affair is always a threat to a traditional relationship. When asked whether a cyber-affair can 'enhance a person's primary relationship', 50 per cent (1,434) responded either 'yes' or 'sometimes', while considerably fewer (35.5 per cent, 1,010) responded 'no'. A final question asked whether the respondents were in favour of 'cyber-affairs'. A majority (61.3 per cent) responded that they were in favour of cyber-affairs.

Why might this be so? First, cybersex (as opposed to a cyberrelationship) does not imply emotional commitment. Research on sexual jealousy suggests, at least for women, that emotional commitment by partners is more problematic than infidelity in itself (a pattern reversed for males). However, for males, the virtual nature of cybersex removes the evolutionary imperative of sexual jealousy that one's genes might not be propagated.

Second, for many couples, the expression (and gratification) of sexual fantasies and desires is inhibited by implicit social norms and control and potential embarrassment. The potentially liberalising and empowering nature of cybersex may well translate to the bedroom in real life, in the same way that, say, coming out in cyberspace is associated with coming out in real life (McKenna and Bargh, 1998). Similarly, the need to express your needs, desires and fantasies verbally during cybersex might lead to an increased willingness to do the same in RL.

Authenticity/written communication

If cybersex offers the opportunity for enhancing relationships, it is reasonable to argue that Internet communication in itself could similarly enhance or develop an existing relationship. For instance, there is evidence that long-distance partners do not suffer because much of their communication is mediated by letter, telephone or e-mail. Indeed, it might heighten a couple's feelings for each other by providing them with the opportunity to put their thoughts and feelings in writing without the inhibitions that constrain face-to-face encounters.

Stevens (1996) argues from a humanistic standpoint that:

> For a relationship with its intersubjectivity to work well, *good communication* is essential. For the humanistic psychologist this means that the partners need to be capable of sharing what each other feels and thinks about what is going on. (p. 359, original emphasis)

As has been argued elsewhere, interaction on the Internet (and to a degree all mediated communication), encourages precisely this kind of 'good communication'. From a humanistic standpoint, the authenticity of communication is based, in part, on the reflexive nature of the participants. Again, if CMC encourages self-focus, this is likely to be enhanced. Finally, the notion of intersubjectivity requires that partners develop joint meanings – something not dissimilar to the development of shared norms (Postmes *et al.*, 2000) and negotiation (Doring, 2000) that are requirements for on-line interaction.

Sharing and Surfing: The Benefits of On-line Communities and Web Browsing

6

Virtual communities: the benefits of belonging on-line

Whether or not 'real' or meaningful communities form in cyberspace is itself a topic worthy of a whole book, never mind a section of a chapter. The notion of 'virtual communities' has variously been criticised as a mirage, as pseudo-communities that give the impression of community, but not the reality. However, for its members, a virtual community is real enough, and to an extent its 'reality' as a social network, community or even mirage is irrelevant. For instance, Rheingold (2000) argues that: 'It's hard to sympathize with the charge that all on-line relationships are unreal when you've stood in front of a person's friends and family at their funeral' (p. 327).

Of course, not all virtual communities develop the kind of close, intimate ties Rheingold describes occurring on the WELL (Whole Earth 'Lectronic Link) community. But the prevalence of virtual communities suggests that for many Internet users, they do fulfil an important social or psychological function. A Pew Internet and American Life report (Horrigan *et al.*, 2001), using telephone survey methodology, reports that 84 per cent of Internet users have used the Internet to contact or gain information from an on-line group. Many of these contacts seem likely to deepen local ties, rather than weaken them: 26 per cent of Internet users used the Internet to get in touch with local groups, and

40 per cent of those reporting using the Internet to join groups have used it to 'become more involved with groups to which they already belong' (Horrigan *et al.*, 2001, p. 3). In light of the trend towards lower levels of social participation in real life (Putnam, 2000), the results of this survey suggest that the Internet may even be reversing this trend. According to Horrigan *et al.*:

> The findings of the Pew Internet and American Life Project survey indicate that something positive is afoot with respect to the Internet and community life in the United States. People's use of the Internet to participate in organizations is not necessarily evidence for a revival in civic engagement, but it has clearly stimulated new associational activity. (2001, p. 10)

This pattern of Internet use increasing community membership and links to one's local community is supported by the follow-up HomeNet research conducted by Kraut *et al.* (2002), and discussed in Chapter 4. In their second study, Kraut *et al.* found that Internet use was associated with greater community involvement and increases in the participants' local social circle. They still caution that the ties in these social networks might be 'weak', although even weak ties might have substantial benefits for Internet users.

The benefits of weak ties and virtual communities

In 1998 I was in the process of designing a study where participants' self-awareness was manipulated experimentally while they communicated electronically. Although I had a reasonable idea how to increase people's private self-awareness (it's usually done with a mirror), I was at a loss when it came to reducing it. In the end, I posted a query to the mailing list for members of the Society for Personality and Social Psychology (SPSP). Within 24 hours I'd got a whole series of different answers, one of which was perfect for the experiment.

The SPSP mailing list experience outlined above is typical of millions of people's experiences of on-line questions. As an academic mailing list, the content tends to be quite businesslike, and I doubt many of the members would term it a community. But, as a loose social network, it proved to be invaluable. At the time of writing (October 2001), British Telecom are running an advertising campaign in the UK for their ISP. In the advert, people stand in the centre of an impossibly large stadium and ask questions (it is supposed to represent the Internet). Of course, they get the answer right away.

Granovetter (1982) proposed a theory of the 'strength of weak ties'. According to Granovetter, the strong ties we have tend to be with similar people, so it is likely that their access to information will be similar. However, weak ties are useful because they provide access to many more people, who tend to be different from ourselves, who might also have access to different (potentially superior) resources.

Constant *et al.* (1997) examined the usefulness of weak ties within a large organisation (Tandem Computers Inc.). Over a period of six weeks, 82 employees broadcast questions on e-mail, and promised to make the replies public. Constant *et al.* report that around half of the queries were solved by the replies, and that the value of the average reply was 11.30 US dollars. And the people asking the questions did not even know the information providers: 81 per cent did not know them at all, and 10 per cent were 'barely acquainted'.

In keeping with some of the predictions of the 'strength of weak ties', the information providers tended to have more access to resources than the information seekers: for instance, 14 per cent of information seekers were based at the HQ compared to 31 per cent of the information providers, and only 2 per cent were managers, compared to 12 per cent of the providers. Moreover, 'the diversity of ties as well as the resources of information providers contributed to whether or not seekers' problems were solved' (Constant *et al.*, 1997, p. 318).

Constant *et al.* conclude that the usefulness of weak ties is in their ability to bridge information across time, location, hierarchy and sub-unit within the organisation, and not simply by providing access to larger numbers of people. They further note that making replies public might increase the pro-social behaviour of information providers.

Emotional support on-line

Once we begin to move from technical advice to emotional support, the nature of weak or strong ties forged on the Internet becomes more important. In the same British Telecom advert discussed earlier, a woman with a young child stands in the centre of the stadium and asks if, as new mothers, does anyone else ever feel 'overwhelmed'? She witnesses a large section of the stadium stand in unison.

Discussions of emotional support on-line tend to be focused on its occurrence within established on-line communities. For instance, Rheingold (1993, 2000) discusses a number of occasions where WELL members sought and received emotional support following the diagnosis of life-threatening illnesses. In several cases, the on-line support also led to social and other support in real life. However, the use of relationships forged on-line for emotional and social support when needed is perhaps one of the least unexpected outcomes of virtual communities. What is more unexpected is that on-line social support has spawned its own communities and environments specifically with the purpose of providing empathy, advice and support to people who have little in common apart from a shared need for support, or willingness to provide it.

On-line social support: content

As we have seen, the Internet can provide an invaluable 'information bridge' for those seeking solutions to technical problems. Similarly, on-line groups dedicated to specific problems or groups might provide a similar resource for people. For instance, Rheingold describes the parenting forum on WELL where parents swapped stories and advice about their children. In a study of on-line and face-to-face support groups, Davidson et al. (2000) provide an example of information provision on-line:

> The reason they are calling your mother a Type II is because the first hour was 212 and the second 183. Two hours after eating is when the sugar levels should peak out. Because her levels were above 120 two hours after eating, she is probably a Type II. Since her bg [blood glucose] levels were down to 11 three hours later, it probably means that your mom has lazy organs like I do. (p. 210)

However, on-line social support might well serve another, just as important function: to provide empathy (Preece, 1999). Jenny Preece notes:

> After lurking on medical support groups ... for several months, it became clear to me that similar questions were asked again and again by different people. Sometimes the questions were phrased slightly differently or included additional information but sometimes they were almost identical. Often these questions were raised by newcomers to the group and were then answered by old timers.

What amazed me was the tolerance of the community. Occasionally someone would refer the questioner back to previous communication but there was no evidence of posting acrimonious replies and very little evidence even of frustration. (p. 64)

Preece notes that her initial reaction was to wonder why there were no FAQs. But then she realised that something more important was happening: the people were not just looking for factual information, they were identifying themselves as suffering from a problem, and communicating with fellow sufferers. *Empathy*, the ability to identify with someone else, is, says Preece, a vital component of psychotherapy. To examine the role of empathy in on-line support groups, Preece studied a community for sports people with anterior cruciate ligament (ACL) injuries. She found that 44.8 per cent of the postings were empathic, while 17.4 per cent were question and answer. A further 32 per cent were personal narratives, while none were non-empathic or non-sympathetic. She suggests that empathy is crucial to understanding the usefulness of on-line support (psychological processes of on-line social support are discussed later in this chapter).

An earlier study of on-line social support groups was conducted by Andrew Winzelberg (1997). Winzelberg analysed 306 messages posted over a three-month period to an eating disorder support group on the Internet. He noted that the majority of messages were posted outside normal office hours, suggesting that use might increase when the usual sources of support are unavailable.

Winzelberg also analysed the messages for content using six main categories. The most common type of message was personal disclosure (31 per cent), followed by providing information (23 per cent), providing emotional support (16 per cent), and requesting information, support or disclosure (7, 5 and 4 per cent respectively). This clearly echoes the findings of Preece that electronic social support is a combination of empathic and information communication. Winzelberg also notes that most of the information provided was medically accurate and appropriate, although 12 per cent was considered to be 'inaccurate and outside the standards of medical and psychological care' (p. 405).

The problem of establishing legitimacy and authority in electronic support groups was studied by Galegher *et al.* (1998). They note that electronic support groups, because of the nature of the medium (i.e. anonymity), face a number of rhetorical challenges and opportunities. One such challenge is for participants to establish legitimacy as people justifying help and support. Galegher *et al.* note that in face-to-face groups, attending the meeting and conforming to the groups' norms are usually enough to make one a legitimate member of the group deserving support. They argue that simply 'showing up' in an electronic support group (ESG) is not a sufficient way of demonstrating commitment or establishing legitimacy. Similarly, as a member moves from being seen as a legitimate recipient of support to being a provider of information and support, Galegher et al. argue that they will be concerned with establishing authority for their contributions. To examine how members of an ESG might try to establish legitimacy and authority, Galegher et al. compared the messages of three Usenet support groups and three hobby groups collected over a three-week period.

Although the support and hobby groups shared many rhetorical features (e.g. a low number of active posters compared to readers, use of emoticons and abbreviations, quoting), there were also some important differences. The average message length was longer in the support groups than in the hobby groups, suggesting the members might be more committed. They also note that many of the question-and-answer threads were anchored in personal experiences, and contained short personal narratives.

The posters created legitimacy in a number of ways. They posted messages appropriate to the group, and used snappy headers to make themselves 'heard'. Galegher et al. (1998) note that often posters refer to their own membership of the electronic group, or how long they have lurked for before asking a question/replying to one. Even frequent posters included references to their membership of the group 80 per cent of the time when asking questions. Posters often signal their membership of the specific problem group (e.g. depression) by introducing information on their diagnosis, prescription or symptoms. For new users, the need to establish legitimacy was felt most strongly. Galegher et al. provide the following example of a new user seeking to establish legitimacy by stating their membership of the electronic group and of the problem group arthritis, or AS, and finally amplifying the claim with information on medication:

Hi. I've been reading/lurking here for a few months. I've been diagnosed with AS and have been taking anti-inflammatories since May. I am wondering what type of side effects others have had with these meds beside ulcers. Currently I am taking Lodine 1200 mg/day. I am wondering if the swelling I've been having with my eyelids has anything to do with this drug. Also, any other common side effects? (1998, p. 513)

In the support groups Galegher *et al.* studied, 80 questions received no reply. Virtually all of these lacked any legitimising information of the type outlined above, and were generally simply requests for information rather like complex database queries. In the hobby groups, evidence of such legitimacy seeking was much less apparent.

For those posting information, seeking to convey authority, or at least limiting the potential reach of any disagreement, seemed to be more important than establishing legitimacy. Galegher *et al.* found that people answering questions used a number of techniques used to either limit the potential comeback on questionable advice, or to establish authority. Many posters included caveats in their replies (e.g. 'here's my two cents worth' or 'YMMV – Your mileage may vary'). These caveats were mainly used when someone's answer was based on their own personal experience. For answers that attempted to establish a scientific or factual authority, the posters would tend to use citations (e.g. to studies or professional organisations) or refer to their own background. If a reply lacked these markers of authority, and was not based on personal experience, it was likely that its authority would be challenged in a follow-up message.

Galegher *et al.* (1998) argue that the processes of establishing legitimacy and authority in electronic social support groups leads to a strengthening of the community and group identity aspect of membership. They further note that ESG membership seems to provide an important function in allowing members to realise that they are 'not alone'. A text search for the phrase 'I am not alone' revealed that it had been used by 39 different authors in the support groups, compared to three in the hobby groups: 'And I am so grateful for this group ... it means so much to me tho I can't always express it ... whenever things get really bad I login and remember I am not alone' (from alt.support.depression: Galegher *et al.*, 1998, p. 521).

Who seeks support on-line?

There has been relatively little empirical research into the types of people who might choose the Internet as a source of support compared with face-to-face support groups or family and RL friends. Davidson *et al.* (2000) compared the prevalence of on-line versus real-life support groups. In the cities they studied, support groups for alcoholism were most prevalent (so much so, they were removed from some analyses for being overly influential), followed by AIDS, cancer (with breast cancer having the most support groups, lung cancer the fewest) and anorexia. There were no support groups for either hypertension or migraines. The pattern of support groups on the Internet broadly followed the same pattern, with some notable exceptions. Alcoholism support groups were relatively few on the ground on the Internet, while the top three diagnoses for establishing support groups were multiple sclerosis, chronic fatigue syndrome and breast cancer.

Of particular interest is the analysis Davidson *et al.* (2000) conducted on support groups and stigma. It is commonly argued that stigmatisation or embarrassing ailments usually mitigate against seeking affiliation with others. To examine this, the researchers had a number of medical professionals rate the various diagnoses on their 'social burden' (how disfiguring, embarrassing, noticeable and stigmatised the illness is). They found that for both face-to-face and on-line social support groups, the number of groups positively correlated with the social burden imposed by the ailment, particularly the embarrassment associated with a particular diagnosis or treatment.

Kristin Mickelson (1997) studied the motivations and existing support networks of parents with learning-disabled children involved in on-line and face-to-face support groups. The two groups differed in a number of ways, including demographically (so any differences need to be taken with a pinch of salt). Compared to the 'nonelectronic' parents, the Internet parents reported a greater perceived stigma associated with their child's diagnosis, greater visibility, and lower expectations of support from their parents and casual friends. This general pattern was also clear at follow-up interviews four months later. Mickelson notes that the association between perceived lack of social support and participation in Internet support groups is difficult to interpret: the parents could turn to the Internet due to lack of 'real' social support, or the Internet could lead to isolation from 'real life' sources of support.

What seems to be important is that people have a source of support, whether virtual or in real life. Many (if not all) of the benefits of support groups can be fulfilled on-line, and some may even be enhanced.

Psychological processes and benefits of on-line social support

For many people, traditional sources of support are not available for a number of reasons. Friends and family may be distant, or professional help might not be available. Even if one does have social support available locally, an unwillingness to burden others, or a belief that only fellow sufferers can understand, or a stigmatised or rare problem, can stop people from seeking the support they need. The growth of self-help books (more than 2,000 are published each year in the USA) testifies to the demand for support by people facing any number of mental or physical problems. There is some evidence that self-help in the form of books can be beneficial in alleviating a number of problems (Marrs, 1995). While there is no certain evidence that on-line social support is similarly beneficial, there are a number of compelling reasons to believe that it should be.

The benefits of being in the same boat

In an unpublished study of on-line social support, Cummings *et al.* (1998) found that, in a survey of posters to a support group, 53 per cent reported that one of the benefits of participation in the group was 'feeling I am not alone'. Misery loves company for a number of psychological reasons, the key being social comparison. Social comparison is a process of comparing ourselves with others. In general, we can compare ourselves with those doing better than ourselves (upward social comparison) or those doing worse (downward social comparison). Within a self-help context, the two forms of comparison serve two independent functions: downward social comparisons may improve a person's mood and self-esteem by showing that there are others worse off (Gibbons, 1986; Wills, 1987), while upward comparisons may provide a guide for action (Wills, 1992; Wood, 1989). The size of on-line support groups also ensures that the likelihood of finding comparison targets who are worse off than yourself is increased.

Social support and information bridges

Just as weak ties can be useful for technical advice, so on-line social support networks similarly provide an 'information bridge' to many other sources of expertise unavailable in real life. Weak ties are particularly useful for the generation of solutions to problems. In the case of a query about sleepless nights on a parenting forum, the variety of advice would be likely to be more varied than that provided by a local 'real life' support network.

Of course, within the context of social support, information in a problem-solving sense will invariably contain a social component as well.

The physical and mental benefits of disclosure

Although much social support on the Internet takes the form of large electronic gatherings on Usenet, there are many instances of social support occurring in other domains; for instance, amongst webloggers and members of a community not focused on social support as a *raison d'être*.

For instance, Stone and Pennebaker (2002) examined chat-room conversations on AOL immediately following the death of Princess Diana. They found that talking about the death of Diana was very high in the first week (at times, up to 48.5 per cent of all conversational topics), but within a week it took up less than 6 per cent of the conversations. Within four weeks, discussion of Princess Diana was almost non-existent. Stone and Pennebaker interpret this pattern as supporting a model of collective coping that moves from an emergency phase (when everyone talks about it constantly) to an inhibition phase (where the topic is still thought about, but discussion is discouraged).

Disclosing emotional feelings and trauma can have marked effects on the disclosers' well-being. Pennebaker *et al.* (1988) found that participants assigned to a trauma-writing condition (where they wrote about a traumatic and upsetting experience for four days), compared to a no-trauma group, showed immune system benefits. Disclosure in this form has also been associated with reduced visits to medical centres and psychological benefits in the form of improved affective states (Smyth, 1998). Although not all people benefit equally from self-disclosure, and some traumas are coped with better than others, the general effect is remarkably strong (Pennebaker *et al.*, 2001). For people using the Internet to talk about their problems (or to publish weblogs), their activities may well have unforeseen, positive, health and psychological benefits.

Anonymity

There is a good reason why Alcoholics Anonymous is not called Alcoholics Identifiable. The assumption of the benefits of anonymity for participation taken for granted by AA has similar ramifications for on-line support groups. As Davidson *et al.* (2000) found, social support seeking is associated with the social burden of a diagnosis. Thus, social support provides an interpersonal function.

In a professional setting, Azy Barak (2001) has argued that anonymity and the disinhibiting effect of on-line communication can be used to enhance counselling on-line. Barak (2001) developed SAHAR, a Hebrew language site for 'support and listening on the net'. SAHAR provides a variety of support environments, including one-to-one chat with 'helpers', bulletin boards and e-mail support. They also provide a 'rescue' operation – Barak (2001) estimates that within the first year of operation, over twenty people have been rescued following a suicide attempt. Barak further notes that the anonymity afforded by SAHAR has seen high levels of usage by adolescents, shy and socially anxious people, and those with a high public profile.

Accessibility

One of the benefits of on-line support is its availability 24 hours a day. For instance, while SAHAR (Barak, 2001) provides a one-to-one chat facility for just a few hours per day, there is also an emergency service available virtually 24 hours a day. Winzelberg (1997) notes that many of the postings on social support sites occur out of hours (e.g. late night or early morning), when both professional and non-professional sources of support are likely to be unavailable.

The Internet and quality of life

As we have seen, the Internet can have benefits for the self, for social interaction and for those with ailments seeking social support. The question then arises as to whether or not this translates into an improvement in the overall quality of life for Internet users. Quality of life is difficult to quantify, but as a rule of thumb, it can be seen as the benefits a person receives from their social environment. There are a number of obvious ways in which Internet use can improve quality of life. For instance, although the Stanford study discussed in the previous chapter (Nie and Erbring, 2000) suggested a decrease in social contact, it also found that Internet use was associated with reduced time spent in traffic jams commuting, and, for users of the Internet for more than five hours a week, 25 per cent reported less time spent shopping in stores (which may well, at least for some, translate into a quality of life issue).

The Pew Internet and American Life Project presents less equivocal data. As we saw, Internet users are more likely to have social contact with family and friends than non-Internet users (Howard *et al.*, 2001). Howard *et al.* also report that daily or experienced Internet users, compared with average users, are more likely to report that the Internet has affected their personal life by improving the way they learn about hobbies, learn about new things, manage their personal finances, get information about health care and do their shopping. Howard *et al.* conclude:

Many Americans report substantial benefits from being connected. Well over half of all Internet users say the Internet has improved their connection to family and friends. Three quarters of them say Internet use has improved their ability to learn about new things. Half say the Internet improves the way they pursue hobbies; 37 percent say it improves the way they do their jobs; 35 percent say the Internet has improved the way they get information about health care; 34 percent say the Internet improves their ability to shop; and 26 percent say it has improved the way they manage their personal finances. (2001, p. 20)

In a comparison of men's and women's Internet use, another Pew Internet report (2000a) reports that 24 million Americans have used the Internet to locate friends and family they had lost touch with. Sixteen million say they have learnt more about their families since they began using e-mail, and 54 million belong to a family where the Internet has been used to research family history or genealogy. The use of e-mail for increasing social connectedness is particularly striking for women on-line: 60 per cent report that e-mail has improved their connection to their family (compared to 51 per cent of men), and 71 per cent say that e-mail has improved their connection to their friends (compared with 61 per cent of men). Women are also more likely to use the Internet as a support mechanism: 50 per cent use e-mail to tell relatives about something they are upset or concerned about, compared with 34 per cent of men. More than half (54 per cent) of e-mail users have a dedicated e-mail group list for family and friends. The use of e-mail has brought 51 per cent of users closer to their friends, and 40 per cent closer to their families.

Rainie and Kohut (2000) claim e-mail is an 'isolation antidote'. They argue that 'the use of e-mail seems to encourage deeper social connectedness' (p. 20). And, the more experienced a user is, the more likely they are to report an improvement in their social connections with family and friends because of e-mail. This increase in social contact does not seem to be to the detriment of 'real life' contacts. Internet users (both new and experienced) are more likely to have called or visited someone the previous day than non-users (see Table 6.1).

Table 6.1   The social connections of Internet users and non-users

Percentage who...	Non-users	New Internet users (<6 months)	Experienced Internet users (3+ years)
Have many people to turn to when they need help	38	43	51
Visited with someone yesterday	61	71	70
Called someone just to talk yesterday	58	61	62

Sources: Pew Internet and American Life, March 2000 Poll; Rainie and Kohut (2000).

A similar pattern of results comes from a Pew study of American teenagers on the Internet (Lenhart *et al.*, 2001). Lenhart *et al.* note that almost half (48 per cent) of teens using the Internet report that it has improved their relationships with their friends. This response increases with the amount of use: around 60 per cent of frequent users report that the Internet has improved their friendships 'some' or 'a lot'.

The use of the Internet to improve 'real life' social connections with family and friends does not preclude the possibility of the Internet for forging new social connections. Lenhart *et al.* (2001) found that 37 per cent of younger teenagers said that the Internet helped them make new friends (compared with 29 per cent of older teens).

This pattern of the Internet being associated with positive outcomes is supported by the follow-up HomeNet studies (Kraut *et al.*, 2002). This work was discussed in more detail in Chapter 4. To recap, in a follow-up of the original HomeNet participants (Kraut *et al.*, 2002, Study 1) and a comparison of new computer versus television purchasers (Kraut *et al.*, 2002, Study 2), increased Internet use was associated with positive outcomes (e.g. decreases in loneliness) and increased social involvement.

Charlotte's web: one woman's story

The use of the Internet to enhance quality of life and social interaction is highlighted in the in-depth case study of one user 'Charlotte' (Biggs, 2000). Charlotte (a pseudonym) is a white, middle-class woman in her thirties. Charlotte's husband discovered that she had been communicating with an unmarried man, and forcefully ejected her from their home. They divorced soon after.

One unique aspect of Charlotte's Internet use is that she kept detailed journals of her on-line activities. Biggs interviewed Charlotte twice for two hours using ICQ chat software, and once over e-mail. Biggs identifies two key themes from his interviews with Charlotte: her relationship with herself, and her relationships with others.

Relationship with self

According to Biggs, Charlotte's use of the Internet has encouraged her to become more reflective, and to discover her own 'voice' and sense of autonomy. She says that rather than acting inauthentically and 'talking herself into a good thing' (i.e. convincing herself that all was well), she had instead begun to be more assertive. Rather than experiment with on-line identities, Charlotte was '100% myself' when on-line: something she was not in real life. In her own words (Biggs, 2000, p. 659): 'It [the Internet] was the catalyst for my emergence into myself. I often reflect that it saved my life. It saved me certainly from living an illusion and helped me to become real.'

Relationships with others

Charlotte's relationships with others on-line had played a similarly critical role in her developing identity. She perceives her connections with men off-line to be lacking – in part due to her upbringing, and her being a 'woman of size'. According to Biggs, the Internet provides a safe place for her to be herself when interacting with others. There was a clear link between her ability to see herself differently on-line and the new opportunities this opened for her to connect with a differing array of people in new ways. The feedback she received from her relations with those who liked or were attracted to her on-line personality positively reinforced the developing identity.

Charlotte formed a number of romantic attachments with men on-line, some of which led to phone and FtF meetings. Unlike her experiences of dating via other media, she 'never had the sense that anyone she met f2f had misrepresented himself on-line' (Biggs, 2000, p. 660).

Biggs argues that the process Charlotte describes has many similarities aimed for in psychotherapy. She used the Internet to reveal aspects of herself to others that even she had not before consciously recognised. Moreover, the task of expressing herself through text, Biggs argues, may have objectified her understanding and experience, in a similar way that therapists may seek to have their clients engage in direct tasks. For instance, there is evidence that keeping a journal can lead to the experience of personal growth (McLennan *et al.*, 1998; Stone, 1998).

Charlotte's experience of the Internet has not only been an exercise in self-understanding, and helped her move out of a difficult relationship, but it has also allowed her to generalise her experiences on-line to her off-line life, 'allowing her to find a voice off as well as on the web' (Biggs, 2000, p. 661).

Positive aspects of motivated web browsing

As we have seen, social support and intimate, empathic communication on-line can have a number of benefits for an individual.

To an extent, the same applies to the seeking of information on the WWW. Although most health-related WWW research has quite rightly focused on the quality of the information available, some has examined the behaviour of users – including the types of health information they seek, and their motives.

Fox and Rainie (2000) report on a further Pew Internet and American Life survey of Internet users' experience of health-care information on the Internet. They report that 55 per cent of all (US-based) Internet users go on-line to access health information. This health-seeking behaviour was more pronounced in women (63 per cent go on-line for health or medical information) than men (46 per cent seek health information on-line). The information this sample found on-line also seemed to be of use: of all those going on-line to look at health information, 41 per cent said it affected their subsequent decisions about, say, whether to see a doctor or what treatment to pursue, and 48 per cent report that the health advice they found on the Internet helped improve the way they take care of themselves.

Fox and Rainie (2000) report that the main attractions of health information on-line are convenience, anonymity and the sheer amount of information available. Overall, 91 per cent of 'health seekers' looked up information about a physical complaint on-line, and 26 per cent have found information about a mental illness. Overall, 16 per cent report that they have 'gotten information about a sensitive topic' on-line. This was increased for people under 40 – 23 per cent found sensitive information. Health information seeking for others usually occurred after the person had seen a doctor (i.e. post-diagnosis). However, when seeking information for their own use, access was fairly evenly divided between before a visit to the doctor, after a visit, and unrelated to a visit to a doctor.

This pattern of health information seeking mirrors the study of a cancer web site by Joinson and Banyard (2002). In this study, we examined the access rates ('hits') to a cancer web site, and compared them with the primary query on a telephone helpline for cancer, and prevalence statistics for the UK population. We found that the hits on the web site seemed to follow the pattern of prevalence in the population more closely than the telephone enquiries, with the exception of potentially embarrassing or stigmatised cancers (testicular and lung), which were overrepresented on the web compared with the telephone and, to an extent, prevalence (see Table 6.2).

Table 6.2 WWW and telephone helpline 'hits' by cancer site						
	Site of cancer					
	Breast	Lung	Colon and rectum	Prostate	Non-Hodgkin's Lymphoma	Testicular
WWW hits (%)	24.20	21.30	15.60	10.70	12.80	11.60
Telephone (% all enquiries)	27.60	7.20	7.60	6.50	<1	1.90
Telephone (% six sites)	53.49	13.95	14.73	12.60	1.55	3.68
Prevalence (% all cancers)	15.60	15.10	13.00	8.40	3.50	0.70
Prevalence (% six sites)	27.71	26.82	23.09	14.92	6.22	1.24
Female prevalence (% six sites)	27.72	9.73	11.03	0	2.79	0
Male prevalence (% six sites)	0	17.11	12.16	14.93	3.36	1.17

Source: Joinson and Banyard (2002).

Joinson and Banyard conclude that much health information seeking on the Internet seems to be post-diagnosis, although the overrepresentation of testicular cancer suggests that it might also be driven by either curiosity or interest in preventative/self-examination procedures.

Fanship on the Internet: evidence for 'safe' environments

The idea that the World Wide Web provides a relatively 'safe' environment in which to seek potentially threatening information receives some empirical support from studies of the behaviour of sports fans on-line. Being a fan of a specific sports team has psychological consequences, with the self-esteem and optimism of the fan affected by the performance of the team (Hirt *et al.*, 1992). When a team is successful, fans tend to proclaim their allegiance to the team (termed 'basking in reflected glory' or BIRGing), whereas when the team loses, they tend to engage in distancing behaviours (termed 'cutting off reflected failure' or CORFing). Although usually seen as impression management techniques, there is some evidence that BIRGing and CORFing occur in an internal audience.

Fanship therefore provides an opportunity to study the effect of the Internet on seeking self-enhancing information (i.e. after a team wins) and self-protective behaviour (after a team loses). In one of the earliest studies of web behaviour, I (Joinson, 2000a) measured the hits on football web sites before and after games during the 1994–5 season. It was predicted that the WWW would provide an opportunity to BIRG through the access of team information following a victory, and that the need to CORF would be reduced due to the relative interpersonal safety of the WWW. The results are illustrated in Figure 6.1. The interaction between the result, and whether the measurement was pre- or post-match, was significant.

This effect was conceptually replicated by End (2001). End studied both the web pages of sports fans, and their postings to bulletin boards. He found that although fans seemed to engage in BIRGing by linking to a successful team's web page from their own, a similar number of fans also provided links to unsuccessful teams, suggesting that CORFing did not occur. The results from the bulletin board postings followed a similar pattern: although overall there were more postings made to the bulletin boards of successful rather than unsuccessful teams, the posters were more likely to identify themselves as a supporter of an unsuccessful team than as a supporter of a successful team.

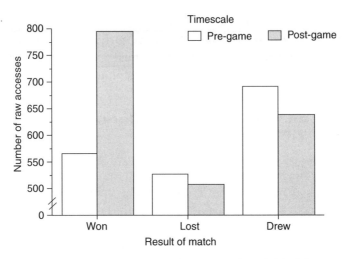

Figure 6.1   Football fans and computer-mediated BIRGing

Source: Joinson (2000a).

Together, the studies of End (2001) and Joinson (2000a) suggest that WWW browsing, while still motivated by self-related goals, also reduces some of the self-presentation requirements following a defeat. Although obviously the social psychological implications of an illness are quite different from fans seeking information about their team, the work on sports fans does suggest that people may seek information on the Internet, or be willing to associate themselves with entities, that present a potential threat to their self-esteem. Although there are a number of explanations for this effect (e.g. anonymity, social support, posting to 'blast' opponents and reduce their opportunity to BIRG), it remains an intriguing effect worthy of future investigation.

Applications and implications of positive Internet use

Throughout this chapter, the discussion of the positive benefits of the Internet has tended to focus on positive outcomes from Internet use *per se*, or through participation in social interaction/information seeking. However, there is every reason to believe that these same benefits of everyday Internet use can be harnessed for more organised interventions – for instance, psychotherapy or beneficial Internet use within an organisation.

Although both these cases are discussed in more detail in the final chapter of this book, it is worth outlining some of the key points here. From a therapeutic view, the Internet would seem to provide an ideal environment for clinical intervention. That people seem to be more willing to open up on-line, and that private self-awareness is encouraged through Internet use, would suggest that on-line therapy will be a worthwhile addition to any therapist's repertoire. Moreover, the very act of on-line counselling or therapy, and the need to express one's feelings through writing, may in itself have a therapeutic effect on the user (Pennebaker *et al.*, 1988). Although there is something of a dearth of outcome evaluations of on-line therapy (although that is beginning to change), some early data support the contention that on-line interventions can be as successful as face-to-face interventions, if not more so. Further, private self-awareness, because of its links to self-regulation, is also associated with greater behavioural control and attitude–behaviour consistency. So, for interventions aimed at changing potentially unhealthy or harmful behaviours, the Internet may actually work better than more traditional methods.

A similar pattern emerges within organisations. For instance, team meetings and brainstorming tend to reduce the number (and sometimes the quality) of ideas produced (Furnham, 2000). However, on-line meetings may improve brainstorming by reducing the ability for social loafing, while at the same time reducing accountability concerns (Furnham, 2000). The key, as ever, is that by understanding the processes that drive Internet behaviour, and designing tools and situations appropriately, then positive behaviours can be encouraged. Similarly, bad design may lead to some of the negative outcomes discussed in previous chapters. And, as should also be clear, many of the psychological processes associated with the more negative outcomes of Internet use are also fundamental to ensuring positive outcomes. In this sense, a division of the Internet into positive and negative outcomes is pointless, although it does serve to illustrate the links between the two. What is important to recognise is that many of the steps to reduce the 'negative' aspects of Internet use will also lead to detriments in the more 'positive' aspects. For instance, the introduction of monitoring software on employees' computers will certainly reduce the accessing of, say, pornographic material. But it may also create an increased sense of accountability and privacy concerns for all Internet behaviours within the organisation. And if this discourages, say, the exchange of social information within teams working on-line, it is possible that the team will not develop the relational skills needed for on-line working (Warkentin and Beranek, 1999). Within an educational setting, Salmon (2000) has argued that social interaction is a necessary precursor to learning-enhancing interaction. If we remove the seemingly wasteful social interaction, we may never reach the more productive heights of group work.

A Framework
for Understanding
Internet
Behaviour

Like other areas of psychology, cyberpsychology draws on many disciplines in its scholarship. Work that can be broadly termed 'cyberpsychological' draws on research and concepts from computer science, linguists, anthropology, sociology, business studies and communication/media studies, to name a few. For instance, two recent edited books on psychology and the Internet (Gackenbach, 1998; Kiesler, 1997) include contributions from authors in a wide variety of university departments, including sociology, communication studies, management and policy, information science, educational anthropology, computer science and human–computer interaction, clinical and social psychology, professional writing and health care. It is this interdisciplinary nature of the emerging field that makes cyberpsychology such an exciting area in which to work. It also poses unique challenges when developing a framework that incorporates the many different approaches and epistemologies of the contributing disciplines. To begin this process, I intend to outline a series of key proposals that form an agenda for the development of a framework for understanding the psychology of the Internet.

Aspects of the user

Strategic use of the Internet

The strategic use of the Internet by users is something that has been somewhat lost in most accounts of CMC. User strategy is commonly applied to their selection of media – so, for instance, someone who does not want to get involved with a lengthy conversation might choose to use e-mail or text messaging. During 2001, Vodafone, one of the UK's leading mobile phone providers, ran a series of adverts extolling the virtues of text messaging when you want to keep it 'short and sweet'. In effect, they are appealing to the strategic user.

However, we also need to recognise that the strategic aspect of Internet use extends beyond media selection. Internet users also use their chosen media in a motivated manner. That is to say, quite apart from the strategic aspect of media choice, users' motives and, to an extent, their more stable characteristics like personality and gender also affect both media choice and usage.

The strategic use of media, and specifically the work of O'Sullivan (2000), was discussed earlier. To recap, O'Sullivan argues that people's self-presentation and impression management needs influence the choice of media, such that people act strategically for instance, to reduce the impact of possible rejection. O'Sullivan asked participants to think about interpersonal situations in which their self-presentation was threatened (e.g. confessing something 'your partner would find repugnant') or boosted (e.g. revealing something that would 'enhance how your partner thinks about you'), and what their favoured communication medium would be for this interaction (telephone, answering machine, letters, e-mail or face to face). O'Sullivan also manipulated whether or not the communication referred to the self (as above) or the person's partner. As predicted, there was a significant tendency for people to prefer mediated channels when the news was bad rather than good, and when the interaction would refer to the self rather than the other person. The 'confess' condition showed significantly higher preference for mediated communication than all other conditions.

O'Sullivan's study illustrates one aspect of the strategic use of media – the tendency to prefer mediated communication when revealing negative aspects of the self. He argues that mediated communication allows for greater control over self-presentation, and so might be preferred in these situations.

In Chapter 1, the use of the telephone in America was discussed. Fischer (1992) reports a number of early users of the telephone recalling that it was little used except for during courtship. There seems to be a similar pattern for SMS text messaging. Culwin and Faulkner (2001) report a survey of 565 students' use of SMS. They found that a sizeable proportion (35.6 per cent females, 17.3 per cent males) would choose SMS for asking someone out on a date, compared with those who would preferentially use the telephone (55.4 per cent females, 74 per cent males; no data were collected for FtF prefer- ences). It would seem, then, that perhaps users choose media strategi- cally – with media allowing reduced bandwidth (and so cues, and also increasing impression management ability) being chosen in situations in which self-presentation and perhaps gender-role concerns are paramount. The management of telephone use also reflects the stra- tegic dimension of media use. Brown and Perry (2000) begin by noting that most telephones do not have off switches (although mobile phones have changed this somewhat). They further note that this effec- tively creates a rule that says 'if the telephone rings, answer it'. But, often we do not want to answer the telephone, and so have appropri- ated other technologies (like Caller ID, voice mail and answer phones) to enable us not to answer the phone automatically. Their point, which is well-made, is that the design of telephones allows for behav- iour according to one rule ('if it rings, answer it'), meaning that other 'deviant' behaviours ('if it rings, screen it') are essentially discouraged (although other technologies are developed to allow users this option). As such, with user adaptations the telephone can become an asyn- chronous device (talking to each other's answer phones). Brown and Perry conclude that the design of communication technology needs to recognise these implicit rules, and provide freedom for users to break them. The example of the ringing, unanswered telephone also illus- trates how, as social communicators, we are able to act strategically when managing our mediated interactions. The growth of call screen- ing and voice mail also suggests that at times we might prefer asyn- chronous interaction over the 'richer' real-time telephone call.

There are other factors besides impression management in the stra- tegic choice of media. One's choice of media does more than convey a message, it is also part of the message itself (McLuhan, 1964). The symbolic meanings associated with media mean that users can suggest meaning simply through their choice of channel. So, for the strategic Internet user, perhaps if they want to convey interpersonal trust, they might switch to the telephone rather than remain using exclusively e-mail communication. This is not so much because of the ability of the media to convey levels of trustworthiness, but rather because of what the choice of media says about the user's intentions.

While O'Sullivan's approach to the strategic use of media makes a positive contribution to understanding impression management goals in close relationships, his focus can be seen as a little too narrow for un- derstanding the full array of Internet interactions and behaviours. I would argue instead that impression management in close relationships is just one element involved in the strategic use of media, albeit a crucial one in many interactions. However, on many occasions we may just be performing to an internal audience, which still has a self-presentational imperative. Moreover, strategy implies some degree of expected outcome of an interaction. Although we might choose a medium because we expect an outcome to result from the interaction, we might also expect an outcome to result from the use of the medium. What is important to recognise is that users can act strategically in their choice of media, or indeed, in their choice of, say, web sites to visit. That Internet behaviour might be goal-driven in some way or another shifts the emphasis from the impact of the media to the user.

User characteristics and Internet use

There has been relatively little empirical research on the users' characteristics and their use of Internet services. One exception is research into the differential use of Internet services by men and women. For instance, the Pew Internet and American Life Project (2000a) reports that women's use of the Internet differs significantly from that of men, particularly their use of e-mail. For instance, more women find e-mail useful for communicating with family (60 per cent) and friends (71 per cent) compared with men (51 per cent and 61 per cent respectively). Women are significantly more likely to look forward to receiving e-mail than men (78 per cent versus 62 per cent), and more women have used e-mail to communicate with distant family (53 per cent) and friends (73 per cent) than men (43 per cent and 65 per cent respectively).

Other Internet-based activities differ too. Women are more likely than men to look for health or medical information on-line (61 per cent of women compared with 47 per cent of men), more likely to look for job information (41 per cent versus 35 per cent), play games on-line (37 per cent versus 32 per cent), and search for religious or spiritual material (23 per cent versus 19 per cent).

On the other hand, men are more likely than women to visit news sites (66 per cent versus 53 per cent), get financial information and trade stocks (52 per cent versus 35 per cent and 16 per cent versus 9 per cent), look up product information (80 per cent versus 67 per cent), take part in on-line auctions (19 per cent versus 11 per cent) and look for information on a hobby or interest (80 per cent versus 71 per cent).

However, some activities, like sending instant messages, using chat rooms and browsing the web for fun, is just as likely to be used by men as by women.

Findings from the HomeNet project also support the contention that men and women differ in their use of the Internet (Boneva *et al.*, 2001). Boneva *et al.* found that women's traditional relationship maintenance role extended to the use of e-mail as well. Women were significantly more likely to spend more time each day talking to family and friends and using e-mail (although these are self-report measures). Women also rated social uses of the Internet (specifically, software that allows you to 'keep in touch with family and friends' and that allows you to 'find new people to communicate with from all over the world') as both significantly more useful and more fun than men did.

Boneva *et al.* (2001) conclude that women's use of e-mail is due to the different ways women and men enact relationships. For men, many relationships are maintained through joint activities (e.g. attending sports events), so the use of e-mail is not a suitable replacement. However, for women relationships are maintained through personal and emotional intimacy and communication. This would explain why Boneva *et al.* found no difference in the use of e-mail for communication with local friends: men were using it as a coordination device (that is, to arrange meetings). It was with the use of e-mail for talking to long-distance friends that the gender gap appeared: because for men, an instrumental relationship is not really possible over a long distance, communication is deemed unnecessary. Conversely for women, distance places little or no barrier to the maintenance of a relationship using expressive means. Boneva *et al.* also note that women tend to prefer 'spurts' of intense communication, compared to men who prefer communication at a more leisurely pace. They hypothesise that because of this, women may be more attracted to instant messaging than men.

So, it is clear that at least one characteristic of the Internet user, gender (and the roles associated with it), will influence the amount and type of Internet use, and the satisfaction gained from that use. Presumably, in this case, use of the Internet is to a degree self-reinforcing. Women report using e-mail more to conduct personal relationships, and report that they get more satisfaction from those relations.

There is also considerable evidence that gender is also associated with the content and style of communication on the Internet (Herring, 1993; Savicki *et al.*, 1999). Again, this characteristic of the user is likely to feed back to their experience of the Internet, and cycle recursively to their own motives and experiences for Internet use.

A somewhat less well-researched, but considerably well-conjectured, aspect of the user is their personality and its implications for the type of Internet activity they choose to engage in. Hamburger and Ben-Artzi (2000) analysed people's Internet activities in light of their scores on Eysenck's personality inventory (EPI). They identified three main types of Internet activity or service: 'Social' (e.g. chat, discussion groups, people-address seeking); 'Information' (e.g. work- or studies-related information seeking); and 'Leisure' (e.g. sex web site and random surfing). In their study, Hamburger and Ben-Artzi asked 72 psychology students to score their level of activity on each Internet activity (using a ten-point scale) and also to complete the EPI. They found that scores on *extraversion* were positively correlated with use of leisure services for men, and negatively correlated with the use of social services for women. Scores on the *neuroticism* scale were positively correlated with use of social services for women, and negatively correlated with the use of information services for men.

So, extravert men are drawn to surfing for fun and for sexual kicks (replicating other studies reporting links between extraversion and sexual sensation seeking). Similarly, extraversion has been associated with uninhibited communication in groups (Smolensky *et al.*, 1990). Meanwhile, introverted and highly neurotic women are drawn to the use of chat, discussion groups and people-seeking, according to the results of Hamburger and Ben-Artzi (2000). Hamburger and Ben-Artzi argue that this may be because women tend to be more self-conscious than men, and as such might be more attuned to signs of psychological distress. As such, they may be more likely to seek support on-line. To be sure, women are somewhat more likely to seek support than men, but there is ample evidence of men using on-line social support as widely as women (Mickelson, 1997). Swickert *et al.* (2002) found only a slight link between neuroticism and Internet use, in that scores on a measure of neuroticism were negatively correlated with 'technical' Internet use (including chat rooms, bulletin boards, web page design and MUDding) and 'information exchange' (e-mail and web use).

A second personality characteristic that has been associated with specific patterns of Internet use is shyness and social anxiety. Because shyness and social anxiety are very much rooted in a person's expectation of a self-presentation failure, it would seem that the Internet should provide an ideal opportunity for socially anxious individuals to control their self-presentation more carefully. It would also be expected that this would be easier to do using an asynchronous medium like e-mail than a synchronous medium like chat or IRC.

There is some suggestive evidence that shy people do find the Internet to be particularly useful for making social contacts, compared with non-shy people. For instance, Scharlott and Christ (1995) studied the users of an early electronic dating system called 'Matchmaker'. They found significant differences between shy and non-shy users of the system. Shy users, compared with non-shy users, were more likely to agree that they used the system to 'explore new aspects of their personalities' and 'explore fantasies in an anonymous, non-threatening environment' (p. 199). Scharlott and Christ also found that self-rated appearance was not associated with the likelihood of starting a romantic relationship on the Matchmaker system. In contrast, they note that users of a video dating system used appearance as their primary criterion for selecting potential partners (Woll and Cozby, 1987). They therefore conclude that 'a CMC system like Matchmaker can be beneficial in helping some individuals meet and form relationships, especially those who have had difficulty doing so because of sex role, shyness or appearance inhibitions' (p. 203).

Again, the user characteristics would seem to interact with Internet use. Kraut *et al.* (2002) found that extraverts seem to benefit more from Internet use than introverts (a rich get richer, poor get poorer hypothesis). Similar concerns have been raised by Shepherd and Edelmann (2001) in their overview of social phobia and Internet use. They propose that social phobics may be attracted to the Internet because it provides a safe, easier environment for social interaction, which in turn places them at risk of excessive Internet use, which then leads to increases in social isolation and damage to real-world interactions.

Motives and Internet use

The array of motives argued to determine behaviour is large, and growing. Because there is limited space here to discuss all motives that might influence the behaviour of Internet users, a selection are considered.

Self-enhancement, self-protection and self-esteem

Self-enhancement refers to people's desire for a positive sense of self-esteem, to present themselves and see themselves in a positive light. For example, McDougall (1933) termed the need for self-regard the 'master motive'. Allport (1937) claimed self-enhancement is a central goal of existence. Kaplan (1975) stated that the self-esteem motive is 'universally and characteristically' dominant (p. 16). It has been argued that there are two ways – protection and enhancement – in which people can promote and maintain a sense of self-worth (Baumeister *et al.*, 1989). People engaged in self-protection 'focus not on their good points but on trying to minimise their weaknesses' (Schlenker *et al.*, 1990, p. 856). Meanwhile, self-enhancement refers to those who 'see ways of drawing attention to their skills and talents' (Wood *et al.*, 1994, p. 713). This view of the bold, self-enhancing individual is closely linked to the possession of high self-esteem (Baumeister *et al.*, 1989). The more cautious, self-protective individual is linked with the possession of low self-esteem (Arkin, 1981; Baumeister *et al.*, 1989).

The desire for positive self-regard has been linked to a series of biases in social perception, as well as being proposed as crucial to understanding group behaviour within social identity theory (Hogg and Abrams, 1993).

For the Internet user, the self-enhancement motive is clearly relevant for both choice of Internet service and behaviour using that service (e.g. lurking on a social support bulletin board to engage in downward comparisons). A self-protection motive might be associated with the use of the Internet by socially anxious and shy people and those with low self-esteem. Preliminary data from Joinson (2002) support this notion. Internet users with low self-esteem were more likely to choose e-mail over face to face when the chances of negative feedback, or the need to disclose intimate details about one's private life, were high.

Self-assessment and uncertainty reduction

Trope (1979) argues that information about the self is sought if it is diagnostic, that is, whether it reduces uncertainty and increases accurate self-assessment in a particular domain. Hogg and Mullin (1999) have extended this motive to social identity theory, arguing that a desire to reduce uncertainty about one's sense of self is a powerful motive in group behaviour.

At times, the self-assessment and enhancement motives may well be in opposition. For instance, wishing to reduce uncertainty about a potential threat to the self (e.g. an illness) would, if confirmed, presumably also threaten self-esteem. To an extent, it is possible that the Internet might reduce this dilemma somewhat – in many cases it provides a 'safe' environment for the seeking of uncertainty-reducing information.

Affiliation

People are motivated to seek the company of others – something called the need for affiliation. Affiliation provides a number of rewards for people, including: enjoyment from the stimulation others provide mentally; self-esteem from the praise of others; an opportunity to socially compare and learn more about the self; and also a source of support or empathy (Hogg and Abrams, 1993). The sub-motives for seeking affiliation will presumably also determine the behaviour of the Internet user – the type of group they choose to join, and the level of commitment they are willing to give to the group.

Meaning

The search for meaning has been implicated in human motivation in many forms, including self-actualisation and existential angst. The loss of certainty and meaning has been associated with the postmodern condition (Gergen, 1992). Indeed, Baumeister (1991) argues that the search for meaning and value leads us towards a state of moral relativism in modern times. The desire for self-understanding has never been more popular – be it in the form of purchasing self-help books or membership of new-age cults. While the role of the Internet in recruiting for these various cults has been well-documented in the popular press (witness the search for the 'Heaven's Gate' web sites), the use of the Internet by people to search for meaning and self-understanding has been somewhat ignored, although case studies do suggest that this might be a motive for Internet use (e.g. Biggs, 2000; Turkle, 1995).

Efficacy

The final motive discussed here is for a sense of control (or efficacy; e.g. Bandura, 1977). A sense of self-efficacy tends to improve self-esteem (Gecas and Schwalbe, 1983). A number of theorists have argued that participation in MUDs gives people a unique sense of control (e.g. Curtis, 1997; Turkle, 1995), something that may be lacking in their everyday lives. While the sense of mastery available on-line has been implicated in Internet addiction (e.g. Morahan-Martin, 2001), it may also motivate non-pathological Internet use, particularly with regard to channel selection.

Conclusions: the role of the user

Thus, there is clear evidence that aspects of the user influence their choice of media, the goals of their media use and the satisfaction they derive from the media. Some of this use may well be strategic: someone who has low self-esteem regarding their appearance may choose a text-based dating service or chat, rather than a picture or video service, because they recognise their inhibitions. However, strategic use extends beyond this. Often, someone might be motivated to keep in touch with family or friends, but not wish to get engaged in a lengthy conversation. In this case, we might expect an e-mail rather than a telephone call. Further, as O'Sullivan has pointed out, people's expectations of an interaction and the likely feedback, as well as the symbolic meaning associated with the media, also influence media choice.

Finally, the self-related motives of an individual will dictate the form and content of an interaction. Just as different social comparison targets seem to be used to fulfil different self-related goals, so it is reasonable to suggest that such goals are transferred to cyberspace.

Media effects

In the past, psychology has tended to ignore the physical environment in favour of laboratory studies which are, by definition, a 'non-environment'. This tendency was noted by Brunswik (1956) who argued that 'Both historically and systematically psychology has forgotten that it is a science of organism–environment relationship, and has become a science of the organism' (p. 6). However, the role of the physical environment on behaviour has been well-documented in the new discipline of environmental psychology (e.g. Bell *et al.*, 1996). Winston Churchill summed up the key premise of environmental psychology in a speech to Parliament in 1943 when he argued that 'we give shape to our buildings and they, in turn, shape us'.

The increased use of technology in everyday life has increased the need for psychology to recognise its role in shaping social behaviour as well as simply mediating this same behaviour. An extreme version of this argument is proposed by Kipnis (1997), who notes that social psychology's reliance on psychological states, because of the difficulties in establishing their existence, leaves theories open to 'continual challenge and replacement' (p. 6). Kipnis argues that technology defines the world in which we live, offering us new and novel choices and experiences, while simultaneously restricting our choices in other areas. He provides a classification of technology to enable its study:

- *Craft technology* Craft technology still requires skill and effort on the part of the person to achieve an outcome – for instance, using a 35 mm camera or cooking from raw ingredients. Technology is integral to the activity, but the person still needs to use their unique skills.

- *Mechanised technology* According to Kipnis, at this level of technology the skill is shifted to the machine rather than the person – for instance, 'point and click' cameras and microwave dinners. The skills needed by the end user to bring about a successful outcome are reduced.
- *Automated technology* At this level, the machine (e.g. a robot or computer) actually takes responsibility for the act – Kipnis argues that television and computing statistics on using a computer package are examples of this level of technology (at least for the user – there is still considerable human skill involved in the programming).

Kipnis argues that the use of different levels of technology influences how successful outcomes are attributed to the person or the technology/tool (e.g. did you cook dinner yourself or was your only involvement putting it in the microwave?), and from that, the level and type of satisfaction people gain from a successful outcome. For instance, a tasty meal cooked by oneself would be attributed to the skill of the cook, and the cook might well feel satisfied with his or her skills. A tasty microwave meal is likely to be attributed to the skills of the technology (i.e. the organisation who produced the meal), and any satisfaction is likely to derive from the time saved rather than one's own skills in piercing the wrapper and using the microwave competently.

The arguments put forward by Kipnis demonstrate the importance of technology in determining psychological outcomes. To return to the use of the Internet, we might also see the impact of the tool chosen as having a number of different effects on behaviour and the user. One method for classifying these is into those effects that are specific to the tool used, and global/symbolic effects of both the tool and the Internet *per se*. A further classification is into those effects that were predicted and expected by the user, and those that emerge through use.

Specific and global effects of Internet use

One way to conceptualise the effects of Internet use on the user is to consider whether they are specific to the tool used, or global (i.e. apply to Internet use *per se* or are culturally grounded). For instance, specific aspects of a tool might be:

- The level and type of anonymity it provides
- Whether interaction is synchronous or asynchronous
- Is interaction text-, voice- or video-based?
- Does the software provide automatic quoting or emoticons?

As has been argued throughout this book, these specific aspects of the tool used have effects on the users' psychological state (e.g. self-awareness or salience of social identity) as well as a direct impact on their behaviour (e.g. in terms of the choice they have and, to an extent, the behaviours they enact).

Internet use also has more global outcomes for the user. One such global outcome might be grounded in the cumulative use of any number of Internet-based services. As we have seen, increased experience or quantity of Internet use has been associated with both positive (e.g. communication with distant family) and negative (e.g. detriments to the psychological well-being of the user) outcomes. Cumulative use also leads to different use of Internet services, and to different levels of linguistic adaptation (Herring, 1999; Utz, 2000).

The global effects of the Internet can also be seen as grounded in a more cultural level. Different media carry with them varying symbolic meanings (Sitkin *et al.*, 1992). For instance, certain media are seen as more intimate or personable, and thus more appropriate for certain types of interaction. So, it would be seen as inappropriate to notify people of a funeral by postcard. However, these symbolic meanings are of course in continual change and flux – witness the current pre-eminence of a handwritten letter for conveying effort and care. However, in a pre-literate time, writing was considerably less trustworthy than a messenger.

Predicted and emergent effects of Internet use

A second classification is whether these specific and global effects were expected (i.e. predicted) by the user, or whether they emerged through the user's interaction with the tool/others.

In many instances, the outcomes of Internet use may well have been expected by the user and, indeed, may have been one factor in the choice of media in the first place. For instance, there are numerous accounts of shy or socially anxious people using the Internet with the express aim of overcoming or routeing around their inhibitions in real life. Similarly, the visual anonymity of Internet romance might be used strategically by people because of concerns about their own appearance or, alternatively, because they want to 'get to know someone' without the 'impediment' of first impressions based on the visual alone. For instance, one of the Internet users who formed relationships on-line studied by Baker (2000) suggests that asking for a photograph too soon is seen as rather shallow. Numerous other cases of people choosing to use the Internet because they expect or predict certain behavioural or psychological outcomes have been documented in the literature (e.g. Turkle, 1995). Of course, many of these outcomes might not be expected when one is a new user – it is likely that they began life as the second class of outcomes: emergent.

Emergent outcomes are those psychological or behavioural outcomes that were not expected or predicted by the user. Importantly, they emerge or are the product of the users' on-going interaction, either with a web site or with other people. It is these emergent outcomes that have been the focus of most CMC research: for instance, changes in the users' self-awareness or social affiliations and identities, hyper-personal interaction and inflated liking and so on. There might also be consciousness-changing emergent outcomes (e.g. experiences of flow or changes in perception of the flow of time), and cumulative emergent outcomes (e.g. changes in identity, in patterns of communication or in mental well-being). As was noted earlier, it is possible for these emergent outcomes to become expected or predicted as the user gains more experience of on-line life. It is also predicted that as cyberspace becomes a more immersive experience (e.g. through VR), so the consciousness-changing emergent effects will increase, although some of the benefits of disclosure/writing might be lost.

Linking predicted and emergent effects

To an extent the differentiation of emergent and predicted effects is problematic in that some outcomes can both be expected and contain emergent aspects. For instance, take a person seeking social support on a bulletin board. The user might well choose this path for seeking support because of the expectation of anonymity. However, the same anonymity could lead to a number of unpredicted effects, ranging from heightened levels of self-awareness, and hence increased self-disclosure and/or a sense of shared social identity with other group members. From

Table 7.1 Emergent effects and technology use	
Level	*Description*
One	Temporary changes in psychological state or behaviour when on-line
Two	Changes in higher-order psychological states or behaviour based on level one changes – some effect/seepage into 'real life'
Three	Transference of level two effects to 'real life' behaviour, identity, health or psychological state

this, we may well see second-order emergent effects like increased psychological well-being (e.g. through the process of sharing, empathy, belonging) and behaviour associated with, say, a social identity based on the membership of the target group. A third level of emergent effects might see the person using this experience for their negotiation of support or identities in real life (McKenna and Bargh, 1998). These levels of emergent effects are outlined in Table 7.1.

While some of these effects might have initially been expected (e.g. that one might feel more 'belonging'), in the main, emergent effects are unexpected. And, importantly, it is through interaction that these outcomes are achieved and voiced. Inherent in this notion is the idea that many aspects of interaction (e.g. power, norms) are socially constructed through the process of interaction, rather than preset for users to adopt as and when needed (Postmes *et al.*, 2000).

In many cases, the user will have anticipated the psychological impact of the mediation tool they chose. However, in some cases, particularly when the user is relatively inexperienced, these effects may well come as a surprise. Through experience, users are more able to control and predict these effects, and so choose their use of the Internet in a more strategic or motivated way.

This basic approach to the interaction on the motivated user and the emergent technology allows one to explain a number of potentially problematic occurrences in Internet use. For instance, many Internet users would be happier sending an e-mail cold to someone they respect or who is important. There are a number of likely reasons for this; for example, the user can spend time editing and reviewing their message, something not possible by, say, telephone. Also, there is still something of an informality/equality norm on the Internet, making such 'cold' e-mails more socially acceptable. Thus, for a strategic and motivated user, we would expect them to choose to use e-mail when circumstances maximised the benefits to them compared to other media.

However, let us say that the important person replies in a very friendly, personable manner. First, the user might respond in kind (for instance, in switching to the use of first names). Second, as an interaction develops, we might expect to see the kind of emergent properties predicted from a technological determinist approach (e.g. increased self-disclosure, liking and so on). But, without the initial essentially strategic decision, this process would not occur. Of course, in the lab, we are less likely to see people acting particularly strategically, although O'Sullivan has shown that in some instances (e.g. when expecting rejection), people do choose media strategically.

The framework provided by the strategic and motivated user, expected and emergent effects approach (SMEE) is schematically illustrated in Figure 7.1.

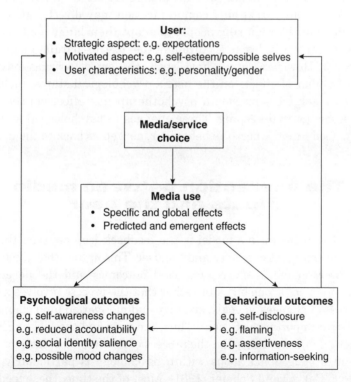

Figure 7.1   The strategic and motivated user, expected and emergent effects (SMEE) framework

As illustrated in Figure 7.1, the various expected and emergent effects of Internet use can be categorised into psychological and behavioural. This approach differs significantly from other models that tend to see the impact of behaviour on the Internet as mediated by changes in psychological states (although the model does allow for this form of interaction). Instead, in some cases, behaviour is seen as directly influenced by media use and the interactions enacted through that media use. This argument is, in part, derived from Gibson's notion of direct cognition through the affordances of the environment (Gibson, 1979). As applied to Internet behaviour, it is argued that the design of the tool, for instance, its affordances and usability, can have a direct impact on behaviour without necessarily requiring changes in psychological states. However, these changes in behaviour can have an effect on the user's psychological state, which then influences subsequent behaviour.

In many cases, specific elements of the media may well have both a direct effect on behaviour and an indirect effect via a psychological state. For instance, text-only communication may directly affect people's behaviour by requiring people to adapt their language to convey interpersonal attitudes (e.g. through the use of paralanguage and emoticons). However, as we have seen, the act of writing may also have a number of effects on the user's psychological states, including changes in self-focus or even a psychotherapeutic effect via the same processes as journal-keeping. These changes in psychological state are likely to feed into the person's behaviour, as well as back to the user.

The interaction between media effects and the user

The final element in this model is the feedback loop between the predicted and emergent outcomes and the user. This argues that the impact of the user on media choice, expected outcomes and the developing interaction is not a 'one-off', but rather that the process involves a cyclical process of changes in goals, strategy and motivation (and changes in the relative importance of each). Thus, the user and the tool are linked together *ad infinitum* through the process of mediated interaction.

The idea of feedback loops within psychology is particularly wellworn (e.g. Carver and Scheier, 1981). Most of the time, these feedback loops are aimed at restoring balance of some sort (e.g. between behaviour and ideal standards), or in the regulation or control of behaviour.

The aim of the feedback loop in SMEE is to provide an explicit ongoing link between the user and their on-line behaviour. That is, the impact of Internet use on the user is seen as more than a one-off occurrence – it is an ongoing process whereby the users' on-line activities feed back to their on-line and real-life characteristics, which then feed back to their mediated behaviour. This pattern of interaction establishes two key propositions. First, that on-line and off-line life cannot be artificially separated, whether through the use of personae or postmodern concepts (e.g. Turkle, 1995). The off-line and on-line worlds are intricately linked through the ongoing process of interaction. The second proposition is that Internet use interacts with user characteristics over time to produce different outcomes for different people. The initial work by Kraut *et al.* (2002) on the differential impact of Internet use on introverts and extraverts supports this argument. Similarly, work on the health and psychological benefits of disclosure has found distinct individual differences (Pennebaker *et al.*, 2001). Even if we assume that Internet use exerts universal effects on people (e.g. an increase in private self-awareness), in the laboratory, individual differences (e.g. self-monitoring) have been found to respond differently to self-awareness manipulations (Webb *et al.*, 1989), suggesting that even universal effects of, say, chat-room use will inevitably interact with individual differences. This is not to say that the study of media effects *per se* is to be discouraged, but rather that a recognition of individual differences will enrich the research programme.

Implications and applications of SMEE

Links to other models

The framework outlined above goes some way to combining a number of differing approaches to cyberpsychology. The first is the distinction between technologically determinist and strategic views of media use (and choice). One of the shortcomings of many strategic approaches to media use is that they focus predominantly on media choice. Although the model proposed by O'Sullivan (2000) goes some way to addressing this by including a feedback system for checking the interaction against the goals, this model is still based on a single interaction-based goal.

However, technologically determinist models can be criticised for similarly ignoring the user in the search for universal effects of the media. And, in many cases, very few aspects of the media (e.g. visual anonymity) are counted. The SIDE approach to CMC promises a further degree of subtlety to this approach by combining both technologically determinist (e.g. anonymity) and context-dependent (e.g. group salience) effects. However, the vast majority of research to examine CMC and SIDE has focused on the 'cognitive' aspect of SIDE as opposed to the strategic aspect. According to the cognitive aspect of SIDE, visual anonymity (as opposed to lack of identifiability) leads to, in certain contexts, the heightening of social identity salience, and hence increased adherence to group norms. Meanwhile, the strategic aspect of SIDE accounts for the role of identifiability and accompanying self-presentation concerns in the presence of powerful outgroups, and the potential supportive role co-present group members can play in the expression of group norms despite possible sanctions (e.g. Reicher and Levine, 1994). The relations between these two aspects of SIDE are not well-developed, although Spears *et al.* (2001) argue that they may well act in a dynamic manner, with the strategic dimension of SIDE feeding into self-definition (Spears, 1995). In this sense then, the SMEE framework echoes the developing work on SIDE. In SMEE the strategic (and motivated) aspects of the user do not simply exert a one-off effect on media choice, but rather go on to influence the effects of the media on behaviour and psychological state, which then feed back and interact with the user. It is only through interaction with others (whether in the form of a web site or CMC) that this process begins cycling between the media effects and the user. To a degree then, the interaction between the strategic, self-presentational dimension of SIDE and the cognitive SIDE can be seen as mirroring the interactions between the user and the media effects in SMEE.

The hyperpersonal model outlined by Walther (1996) is also congruent with SMEE, although SMEE also serves to answer some of the seeming contradictions within the model. At a general level, hyperpersonal interaction also includes the three key elements of SMEE: the user presenting the self strategically or at least positively, media effects (e.g. similarity), and effects due to the process of interaction (e.g. self-fulfilling prophecy, behavioural confirmation). However, hyperpersonal interaction also includes some seemingly contradictory elements, like increases in self-awareness and self-presentation, without a strategy for indicating how they might interact. It also relies heavily on asynchronous CMC, which allows users the time to craft self-enhancing messages. However, high levels of self-disclosure (Joinson, 2001a) and idealisation of communication partner (McKenna *et al.*, 2002) have been demonstrated experimentally in short-term, synchronous dyads, suggesting that at least some elements of Walther's model (e.g. cognitive load, asynchronous discussion) might not be supported by laboratory research. However, the general theme of hyperpersonal interaction, that media effects are accelerated (and indeed grounded in some respects) in the process of interaction itself is also argued in the SMEE framework. The SMEE framework extends this notion beyond one-to-one interaction to mediated behaviour *per se*.

The SMEE framework outlined here goes a significant way towards explaining how technologically determinist (media effects) and strategic/media choice models could be integrated. By adopting an idiographic approach to Internet use, the framework suggests that the impact of Internet use on both psychological states and behaviour needs to be understood in terms of three key elements: the user, the media, and the ongoing interaction. The argument presented here is that the psychological and behavioural effects of the media outlined by the various technologically determinist models (1) emerge through the process of interaction with the media (and others) and (2) feed back to the user which then leads to both changes in self-definition, motives and strategy, and eventually to later behaviours both on- and off-line.

So, for instance, self-awareness manipulations have quite different impacts on the person depending on aspects of their personality like self-monitoring. One would assume that a media use that led to increases in private self-awareness would lead to differential effects for different people. Presumably, it would also lead to changes in the goals for the interaction for different levels of self-monitoring.

A similar demonstration of the importance of an ongoing feedback cycle is the role of self-esteem. For people with low self-esteem or negative self-views, increasing self-awareness can have a detrimental effect by increasing the salience of those negative aspects of the self. However, one would assume that this would in part be determined by the nature of the negativity and the use of the media. While shyness might be contributory to low self-esteem, Internet use might provide succour to a possible self as 'non-shy'. Only by adopting an idiographic approach to Internet use can such effects be mapped and identified.

The framework proposed in the SMEE approach can be applied to a variety of Internet phenomena as outlined in previous chapters. At the least, the framework raises a number of questions about the areas.

Internet addiction and SMEE

SMEE proposes that Internet use needs to be seen as psychologically rewarding and strategically chosen. In keeping with a technologically determinist approach, many models of IAD propose elements of the media that cause addiction. For instance, Young (1997) proposes that the Internet is addictive because of Anonymity, Convenience and Escape. While these aspects of the Internet are certainly appealing to many users, to ascribe an outcome (whether it is addiction or increased loneliness) to the characteristics of the medium is too simplistic and untenable. The SMEE framework suggests that any consideration of IAD needs to consider both the user and the medium, and the interaction between the two. It is clear from the various case studies of Internet addiction (or at least excessive Internet use), that high levels of Internet use tend to be associated with a variety of pre-existing problems, both psychological (for instance, chronic social anxiety, social isolation) and social (for instance, disability, stammering, weight problems, marital problems). In this sense, excessive Internet use is providing an escape, but in many cases we could see excessive Internet use as a logical move to use a medium that is psychologically and socially rewarding in the face of a society that stigmatises or shuns some people. While Internet addiction researchers recognise that excessive Internet use is linked to pre-existing problems experienced by the individual (e.g. Davis, 2001), little explicit consideration is given to the interaction between the individual and their use of the medium (and the effects of that use) in creating a loop where Internet use feeds back to the user and reinforces certain behaviours based on those effects (and their interaction with the individual's characteristics). The framework proposed in SMEE provides a system for conceptualising how aspects of the user and their choice of media might interact to produce excessive Internet use.

Uninhibited communication

According to the SMEE framework, uninhibited communication on the Internet is not due entirely to the effects of, say, CMC on public and private self-awareness. Rather, the analysis begins with the user, and their characteristics, motives and strategies. To take the example of self-disclosure, a user might choose to use the Internet to communicate or post on a web site because they are actively seeking the opportunity to disclose in a relatively safe (in an interpersonal sense) environment. They may choose to disclose on-line because they are more able to control their self-presentation or because they fear negative feedback (O'Sullivan, 2000). Alternatively, they might be on-line looking for affiliation or belonging, social support or self-enhancement. Whatever the reason, to understand fully why people disclose more on-line, we need to understand that their choice of the Internet in the first place might be motivated in some form that already predisposes them towards self-disclosure.

Once interacting on the Internet, they may well find that disclosure is easier than it would be face to face because of the reduced accountability concerns that come from anonymity. Thus, the willingness of the person to divulge information about the self comes under the rubric of an expected effect. However, SMEE also predicts that there will be emergent effects that come from the process of interaction. The user may become more privately self-aware because of the visual anonymity and physical isolation. The act of writing and associated need to focus on their own emotions and feelings might heighten this impact. We might then see further emergent effects at a self-definition or understanding level, where the act of disclosure feeds back to the user, leading to changes in how they see themselves (and their strategy, motives and so on). Thus, a cycle is enacted that links the off-line person with the on-line interaction.

So, according to the SMEE framework, heightened self-disclosure is not a universal effect of the Internet, or indeed CMC. Rather, it is an outcome of the ongoing interaction between the user, the tool and the process of interaction itself. To give a further example, an often cited benefit of on-line psychological experimentation is increased self-disclosure and reduced social desirability (Buchanan, 2001). However, as I have shown in a series of studies, it is possible to design out this effect, for instance, by removing visual anonymity or providing accountability cues (Joinson, 2001a, Studies 2 and 3), as well as to 'design in' self-disclosure in web surveys (Joinson, 2001b). So, just as traditional psychological research goes to some length to ensure that participants are anonymous through the design of experimental procedure and materials, so the same process is needed for psychological research on-line. In a similar vein, there is considerable interest within e-commerce in ways both to encourage customer disclosure to web sites (Moon, 2000) and the links between trust and self-disclosure (Olivero and Lunt, 2001). However, the design of accountability cues into many commercial web sites (e.g. registration forms, cookies, profiling), especially as users become more experienced, may well mitigate any tendency to disclose more on-line than off-line. If a user visits an e-commerce site precisely because they are looking for a degree of anonymity, then design that discourages this belief may well lead to the loss of custom. To conclude, on the Internet heightened self-disclosure is not the birthright of all on-line services – it is something that can be encouraged by good design, and discouraged by bad design.

Internet use and mental health

The SMEE framework suggests that the impact of Internet use on the psychological well-being of users requires a consideration of both the user and the potential media effects. This approach is congruent with the follow-up of the HomeNet sample (Kraut *et al.*, 2002) that suggests quantifiable benefits of the Internet use for extraverts, and possible contraindications for introverts. Bargh *et al.* (in press) characterise this as the 'Person × Internet interaction', with any impact of the media depending upon the person's goals of Internet use and their personality and perhaps social skill level. In comparison to the Person × Internet approach, SMEE suggests a pattern whereupon the 'Person' is involved in media choice, which then feeds back to the user via a series of different levels and types of media effects (as well as having a direct impact on behaviour). SMEE also keeps open the possibility that media use, through interaction with the user's characteristics, can lead to widescale, fundamental changes in, for instance, their self-image, sense of efficacy, social isolation and mental well-being.

Looking to the Future, Learning from the Past

8

As I write (late 2001 and early 2002), the bubble has burst for many dotcoms, with a whole series of high-profile crashes (e.g. http://www.boo.com/), and whole sites dedicated to rumours and predictions for the next major casualty (e.g. http://www.fuckedcompany.com/). Recent articles (for instance, in the UK broadsheet the *Guardian*) have argued for a 'postmodern' return of the face to face, while *The Sunday Times* (4 March 2001) reports that some companies are adopting 'e-mail free' Fridays to 'enhance creativity'. In the UK, the number of people with access to the Internet dropped for the first time since they began counting, and attempts at various e-university ventures seem to be ending in acrimony.

The Internet is about communication, not content

Is the Internet really an 'information superhighway'? Visions of the Internet as a place for the essentially passive acquiring of information have tended to dominate both government policy, the advertising of ISPs and the terminology used to describe Internet behaviour. For instance, in the UK most of the advertising for ISPs (dominated by British Telecom and AOL) is characterised by a propounding of the benefits to be gained through the access to information. AOL even has a female seemingly representing the Internet who consists of web pages full of information. That many attempts to widen access to the Internet have seen computers installed in libraries rather than, say, community centres, speaks loudly of the underlying assumption of the Internet as an information technology, rather than as a social technology. The terms 'surfing' or 'browsing' the Internet suggest an activity akin to surfing TV channels, similar in levels of social involvement and passivity (Johnson, 1997). Johnson also notes that most technological development of WWW tools has focused on the provision and design of content (e.g. frames, tables, Flash), rather than on hypertext links, which have effectively remained unchanged since the first version of HTML. Sproull and Faraj (1997) argue that the metaphors we employ to describe Internet users have wide-ranging implications for the kind of tools (and policy) we develop. They contrast the popular notion of Internet users as information processors with evidence that users are, in fact acting as social beings. If we assume that Internet users are information processors we see the outcome of Internet use to be individual knowledge acquisition, with the inevitable conclusion being that financing of the Internet comes from charging for access to the content. Alternatively, if we see the Internet user as a social being, the outcome of Internet use is affiliation, with money coming from membership fees, rather than content. Rheingold (2000) came to a similar conclusion in his arguments for a 'social web', where web tools are developed to create social connections, rather than links to information.

The idea of the Internet as a social technology may also go some way to explaining why so few organisations are able to make money by charging for content. When the telephone was seen as an information-broadcasting device, various attempts were made both to inhibit social communication and produce 'content' and uses worth paying for (Fischer, 1992). In Budapest, the telephone newspaper Telefon Hirmondo broadcast daily from 1893 till 1919. An attempt to develop a telephone newspaper in the USA (the Telephone Herald in New Jersey) shut down soon after it launched in 1911 (Briggs, 1977).

Financial aspects of the social/information metaphor

Odlyzko (2001) notes that for many Internet industry executives, the metaphor of the Internet as a delivery device is widespread. The chairman of Sony, Norio Ohga, is quoted as saying that 'without content, the network is nothing' (Schlender, 2000). Bronfman (2000), the head of a music production and distribution company, expounds an extreme version of the 'content is king' position:

What would the Internet be without 'content'? It would be a value-less collection of silent machines with gray screens. It would be electronic equivalent of a marine desert – lovely elements, nice colors, no life. It would be nothing. (Bronfman, 2000)

In a comparison of the revenues of content and network providers, Odlyzko (2001) argues that although content may be glamorous, it is not the key to financial success. For instance, the US telephone industry (providing connectivity rather than content) had revenues of $256.1 billion in 1997. In comparison, the whole of the US motion picture industry had revenues of $63 billion. While Odlyzko is not arguing that connectivity is the largest part of the US economy, he does point out that people tend to spend more on connectivity than on content. To take the example of the Budapest telephone newspaper, the annual cost of the newspaper was 18 forints, while the telephone service cost 150 forints. And yet the telephone has flourished, while telephone newspapers have not. Although content, in the form of Internet traffic, would seem to be king, according to Odlyzko, this is misleading. True, web traffic does take up the majority of bandwidth (about twenty times as many bytes as e-mail), but it is not the most popular or prevalent use (e-mail is). The development of new technologies and tools (e.g. WAP and 3G mobile phones, WebTV) tends to be based on the faulty assumption that content drives Internet access and usage. And yet, it is point-to-point communication, particularly SMS text messaging, that has driven increased mobile phone use. It is perhaps not surprising that WAP is generally judged to be a spectacular failure, while the enthusiasm for 3G mobile phones (promising more content) is waning. Nokia, the mobile phone manufacturer, has developed a broadband version of SMS called 'Multimedia Messaging System' (MMS). MMS allows mobile phone users to send pictures (via digital cameras linked to mobile phones), voice and potentially video messages to other MMS users. In part, the aim of MMS is to encourage greater use of mobile phone networks (and so greater revenues for network providers). It is also, according to a Nokia press release, the next step in the evolution of mobile phones:

Nokia's approach is based upon a series of evolutionary steps: text messaging (text only), picture messaging (text and graphics), MMS – Multimedia Messaging System (first phase: still images, graphics, voice or audio clips and text, later also video clips). (Nokia.com, 15 November 2001)

That a preoccupation with content rather than connectivity is driving the design of Internet network tools is evident in the development of broadband connectivity that emphasises high bandwidth links to the home, with lower bandwidth links out of the home (e.g. ADSL).

Tools to enhance the social nature of the Internet have also tended to emerge through user demand rather than a business decision about the nature of the Internet. For instance, the 'portal' e-commerce model hyped in the mid-1990s followed the notion that access to content would be a viable business model. However, the development of these portals illustrates the importance of connectivity: Yahoo! now provides e-mail, chat rooms, e-groups, instant messaging and personal spaces, with web directories and directed access to content seemingly relegated to a more minor role. Google, another search engine, has purchased the Usenet archive and posting system DejaNews, again, showing a shift towards connectivity. And the Microsoft portal (MSN) provides links to hotmail e-mail, MSN communities and chat. No doubt the value of connectivity will soon lead to the charging of fees for at least some of these services.

So, it may not be worth bemoaning a preoccupation with content and broadcasting rather than interaction when dotcom companies would seem required to respond to the demands and needs of Internet users for social interaction to ensure their financial survival. But the experience of peer-to-peer applications like Napster, and additions to AOL's instant messenger that enable peer-to-peer sharing (Aimster) suggest that the Internet industry still views the behaviour of users with some trepidation and wariness (Napster was effectively shut down following legal action, and Aimster is, at the time of writing, facing a legal challenge from AOL). Third Wave, software that allowed users to communicate and overlay comments on web sites, was shut down following campaigns by large companies. The early implementations of interactive TV were also based on the assumption that interactivity is between people and information, not between people. So, it was possible to change camera angles or select sports players to focus on during a match, but not to communicate with fellow viewers.

Like the discovery of sociability by the telephone industry that previously discouraged it (Fischer, 1992), no doubt the WWW industry will eventually begin to develop tools to enhance links between people, rather than the broadcasting of content.

Bandwidth and the psychology of the Internet

I was always puzzled why the original *Star Trek* seemed to represent the cutting edge of future technology (transporting, warp drives and so on), and yet Captain Kirk, when exploring a planet, would always communicate by voice rather than videophone.

In their encyclopaedia of communications technology, Gardner and Shortelle (1997) note:

> It is possible to install videophones ... It is questionable whether videophones will ever become popular. Many people would prefer to be heard and not seen, and the purpose of most telephone calls is to convey a message; visual images are not essential to the process. (pp. 284–5)

Putting aside the assumption that the use of the telephone is simply to 'convey a message', Gardner and Shortelle are right in questioning the potential popularity of the videophone. Increasing the amount of cues conveyed during an interaction does not guarantee a more meaningful or successful interaction. Joinson (2001a, Study 2) compared the communication of pairs of participants using a chat program, half of whom were also linked via a webcam that provided real-time video of the interaction partner. The impact of the video link was substantial: it retarded the amount of self-disclosure in the interaction, and tended to reduce the amount of time spent talking. The data of one participant had to be discarded after he covered the webcam because he felt 'uncomfortable', and the debriefing of the remaining participants in the video-conferencing condition revealed many similar concerns (although thankfully they did not cover the camera).

The apparent evolution of messaging services using mobile phones towards full video messages poses an interesting question about the different roles of bandwidth and synchronicity. The assumption within the mobile phone industry is that wider bandwidth (like MMS) will lead to better communication. For instance, Ron Sommer, CEO of Deutsche Telecom, is quoted in a Nokia press release (19 November 2001) as saying:

> It's good that MMS has arrived. Most of our customers, especially the young users have come to love using SMS – it's often their preferred means of communication. Now their experience can be

enriched as MMS is a natural extension of texting. As the content becomes richer, the way towards mobile multimedia is made smooth – it's a natural progression.

Another telling comment on the development of MMS, in the same press release, comes from Graham Howe, the Deputy Chief Executive Officer at Orange:

> You see how people are no longer simply communicating with voice – now I can see what someone else sees and means, at the same time. Orange customers can now create, share and understand; communication is therefore becoming complete.

Like the development of the telephone, many of the developments in mobile telephony are seemingly aimed at *finding uses* for the 3G bandwidth the network providers spent billions purchasing. Text messaging, a use the industry did not predict, helped mobile phones reach close to saturation point in many European markets. But the low-bandwidth, relatively inexpensive text messaging systems are not generally pushing increased voice calls on the same networks. Hence, the development of potentially 'enriched', more expensive messaging systems that seem to be coming closer to the videophone than would seem to be wise, given the lack of enthusiasm for such technology in the past. However, if the asynchronous aspect of messaging is retained, and with it users' ability to control the interaction and their channel and cues (and so their impression), then MMS might prove to be popular with mobile phone users some of the time.

The effects of the Internet on behaviour and psychological processes reported in this book are as current as the Internet is now. However, changes in, say, the tools used to communicate (e.g. a sudden expansion of videoconferencing) would most likely lead to substantial changes in Internet behaviour. By increasing bandwidth, we risk losing much of what makes the Internet such an enjoyable place to be, which in itself suggests that increased bandwidth is unlikely to yield particularly substantial changes in the nature of Internet communication. Just as videophones have failed to prove a success, so Internet tools that heighten users' self-consciousness, while removing their reduced sense of accountability or shared group memberships, are likely to be rejected by consumers. As demonstrated in the previous section on content versus connectivity, people will choose which services and tools they wish to use and will pay for, and which best suits their psychological requirements. In a discussion of Internet addiction, Morahan-Martin

(2001) argues that 'High-speed access promises to change the delivery of entertainment as well, and to make text-based communication obsolete' (p. 215). While high-speed access may well reduce the time spent downloading MP3s, the lessons of WAP and 3G compared with SMS, and the lack of enthusiasm for videophones, strongly suggest that the assumption that text-based communication is an inferior product, chosen only until a 'richer' alternative is offered, is wrong. Morahan-Martin also predicts that, come the end of text-based communication, 'Social presence will increase and anonymity will decrease with the addition of voice and visual cues' (2001, p. 215).

However, the SMEE framework outlined in the previous chapter predicts the opposite to Morahan-Martin's (2001) assumed slide towards richer media. SMEE argues that the choice of media, including issues surrounding bandwidth, are both motivated and strategic. So, for a mobile phone user, the choice of SMS or voice interaction provides an ideal case study for the strategic and motivated aspects of media choice. And the availability of a wider bandwidth option (voice) does not automatically preclude the choice of a lower bandwidth alternative (SMS). So, the availability of wider bandwidth interaction will not lead to an automatic slide to more 'rich' services. But we may well see much more varied shifts within Internet services as an interaction develops. The drift of on-line interactions from chat to e-mail to the telephone to face to face has been widely reported (e.g. Baker, 2000; Parks and Floyd, 1996; Chapter 5, this book). The development of richer, more immersive Internet services (including VR) may well see changes to this pattern. However, in certain circumstances, the desire for low-bandwidth communication (i.e. text only) will remain, assuming it remains available to users.

Designing Internet behaviour

While the predominant view of the Internet user is as an information gatherer rather than as a social being, the majority of tools are aimed at enhancing the provision of information, the usability of web sites, and, from a knowledge management perspective, the links between information. At the same time, people's interactions with essentially information-driven web sites are viewed as occurring in a social vacuum. The widespread use of registration forms, cookies and, increasingly, spyware and tracking devices, suggests that many information providers are in danger of designing out everyday use of their systems. At the same time, revenue from private organisations is funding research into designing into web sites trust and increased consumer disclosure (Briggs *et al.*, 2002).

However, attempts to design social interaction into computer software is nothing new (Ackerman, 2000). Ackerman describes the gap between the social requirements of the users and the technical feasibility of the systems. Although many attempts (with varying levels of success) have been made to bridge this social–technical gap, Ackerman argues that it still remains the key issue in designing computer-supported cooperative work (CSCW) systems. One such gap is actually knowing when other users are on-line on a web site (You and Pekkola, 2001), or indeed, when they are using an asynchronous CSCW system (Ackerman, 2000). Situational awareness has been implicated in the efficiency of cooperative work (You and Pekkola, 2001), and it is possible to design it into Internet software (chat servers have high situational awareness, whereas bulletin boards tend to be quite low). A number of WWW systems are now available that reveal users of a web site, and allow communication between those same users (e.g. Cobrow and Gooey). You and Pekkola (2001) evaluated the People Awareness Engine (http://www.crackatit.com/). The People Awareness Engine is software that provides situational awareness and a communication facility on web pages. The software is embedded on every page of a web site, meaning that users can talk to people interested in the same information without needing to leave to visit a specific communication page. You and Pekkola conclude that the People Awareness Engine provides a method for bridging the information provision aspect of the WWW, and the need for a workspace or communication on these same web sites. It would seem, then, that the idea of a social web first proposed by Rheingold (2000) is now coming to fruition.

Applying psychological research on Internet behaviour

In many cases, psychological research investigating Internet behaviour is directly applicable to applied settings, including counselling and therapy on-line, education and e-commerce ventures. Although the limited space available precludes a detailed consideration, some key pointers are outlined below.

On-line counselling and support

Despite its apparent facelessness, the Internet might provide a uniquely valuable arena for the provision of mental health services, from clinical assessment to treatment. There is considerable evidence that clinical assessments conducted electronically yield higher levels of self-disclosure and more candid responses than those conducted face to face (Budman, 2000). For instance, De Jarlais *et al.* (1999) found that more injecting drug users reported HIV risky behaviour (e.g. sharing needles) when interviewed by audio computer-assisted self-interview than face to face. The general finding that computerised assessments lead to the reporting of more socially undesirable behaviours or more self-disclosure has been replicated enough times to be considered robust across situations and, to a degree, specific technologies (e.g. Barak, 1999; Ferriter, 1993; Greist *et al.*, 1973; Joinson, 1999; Kissinger *et al.*, 1999; Robinson and West, 1992). While concerns still remain about the equivalence of computer and face to face assessment tools, as well as security (Epstein and Klinkenberg, 2001), the benefits are generally thought to outweigh potential problems (Budman, 2000).

The use of the Internet to conduct one-to-one therapy or counselling is, however, less well-developed and researched. As Suler (2000) notes, psychotherapy on-line can be varied on (at least) five dimensions: synchronous/asynchronous, text/sensory, actual/imaginary, automated/interpersonal and invisible/present. Suler argues that the different elements can be varied to 'design a therapeutic encounter that addresses the specific needs of individual clients' (p. 151).

For instance, the SAHAR site described in a previous chapter (Barak, 2001) is founded on the principle that anonymity (and increased self-disclosure) on the Internet can be harnessed to provide an effective counselling environment. Barak (2001) notes:

> The basic premise guiding SAHAR is that in social meeting points on the Internet – whether for the individual or for groups – many people tend to disclose personal information and share their difficulties ... The idea behind SAHAR was to initiate a cyberplace that would drain people in a crisis situation and offer them – while assuring them anonymity – a virtual listening ear. (Barak, 2001, pp. 1–2)

So, in the case of SAHAR, the development of the service, and the design of the system, is informed by the psychological processes operating on-line. Where one-to-one counselling is unwanted or unavailable, then social support is available on bulletin boards.

Budman (2000) argues that the Internet offers a number of advantages for the provision of behavioural health care, particularly an ability to tailor programmes according to the users' needs, reduced cost, increased self-disclosure, and convenience. Clearly, these benefits need to be designed into a system. Increased self-disclosure and candidness are unlikely if a workplace programme is run on-line while the network is closely monitored. Tailoring interventions for the individual also requires specific design. And if concerns about confidentiality and privacy are to be addressed, then a system needs to take care to protect not only any data submitted, but also the users' own privacy, for instance, through the use of encryption. Similarly, Grohol (1998) notes that with the increase in the use of videoconferencing or audio links, 'more behavioral health-care professionals may feel comfortable exploring on-line modalities because of the restoration of non-verbal cues and the increased degree of telepresence' (p. 131). But, as Grohol also notes, increasing the non-verbal cues available to the therapist (and so perhaps making them feel more comfortable) might remove the attraction of on-line therapy to the client (e.g. anonymity, disinhibition).

A wealth of other, unresolved issues remain with regard to on-line therapy, including ethical and legal issues (Manhal-Baugus, 2001), the usefulness of various tools, and how the choice of tool should match the needs of the client (Castelnuovo et al., 2001; Suler, 2000). I would also add that, as the SMEE framework predicts, the use of the Internet might have quite unexpected effects, dependent upon the characteristics of the user and the ensuing interaction. Is it possible that Internet therapy is actually detrimental to some people? There is an implicit assumption that revealing the 'true self' (McKenna et al., 2002) or an increase in self-awareness (Joinson, 2001a) is beneficial, and in the hands of a skilled therapist this may well be so. But it might also lead to self-revelations that have negative effects on the individual, or might even encourage rumination, which can accentuate depression. In the UK, the Samaritans report that around 50 per cent of people e-mailing them mention suicide, compared to around 20 per cent of telephone sessions (*The Scotsman*, 24 February 1999). While this increased self-disclosure may well be beneficial in a counselling session, there is also the possibility that Internet use encourages a journey of self-discovery that leads to more detrimental outcomes.

Educational technology

Computer-mediated communication (CMC) has been widely adopted by both distance and local educators. The growth of 'virtual learning environments' (VLEs) within universities has led to the widescale implementation of bulletin boards linked to course web sites within traditional universities. While in part this growth is based, at least in the UK, on increasing student numbers, it is also based on the theoretical possibility that CMC presents a number of potentially beneficial pedagogical advantages. These benefits derive from both the affordances CMC offers for peer-to-peer communication, and the potential psychological benefits of CMC over face-to-face teaching. Often the pragmatic advantages (e.g. archiving, increased opportunity for peer-based communication) are used to imply psychological benefits (e.g. disinhibition, equality of participation and so on).

Benefits of CMC in education

It was originally thought that CMC will serve to 'flatten' student discussions, both by encouraging more equal participation and reducing the influence of the tutor on student learning. The traditional classroom interaction has been characterised as following an 'initiation–response–evaluation' (IRE) sequence, wherein the tutor asks a student a question, the student replies, and the tutor comments on that answer (Beattie, 1982). In this traditional model, other forms of interaction (for instance, with one's peers) are minimal. A number of researchers have argued that (1) CMC encourages higher levels of peer-based interaction and (2) this type of interaction is particularly valuable for learning. To take each point at a time, it is perhaps not surprising that CMC seems to encourage more student–student interaction. Not only does the design of CMC systems allow more student–student interaction (Tolmie and Boyle, 2000), but most tutors who set up CMC systems explicitly set out to create peer-based interaction. One would imagine that if a similar norm was established within a FtF tutorial (e.g. students working in small groups), then high levels of student interaction would also be similarly high. When CMC systems are not set up explicitly to encourage student–student interaction, it is not uncommon for the tutor to contribute up to 50 per cent of postings, and for the IRE model to establish itself equally well in a CMC environment as FtF (Light and Light, 1999). The second point is that peer–peer interaction encourages learning. For instance, Tolmie and Boyle (2000) argue that disagreements amongst peers mean that, because there is no authority source, students have to 'make explicit the basis for their ideas' (p. 121). This type of discussion may lead to 'conceptual growth'. Tolmie and Boyle (2000) conclude that 'This framework pinpoints the value of asynchronous e-mail exchange: it is not just that it facilitates discussion between students, but that any disagreements which occur will promote growth in understanding' (p. 121). A final observation about classroom interaction during CMC is that students may be more willing to challenge the tutors' opinion (Reader and Joinson, 1999). Whether this is a good thing remains to be seen.

It has also been proposed that CMC systems can be used to improve students' argumentation skills (Reader and Joinson, 1999). Reader and Joinson argue that what students usually take from a tutorial discussion are just the conclusions (which, after all, are what seem to be important). Of perhaps greater pedagogical importance is an understanding of the actual process that led to these conclusions, even as an observer rather than a participant (McKendree *et al.*, 1998). It could be argued that the transparency of CMC discussions, and the ability for students to review arguments, will improve students' own argumentation skills. A final potential pedagogical benefit is that students might learn vicariously by observing others' discussions (McKendree *et al.*, 1998).

Problems with teaching using CMC

However, in tandem with the theoretical advantages of CMC, a number of problems occur with alarming frequency in reported CMC in an educational setting. Only a relatively small proportion of students with access to the CMC systems usually post, and most posts can usually be attributed to the tutor (Light and Light, 1999). For instance, Light and Light report that 50 per cent of the posts to their CMC system were by the tutor. Joinson (2000b) reports that only around a third of students could be classified as 'active' participants in a CMC system. Morris and Naughton (1999) report that from a population of 3,000 on-line students, in any one month there tended to be only around 100 active contributors to the CMC-based discussions. Low participation rates are reported across CMC experiences (see Tolmie and Boyle, 2000, for a review). When students do post the majority of messages, they often take the form of unrelated postings, often to gain credit for a course (Reader and Joinson, 1999).

While accounts of flaming are relatively low in educational CMC (but see Light *et al.*, 2000, and Morris and Naughton, 1999, for mentions), it is common for reports of CMC implementations to complain that 'students spent a lot of time "off task" ' (Light *et al.*, 2000, p. 265). Morris and Naughton (1999) conclude that, 'While the expected academic use of the medium was less than expected, it was clear that students found CMC very valuable as a source of support and motivation' (p. 151).

Using psychological processes to enhance educational CMC

There have been relatively few attempts to enhance educational CMC using theories of social or everyday Internet use. One exception is the work of Chester and Gwynne (1998) who attempted to encourage 'hyperpersonal' interaction in an educational setting. To achieve this, Chester and Gwynne encouraged a sense of anonymity by allowing students to use pseudonyms in their CMC interactions. They reported that anonymity 'allowed students to find a strong and confident voice', and that 'two-thirds of the students rated their participation in the subject as greater than face-to-face classes' (1998, p. 6). Whilst in general there was a strong sense of community and a relative lack of antisocial behaviour among these students, there were also some problems. For example, one student using the pseudonym 'Hashmann' adopted the persona of a rapper with black American slang who 'swore, wrote in capitals, and flamed other students who made moderate and sensible suggestions' (p. 8).

Utz and Sassenberg (2001) studied the correlates of social identification with a virtual seminar. They found that the students' level of motivation, attitude to the use of the new technology and the degree of fulfilment of their expectations all correlated with their level of social identification with the virtual seminar. If the students' positive expectations are met, they identify more with the virtual seminar, while if they are disappointed, this reduces their level of identification. Although this study does not suggest specific design issues for encouraging social identifications, it does show the importance of students' motivations on social identification processes.

Joinson and Buchanan (2001) argue that theories of psychological processes on-line can be used to develop specific types of behaviour in educational CMC. They state:

Perhaps more importantly, the use of CMC in education can encourage the development of highly affiliated groups when students are visually anonymous and share a social identity (Lea and Spears, 1992). This potential for CMC to create on-line communities rather than on-line tutorials has been overlooked by most educators. Indeed, the tendency amongst many academics is to discourage social communication with the intention of encouraging course-based discussions. We would argue that the two go hand in hand, and that CMC facilitators risk reducing CMC use to a mere trickle if genuine social interaction, and the resulting on-line communities, are not allowed to develop naturally. (p. 233)

E-commerce

The potential for commercially exploiting the tendency to reveal more about oneself on the Internet than face to face also has implications for the design of e-commerce sites, especially the gathering of customer information (Moon, 2000) and the development (and design) of trust (Briggs *et al.*, 2002). However, just as organisations aim to amplify (or at least maintain) certain on-line behaviours, so it is common for organisations to design systems that attempt to reduce these same behaviours. A large number of security companies now offer monitoring software with the aim of reducing on-line misbehaviour amongst employees. These range from systems tracking network traffic to those that scan employees' hard drives to those that record the keystrokes on employees' computers. In these cases, it is reasonable to assume that the software is providing constant accountability cues to employees, which will presumably provide a strong psychological imperative to monitor their own behaviour. However, although the impact of these strategies on employee morale and stress levels is not known, one would expect that higher levels of monitoring (e.g. of keystrokes or hard-drive scanning) would be potentially counterproductive in the long run. The seemingly constant battle between software that enhances anonymity and privacy (e.g. encryption), and the development of both government policy and commercial software to inhibit privacy (e.g. cookies) is likely to continue. The point I would make is that the collection of user information is not likely to be done without a cost to the types of behaviour we see on-line, including behaviours that are potentially useful within organisations (e.g. brainstorming, knowledge-sharing and suggestion schemes).

Future technological developments, past behaviour

With Internet technology developing so quickly, much of the research cited in this book is in danger of becoming redundant within a few years. The rapid rise, and continued development, of the Internet provides a unique opportunity for the psychological study of behaviour on a new medium that will hopefully inform the develop of the Internet as a social technology. Just as importantly, increased research into the impact of Internet use on different people should inform the development of tools that extend the social and psychological benefit of Internet use to all types of people.

At some time in the future, Internet technologies will no doubt become as unremarkable as the telephone is now. One of the interesting aspects of increased research into the Internet is that it has also brought increased attention to earlier forms of communication technology, including the telegraph (e.g. Standage, 1999), the telephone (e.g. Brown and Perry, 2000) and the radio (Gackenbach and Ellerman, 1998). What is clear from these looks at old technology as used today (Brown and Perry, 2000) or when it was 'new' (Gackenbach and Ellerman, 1998; Standage, 1999) is that (1) there are many similarities and links to be made between behaviour on new and 'old' technologies, and (2) when old technologies become everyday, interesting behavioural characteristics remain (see also Short *et al.*, 1976).

The traditional way to forecast future trends is to draw a line from the past to the present, and continue the trajectory to the future. While this works in some cases, much of the time it is likely to fail. In the case of psychology and the Internet, there is a strong case to be made that while the trajectory might not be stable, there is a clear line between the past and the present, and perhaps the future. What is unique about the Internet is the possibility that wholly new, unforeseen ways of interacting will develop. While in some cases the psychological processes associated with Internet use may well become obsolete, in many other cases research on current Internet behaviour will inform, and at best perhaps predict, behaviour using future communication technologies. In a best-case scenario, research into the psychology of the Internet might even inform the design of these future technologies.

References

Ackerman, M. S. (2000). The intellectual challenge of CSCW: the gap between social requirements and technical feasibility. *Human–Computer Interaction*, 15, 179–203.

Aiken, M. and Waller, B. (2000). Flaming among first-time group support system users. *Information and Management*, 37, 95–100.

Allport, G. W. (1937). *Pattern and Growth in Personality*. London: Holt, Rinehart & Winston.

Amateur Radio Newsline (1998, February 13). Available on-line at http://www.arnewsline.org/newsline_archives/cbbs1070.txt

Archer, J. L. (1980). Self-disclosure. In D. Wegner and R. Vallacher (eds), *The Self in Social Psychology*. London: Oxford University Press, 183–204.

Argyle, M. and Dean, J. (1965). Eye-contact, distance and affiliation. *Sociometry*, 28, 289–304.

Arkin, R. M. (1981). Self-presentational styles. In J. T. Tedeschi (ed.), *Impression Management Theory and Social Psychological Research*. New York: Academic Press, 311–33.

Baker, A. (2000). Two by two in cyberspace: getting together and connecting online. *Cyberpsychology and Behavior*, 3, 237–42.

Bandura, A. (1977). Self-efficacy: toward a unifying theory of behavioral change. *Psychological Review*, 84, 191–215.

Barak, A. (1999). Psychological applications on the Internet: a discipline on the threshold of a new millennium. *Applied and Preventive Psychology*, 8, 231–46.

Barak, A. (2001). SAHAR: an Internet-based emotional support service for suicidal people. Paper presented at the British Psychological Society 'Psychology and the Internet: A European Perspective' conference, November 2001, Farnborough, UK. Available on-line at http://construct.haifa.ac.il/~azy/sahar02.htm

Bargh, J. A., Fitzsimons, G. M. and McKenna, K. Y. A. (in press). The self, online: free to be the 'real me' on the Internet. In S. J. Spencer, S. Fein, M. P. Zanna and J. M. Olson (eds), *Motivated Social Perception: The Ontario Symposium*, vol. 9. Nahwah, NJ: Erlbaum.

Bargh, J. A., McKenna, K. Y. A. and Fitzsimons, G. M. (2002). Can you see the real me? Activation and expression of the 'true self' on the Internet. *Journal of Social Issues*, 58(1), 33–48.

Baumeister, R. F. (1991). *Meanings of Life*. New York: Guilford Press.

Baumeister, R. F., Tice, D. M. and Hutton, D. G. (1989). Self-presentational motivations and personality differences in self-esteem. *Journal of Personality*, 57, 547–79.

Beattie, G. W. (1982). The dynamics of university tutorial groups. *Bulletin of the British Psychological Society*, 35 (April), 147–50.

Bechar-Israeli, H. (1998). From <Bonehead> to <cLoNehEAd>: nicknames, play, and identity on Internet relay chat. *Journal of Computer-mediated Communication*, 1(2) (on-line journal). Available at: http://www.ascusc.org/jcmc/vol1/issue2/bechar.html

Bell, P., Greene, T. C., Fisher, J. and Baum, A. (1996). *Environmental Psychology*. London: Harcourt Brace.

Beniger, J. (1987). Personalization of mass media and the growth of pseudo-community. *Communication Research*, 14, 352–71.

Berger, P. (1979). *The Heretical Imperative*. Garden City, NY: Doubleday.

Biggs, S. (2000). 'Charlotte's Web': how one woman weaves positive relationships on the Net. *Cyberpsychology and Behavior*, 3, 655–63.

Birnbaum, M. H. (ed.) (2000). *Psychological Experiments on the Internet*. San Diego: Academic Press.

Boneva, B., Kraut, R. and Frohlich, D. (2001). Using e-mail for personal relationships: the difference gender makes. *American Behavioral Scientist*, 45(3), 530–49.

Briggs, A. (1977). The pleasure telephone: a chapter in the prehistory of the media. In I. de Sola (ed.), *The Social Impact of the Telephone*. Cambridge, MA: MIT Press, 40–65.

Briggs, P., Burford, B. and De Angeli, A. (2002). Trust in online advice. *Social Science Computer Review*, 20, 321–32.

Bronfman, E. (2000). Remarks as prepared for delivery at the Real Conference 2000, San Jose. Retrieved 31 July 2001 from the WWW: http://www.mpaa.org/copyright/EBronfman.htm

Brown, B. A. T. and Perry, M. (2000). Why don't telephones have off switches? Understanding the use of everyday technologies. A research note. *Interacting with Computers*, 12, 623–34.

Bruckman, A. (1993). Gender swapping on the Internet. Available from ftp://media.mit.edu/pub/asb/papers/gender-swapping.txt

Brunswik, E. (1956). Perception and the Representative Design of Psychological Experiments. Berkeley: University of California Press.

Buchanan, T. (2001). Online personality assessment. In U. Reips and M. Bosnjak (eds), *Dimensions of Internet Science*. Lengerich, Germany: Pabst Science Publishers, 57–74.

Buchanan, T., Ali, T., Hefferman, T. M., Ling, J., Parrott, A., Rodgers, J. and Scholey, A. B. (2001). Online research on 'difficult' topics: MDMA, memory and methodology. Paper presented at the British Psychological Society

'Psychology and the Internet: A European Perspective' conference, November 2001, Farnborough, UK.

Buchanan, T. and Smith, J. L. (1999). Using the Internet for psychological research: personality testing on the World-Wide Web. *British Journal of Psychology*, 90, 125–44.

Budman, S. (2000). Behavioral health care dot-com and beyond: computer-mediated communications in mental health and substance abuse treatments. *American Psychologist*, 55, 1290–300.

Burke, J. (1991). Communication in the Middle Ages. In D. Crowley and P. Heyer (eds), *Communication in History*. White Plains, NY: Longman, 67–76.

Buss, D. M. (1988). The evolution of human intrasexual competition: tactics of male attraction. *Journal of Personality and Social Psychology*, 54, 616–28.

Canary, D. J. and Spitzberg, B. H. (1993). Loneliness and media gratification. *Communication Research*, 20, 800–21.

Carver, C. S. and Scheier, M. F. (1981). Attention and self-regulation: a control theory approach to human behavior. New York: Springer-Verlag.

Carver, C. S. and Scheier, M. F. (1987). The blind men and the elephant: selective examination of the public–private literature gives rise to faulty perception. *Journal of Personality*, 55, 525–41.

Castellá, V. O., Abad, A. M. Z., Alonso, F. P. and Silla, J. M. P. (2000). The influence of familiarity among group members, group atmosphere and assertiveness on uninhibited behavior through three different communication media. *Computers in Human Behavior*, 16, 141–59.

Castelnuovo, G., Gaggioli, A. and Riva, G. (2001). Cyberpsychology meets clinical psychology: the emergence of e-therapy in mental health care. In G. Riva and C. Galimberti (eds), *Towards Cyberpsychology: Mind, Cognitions and Society in the Internet Age*. Amsterdam: IOS Press, 229–52.

Chester, A. and Gwynne, G. (1998). On-line teaching: encouraging collaboration through anonymity. *Journal of Computer Mediated Communication*, 4, 2. Available on-line at: http://jcmc.huji.ac.il/vol4/issue2/chester.html

Chilcoat, Y. and DeWine, S. (1985). Teleconferencing and interpersonal communication perception. *Journal of Applied Communication Research*, 18, 14–32.

Cohen, J. (1977). *Statistical power analysis for the behavioral sciences*, rev. edn. New York: Academic Press.

Coleman, L. H., Paternite, C. E. and Sherman, R. C. (1999). A reexamination of deindividuation in synchronous computer-mediated communication. *Computers in Human Behavior*, 15, 51–65.

Collot, M. and Belmore, N. (1996). Electronic language: a new variety of English. In S. Herring (ed.), *Computer-mediated Communication: Linguistic, Social and Cross-Cultural Perspectives*. Amsterdam: John Benjamins, 13–28.

Constant, D., Sproull, L. and Kiesler, S. (1997). The kindness of strangers: on the usefulness of electronic weak ties for technical advice. In S. Kiesler (ed.), *Culture of the Internet*. Nahwah, NJ: Lawrence Erlbaum, 303–22.

Cooper, A. (1998). Sexuality and the Internet: surfing into the new millennium. *Cyberpsychology and Behavior*, 1, 181–7.

Cornwell, B. and Lundgren, D. C. (2001). Love on the Internet: involvement and misrepresentation in romantic relationships in cyberspace vs. real-space. *Computers in Human Behavior*, 17, 197–211.

Cronin, B. and Davenport, E. (2001). E-rogenous zones: positioning pornography in the digital economy. *The Information Society*, 17, 33–48.

Culwin, F. and Faulkner, X. (2001). SMS: users and usage. Presentation at UPA/Design Council seminar, 25 October 2001.

Cummings, J., Sproull, L. and Kiesler, S. (1998). On-line help: using electronic support groups on the Internet. Unpublished manuscript, University of Boston.

Curtis, P. (1997). Mudding: social phenomena in text-based virtual realities. In S. Kiesler (ed.), *Culture of the Internet*. Nahwah, NJ: Lawrence Erlbaum, 121–42.

Daft, R. L. and Lengel, R. H. (1984). Information richness: a new approach to managerial behavior and organization design. *Research in Organizational Behavior*, 6, 191–233.

Daily Telegraph (14 September 2001). Available on-line at: http://www.dailytelegraph.co.uk/dt?ac=006026230637643&rtmo=k7CAx7ep&atmo=rrrrrrrq&pg=/01/9/14/do01.html

Danet, B. (1998). Text as mask: gender, play, and performance on the Internet. In S. Jones (ed.), *Cybersociety 2.0: Revisiting Computer-mediated Communication and Community*. London: Sage, 129–58.

Davidson, K. P., Pennebacker, J. W. and Dickerson, S. S. (2000). Who talks? The social psychology of illness support groups. *American Psychologist*, 55, 205–17.

Davis, R. A. (2001). A cognitive-behavioral model of pathological Internet use. *Computers in Human Behavior*, 17, 187–95.

De Jarlais, D. C., Paone, D., Milliken, J., Turner, C. F., Miller, H., Gribble, J., Shi, Q., Hagan, H. and Friedman, S. (1999). Audio-computer interviewing to measure risk behaviour for HIV among injecting drug users: a quasi-randomised trial. *Lancet*, 353, 1657–61.

Deiner, E. (1980). Deindividuation: the absence of self-awareness and self-regulation in group members. In P. B. Paulus (ed.), *Psychology of Group Influence*. Hillsdale, NJ: Lawrence Erlbaum, 209–42.

Derlega, V. J., Metts, S., Petronio, S. and Margulis, S. T. (1993). *Self-disclosure*. Newbury Park, CA: Sage.

Deuel, N. R. (1996). Our passionate response to virtual reality. In S. Herring (ed.), *Computer-mediated Communication: Linguistic, Social and Cross-cultural Perspectives*. Amsterdam: John Benjamins, 129–46.

Dibbell, J. (1993). A rape in cyberspace. *The Village Voice*, 21 December.

Dietz-Uhler, B. and Bishop-Clark, C. (2001). The use of computer-mediated communication to enhance subsequent face-to-face discussions. *Computers in Human Behavior*, 17, 269–83.

Donath, J. (1999). Identity and deception in the virtual community. In M. A. Smith and P. Kollock (eds), *Communities in Cyberspace*. London: Routledge, 29–59.

Doring, N. (2000). Feminist views of cybersex: victimization, liberation and empowerment. *Cyberpsychology and Behavior*, 3, 863–84.

Douglas, K. and McGarty, C. (2001). Identifiability and self-presentation: computer-mediated communication and intergroup interaction. *British Journal of Social Psychology*, 40, 399–416.

Douglas, K. and McGarty, C. (2002). Internet identifiability and beyond: a model of the effects of identifiability on communicative behaviour. *Group Dynamics: Theory, Research and Practice*, 6(1), 17–26.

Drees, D. (2001). E-mail use in personal relationship development. Paper presented at the British Psychological Society 'Psychology and the Internet: A European Perspective' conference, November 2001, Farnborough, UK.

Duval, S. and Wicklund, R. A. (1972). *A Theory of Objective Self-awareness*. New York: Academic Press.

Eichhorn, K. (2001). Re-in/citing linguistic injuries: speech acts, cyberhate and the spatial and temporal character of networked environments. *Computers and Composition*, 18, 293–304.

Electronics Museum Amateur Radio Club's Newsletter (1996, Feb.). Available on-line at http://www.fars.k6ya.org/relay/9602.html

End, C. (2001). An examination of NFL fans' computer mediated BIRGing. *Journal of Sport Behavior*, 24(2), 162–81.

Epstein, J. and Klinkenberg, W. D. (2001). From Eliza to Internet: a brief history of computerized assessment. *Computers in Human Behavior*, 17, 295–314.

Exline, R. V., Gray, D. and Winter, L. C. (1965). Affective relations and mutual glances in dyads. In S. S. Tomkins and C. E. Izard (eds), *Affect, Cognition and Personality*. New York: Springer.

Feldman, M. D. (2000). Munchausen by Internet: detecting factitious illness and crisis on the Internet. *Southern Medical Journal*, 93, 669–72.

Ferriter, M. (1993). Computer aided interviewing and the psychiatric social history. *Social Work and Social Sciences Review*, 4, 255–63.

Finn, J. and Banach, M. (2000). Victimization online: the downside of seeking human services for women on the Internet. *Cyberpsychology and Behavior*, 3, 243–54.

Fischer, C. S. (1992). *America Calling: A Social History of the Telephone to 1940*. Berkeley, CA: University of California Press.

Fox, S., Horrigan, J., Spooner, T. and Carter, C. (2001). Teenage life online: the rise of the instant message generation and the Internet's impact on friendships and family relationships. Retrieved from the WWW 21 June 2001 from http://www.pewinternet.org/

Fox, S. and Rainie, L. (2000). The online health care revolution: how the Web helps Americans take better care of themselves. Available on-line at http://www.pewinternet.org/

Furnham, A. (2000). The brainstorming myth. *Business Strategy Review*, 11, 21–8.

Gackenbach, J. (1998). *Psychology and the Internet*. New York: Academic Press.

Gackenbach, J. and Ellerman, E. (1998). Introduction to psychological aspects of Internet use. In J. Gackenbach (ed.), *Psychology and the Internet*. New York: Academic Press, 1–28.

Galegher, J., Sproull, L. and Kiesler, S. (1998). Legitimacy, authority, and community in electronic support groups. *Written Communication*, 15, 493–530.

Garcia, L. T. and Milano, L. (1990). A content analysis of erotic videos. *Journal of Psychology and Human Sexuality*, 3, 95–103.

Gardner, R. and Shortelle, D. (1997). *An Encyclopaedia of Communications Technology*. Santa Barbara, CA: ABC-Clio Inc.

Gecas, V. and Schwalbe, M. L. (1983). Beyond the looking glass self: social structure and efficacy-based self-esteem. *Social Psychology Quarterly*, 46, 77–88.

Gergen, K. (1992). *The Saturated Self: Dilemmas of Identity in Contemporary Life*. New York: Basic Books.

Gibbons, F. X. (1986). Social comparison and depression: company's effect on misery. *Journal of Personality and Social Psychology*, 51, 140–8.

Gibson, J. J. (1979). *The Ecological Approach to Visual Perception*. Boston: Houghton Mifflin.

Goldberg, J. (1995). Why web usage statistics are (worse than) meaningless. Retrieved on 16 Feb. 2000 from the WWW: www.cranfield.ac.uk/docs/stats/

Granovetter, M. (1982). The strength of weak ties: a network theory revisited. In P. Marsden and N. Lin (eds), *Social Structure and Network Analysis*. New York: Wiley, 105–30.

Greist, J. H., Klein, M. H. and VanCura, L. J. (1973). A computer interview by psychiatric patient target symptoms. *Archives of General Psychiatry*, 29, 247–53.

Griffiths, M. D. (1998). Internet addiction: does it really exist? In J. Gackenbach (ed.), *Psychology and the Internet*. New York: Academic Press, 61–75.

Griffiths, M. D. (2000a). Does Internet and computer addiction exist? Some case study evidence. *Cyberpsychology and Behavior*, 3, 211–18.

Griffiths, M. D. (2000b). Excessive Internet use: implications for sexual behavior. *Cyberpsychology and Behavior*, 3, 537–52.

Grohol, J. (1998). Future clinical directions: professional development, pathology and psychotherapy on-line. In J. Gackenbach (ed.), *Psychology and the Internet*. New York: Academic Press, 111–40.

Grohol, J. (1999). Too much time on-line: Internet addiction or healthy social interactions. *Cyberpsychology and Behavior*, 2, 395–402.

Hamburger, Y. A. and Ben-Artzi, E. (2000). The relationship between extraversion and neuroticism and the different uses of the Internet. *Computers in Human Behavior*, 16, 441–9.

Hancock, J. T. and Dunham, P. J. (2001). Impression formation in computer-mediated communication revisited: an analysis of the breadth and intensity of impressions. *Communication Research*, 28, 325–47.

Harmon, A. (1998, 30 August). Sad, lonely world discovered in cyberspace. *New York Times*, A1.

Haythornthwaite, C., Wellman, B. and Garton, L. (1998). Work and community via computer-mediated communication. In J. Gackenbach (ed.), *Psychology and the Internet*. New York: Academic Press, 199–226.

Herring, S. C. (1999). Interactional coherence in CMC. *Journal of Computer-Mediated Communication (4)*, 4. Available on-line at htpp://jcmc.huji.ac.il/vol4/issues4/herring.html

Herring, S. C. (1993). Gender and democracy in computer-mediated communication. Electronic Journal of Communication (on-line). Available at http://www.cios.org/getfile/Herring_v3n293

Hilgers, T. L., Hussey, E. L. and Stitt-Berg, M. (1999). 'As you're writing, you have these epiphanies': what college students say about writing and learning in their majors. *Written Communication*, 16, 317–53.

Hiltz, S. R. and Turoff, M. (1978). *The Network Nation: Human Communication via Computer*. Reading, MA: Addison-Wesley.

Hirt, E. R., Zillmann, D., Erickson, G. A. and Kennedy, C. (1992). Costs and benefits of allegiance: changes in fans' self-ascribed competencies after victory versus defeat. *Journal of Personality and Social Psychology*, 63, 724–38.

Hogg, M. A. and Abrams, D. (1993). Towards a single-process uncertainty-reduction model of social motivation in groups. In M. A. Hogg and D. Abrams (eds), *Group Motivation: Social Psychological Perspectives*. London: Harvester Wheatsheaf.

Hogg, M. A. and Mullin, B. (1999). Joining groups to reduce uncertainty: subjective uncertainty reduction and group identification. In D. Abrams and M. A. Hogg (eds), *Social Identity and Social Cognition*. Oxford: Blackwell, 249–79.

Horrigan, J. B., Rainie, L. and Fox, S. (2001). Online communities: networks that nurture long-distance relationships and local ties. Available on-line from http://www.pewinternet.org/

Howard, P. E. N., Rainie, L. and Jones, S. (2001). Days and nights on the Internet: the impact of a diffusing technology. *American Behavioral Scientist*, 45, 383–404.

Johnson, S. (1997). *Interface Culture*. New York: Basic Books.

Joinson, A. N. (1998). Causes and implications of disinhibition on the Internet. In J. Gackenbach (ed.), *Psychology and the Internet*. New York: Academic Press 43–60.

Joinson, A. N. (1999). Anonymity, disinhibition and social desirability on the Internet. *Behaviour Research Methods, Instruments and Computers*, 31, 433–8.

Joinson, A. N. (2000a). Information seeking on the Internet: a study of soccer fans on the WWW. *Cyberpsychology and Behavior*, 3(2), 185–91.

Joinson, A. N. (2000b). Computer-conferencing to the converted: an evaluation of E211. Unpublished manuscript, The Open University.

Joinson, A. N. (2001a). Self-disclosure in computer-mediated communication: the role of self-awareness and visual anonymity. *European Journal of Social Psychology*, 31(2), 177–92.

Joinson, A. N. (2001b). Knowing me, knowing you: reciprocal self-disclosure in Internet-based surveys. *Cyberpsychology and Behavior*, 4, 587–91.

Joinson, A. N. (2002). Self-esteem, interpersonal risk and preference for e-mail over face-to-face communication. Paper presented at *German Online Research*, Hohenheim, October 2002.

Joinson, A. N. and Banyard, P. (1998). Disinhibition and health information seeking on the Internet. Paper presented at The World Congress of the Society for the Internet in Medicine, St Thomas' Hospital, London.

Joinson, A. N. and Banyard, P. (2002). Psychological aspects of information seeking on the Internet. ASLIB Proceedings, *New Information Perspectives*, 54(2), 95–102.

Joinson, A. N. and Buchanan, T. B. (2001). Doing educational research on the Internet. In C. Wolfe (ed.), *Learning and Teaching on the World-Wide Web*. New York: Academic Press, 221–42.

Joinson, A. N. and Dietz-Uhler, B. (2002). Explanations for the perpetration of and reactions to deception in a virtual community. *Social Science Computer Review Special Issue on Psychology and the Internet*, 20(3), 275–89.

Jones, S. (1995). Community in the information age. In S. Jones (ed.), *Cybersociety: Computer-mediated Communication and Community*. London: Sage.

Kaplan, H. B. (1975). Prevalence of the self-esteem motive. In H. B. Kaplan (ed.), *Self-attitudes and Deviant Behaviour*. Pacific Palisades, CA: Goodyear Publishing.

Kiesler, S. (1997). Preface. In S. Kiesler (ed.), *Culture of the Internet*. Nahwah, NJ: Lawrence Erlbaum, ix–xvi.

Kiesler, S. and Kraut, R. (1999). Internet use and the ties that bind. *American Psychologist*, 54, 783–4.

Kiesler, S., Siegal, J. and McGuire, T. W. (1984). Social psychological aspects of computer mediated communication. *American Psychologist*, 39, 1123–34.

Kiesler, S. and Sproull, L. S. (1986). Response effects in the electronic survey. *Public Opinion Quarterly*, 50, 402–13.

Kiesler, S., Zubrow, D., Moses, A. and Geller, V. (1985). Affect in computer-mediated communication: an experiment in synchronous terminal-to-terminal discussion. *Human–Computer Interaction*, 1, 77–104.

Kipnis, D. (1997). Ghosts, taxonomies, and social psychology. *American Psychologist*, 52, 205–11.

Kissinger, P., Rice, J., Farley, T., Trim, S., Jewitt, K., Margavio, V. and Martin, D. H. (1999). Application of computer-assisted interviews to sexual behavior research. *American Journal of Epidemiology*, 149, 950–4.

Kling, R. (1980). Social analyses of computing: theoretical perspectives in recent empirical research. *ACM Computing Surveys*, 12, 61–110.

Kraut, R., Kiesler, S., Boneva, B., Cummings, J., Helgeson, V. and Crawford, A. (2002). Internet paradox revisited. *Journal of Social Issues*, 58(1), 49–74.

Kraut, R., Patterson, M., Lundmark, V., Kiesler, S., Tridas, M. and Scherlis, W. (1998). Internet paradox: a social technology that reduces social involvement and psychological well-being? *American Psychologist*, 53, 1017–31.

La Fanco, R. (1999). The playboy philosophy. *Forbes*, 14 June, 200.

LaRose, R., Eastin, M. S. and Gregg, J. (2001). Reformulating the Internet paradox: social cognitive explanations of Internet use and depression. *Journal of Online Behavior*, 1(2). Retrieved 3 October 2001 from the WWW: http://www.behavior.net/JOB/v1n2/paradox.html

Laurenceau, J. P., Barrett, L. F. and Pietromonaco, P. R. (1998). Intimacy as an interpersonal process: the importance of self-disclosure, partner disclosure, and perceived partner responsiveness in interpersonal exchanges. *Journal of Personality and Social Psychology*, 74, 1238–51.

Lawrence, S. and Giles, C. L. (1999). Accessibility of information on the web. *Nature*, 8 July, 107–9.

Le Bon, G. (1890, trans. 1947). *The Crowd: A Study of the Popular Mind*. London: Ernest Benn.

Lea, M., O'Shea, T., Fung, P. and Spears, R. (1992). 'Flaming' in computer-mediated communication. In M. Lea (ed.), *Contexts in Computer-mediated Communication*. London: Harvester Wheatsheaf, 89–112.

Lea, M., Spears, R. and de Groot, D. (2001). Knowing me, knowing you: anonymity effects on social identity processes within groups. *Personality and Social Psychology Bulletin*, 27, 526–37.

Lenhart, A., Rainie, L. and Lewis, O. (2001). Teenage life online: the rise of the instant-message generation and the Internet's impact on friendships and family relationships. Available online from http://www. pewinternet.org

Levine, D. (1998). *The Joy of Cybersex: A Guide for Creative Lovers*. New York: Ballantine Books.

Lewis, R. and Spanier, G. B. (1979). Theorizing about the quality and stability of marriage. In W. Burr, R. Hill, F. Nye and I. Reiss (eds), *Contemporary Theories about the Family*, vol. 1. New York: The Free Press, 286–93.

Licklider, J. C. R. and Taylor, R. W. (1968). The computer as a communication device. *Science and Technology*, 76, 21–31.

Light, P. and Light, V. (1999). Analysing asynchronous learning interactions: computer-mediated communication in a conventional undergraduate setting. In K. Littleton and P. Light (eds), *Learning with Computers: Analysing Productive Interaction*. London: Routledge, 162–78.

Light, P., Nesbitt, E., Light, V. and White, S. (2000). Variety is the spice of life: student use of CMC in the context of campus based study. *Computers and Education*, 34, 257–67.

Mabry, E. A. (1997). Frames and flames: the structure of argumentative messages on the Net. In F. Sudweeks, M. McLaughlin and S. Rafaeli (eds),

Networks and Netplay: Virtual Groups on the Internet. Cambridge, MA: MIT Press, 13–26.

MacKinnon, R. C. (1995). Searching for the Leviathan in Usenet. In S. Jones (ed.), *Cybersociety: Computer-mediated Communication and Community.* London: Sage, 112–37.

MacKinnon, R. C. (1997). Punishing the persona: correctional strategies for the virtual offender. In S. Jones (ed.), *Virtual Culture: Identity and Communication in Cybersociety.* London: Sage, 206–35.

Maheu, M. M. (2001). *Cyber-affairs survey answers.* Retrieved from the WWW 31 October 2001 from http://www.self-helpmagazine.com/cgibin/cyber-survey.cgi?results=go

Manhal-Baugus, M. (2001). E-therapy: practical, ethical, and legal issues. *Cyberpsychology and Behavior,* 4, 551–63.

Manning, J., Scherlis, W., Kiesler, S., Kraut, R. and Mukhopadhyay, T. (1997). Erotica on the Internet: early evidence from the HomeNet trial. In S. Kiesler (ed.), *Culture of the Internet.* Nahwah, NJ: Lawrence Erlbaum, 68–9.

Mantovani, G. (1996). Social context in HCI: a new framework for mental models, cooperation and communication. *Cognitive Science,* 20, 237–96.

Markus, H. and Nurius, P. (1986). Possible selves. *American Psychologist,* 41, 954–69.

Markus, M. L. (1994). Finding a happy medium: explaining the negative effects of electronic communication on social life at work. *ACM Transactions on Information Systems,* 12, 119–49.

Marrs, R. W. (1995). A meta-analysis of bibliotherapy studies. *American Journal of Community Psychology,* 23, 843–70.

Matheson, K. (1992). Women and computer technology. In M. Lea (ed.), *Contexts in Computer-mediated Communication.* London: Harvester Wheatsheaf, 66–88.

Matheson, K. and Zanna, M. P. (1988). The impact of computer-mediated communication on self-awareness. *Computers in Human Behavior,* 4, 221–33.

McDougall, W. (1933). *The Energies of Man: A Study of the Fundamentals of Dynamic Psychology.* New York: Scribner's.

McKendree, J., Stenning, K., Mayes, T., Lee, J. and Cox, R. (1998). Why observing a dialogue may benefit learning. *Journal of Computer Assisted Learning,* 14, 110–19.

McKenna, K. Y. A. and Bargh, J. (1998). Coming out in the age of the Internet: identity 'demarginalization' through virtual group participation. *Journal of Personality and Social Psychology,* 75, 681–94.

McKenna, K. Y. A. and Bargh, J. (2000). Plan 9 from Cyberspace: the implications of the Internet for personality and social psychology. *Personality and Social Psychology Review,* 4, 57–75.

McKenna, K. Y. A., Green, A. S. and Gleason, M. E. J. (2002). Relationship formation on the Internet: what's the big attraction. *Journal of Social Issues,* 58(1), 9–31.

McLennan, M. L., Schneider, M. F. and Perney, J. (1998). Rating (life task action) change in journal excerpts and narratives using Prochaska, DiClementa, and Norcross' five stages of change. *Journal of Individual Psychology*, 54, 546–59.

McLuhan, M. (1964). *Understanding Media*. New York: McGraw–Hill.

McLaughlin, M. L., Osborne, K. K. and Smith, C. B. (1995). Standards of conduct in Usenet. In S. Jones (ed.), *Cybersociety: Computer-mediated Communication and Community*. London: Sage, 90–111.

Mehta, M. D. and Plaza, D. E. (1997). Pornography in cyberspace: an exploration of what's in USENET. In S. Kiesler (ed.), *Culture of the Internet*. Nahwah, NJ: Lawrence Erlbaum, 53–67.

Metts, S. (1989). An exploratory investigation of deception in close relationships. *Journal of Social and Personal Relationships*, 6, 159–79.

Mickelson, K. D. (1997). Seeking social support: parents in electronic support groups. In S. Kiesler (ed.), *Culture of the Internet*. Nahwah, NJ: Lawrence Erlbaum, 157–78.

Moody, E. (2001). Internet use and its relationship to loneliness. *Cyberpsychology and Behavior*, 4, 393–401.

Moon, Y. (2000). Intimate exchanges: using computers to elicit self-disclosure from consumers. *Journal of Consumer Research*, 27, 323–39.

Moore, P. (2001). Dangerous liasons? A technique for thematic mapping applied to pro-anorexia Internet groups. Paper presented at the British Psychological Society 'Psychology and the Internet: A European Perspective' conference, November 2001, Farnborough, UK.

Morahan-Martin, J. (2001). Caught in the Web: research and criticism of internet abuse with application to college students. In C. Wolfe (ed.), *Learning and Teaching on the World-Wide Web*. New York: Academic Press, 191–219.

Morahan-Martin, J. and Schumacher, P. (2000). Incidence and correlates of pathological Internet use among college students. *Computers in Human Behavior*, 16, 13–29.

Morais, R. C. (1999). Porn goes public. *Forbes*, 14 June, 214–20.

Morris, D. and Naughton, J. (1999). The future's digital, isn't it? Some experience and forecasts based on the Open University's technology foundation course. *Systems Research and Behavioural Science*, 16(2), 147–55.

Nie, N. H. and Erbring, L. (2000). *Internet and Society: A Preliminary Report*. Stanford, CA: Stanford Institute for the Quantitative Study of Society. Available on-line at http://www.stanford.edu/group/siqss

Niederhoffer, K. G. and Pennebaker, J. W. (2001). Linguistic synchrony in social interaction. Manuscript submitted for publication.

Norman, D. A. (1988). *The Psychology of Everyday Things*. New York: Basic Books.

O'Brien, J. (1999). Writing in the body: gender (re)production in online interaction. In M. A. Smith and P. Kollock (eds.), *Communities in Cyberspace*. London: Routledge, 76–106.

Odlyzko, A. (2001). Content is not king. *First Monday*, Issue 6 (on-line). Available at http://firstmonday.org/issues/issue6_2/odlyzko/

Olivero, N. and Lunt, P. (2001). Self-disclosure in e-commerce exchanges: relationships among trust, reward and awareness. Paper presented at the British Psychological Society 'Psychology and the Internet: A European Perspective' conference, November 2001, Farnborough, UK.

Ong, W. J. (1982). *Orality and Literacy*. London: Methuen.

Ong, W. J. (1986). Writing is a technology that restructures thought. In G. Baumann (ed.), *The Written Word: Literacy in Transition*. Oxford: Clarendon Press, 23–50.

O'Sullivan, P. (2000). What you don't know won't hurt me: impression management functions of communication channels in relationships. *Human Communication Research*, 26, 403–31.

Parks, M. R. and Floyd, K. (1996). Making friends in Cyberspace. *Journal of Computer-mediated Communication*, 1(4). Retrieved 10 December from the WWW: http://jmc.huji.ac.il/vol1/issue4/parks.html

Pennebaker, J. W., Kiecolt-Glaser, J. K. and Glaser, R. (1988). Disclosure of traumas and immune function: health implications for psychotherapy. *Journal of Consulting and Clinical Psychology*, 56, 239–45.

Pennebaker, J. W., Zech, E. and Rimé, B. (2001). Disclosing and sharing emotion: psychological, social, and health consequences. In M. S. Stroebe, R. O. Hansson, W. Stroebe and H. Schut (eds), *Handbook of Bereavement Research: Consequences, Coping, and Care*. Washington, DC: American Psychological Association, pp. 517–44.

Petrie, H. (1999). Report of the MSN Hotmail Study. Available from http://www.netinvestigations.net

Pew Internet and American Life Project (2000a). Tracking on-line life: how women use the Internet to cultivate relationships with family and friends. Available on-line from http://www.pewinternet.org

Pew Internet and American Life Project (2000b). The online health care revolution: how the web helps Americans take better care of themselves. Available on-line from http://www.pewinternet.org

Pfeffer, J. (1982). *Organizations and Organization Theory*. Marshfield, MA: Pitman.

Postmes, T. and Brunsting, S. (2002). Collective action in the age of the Internet: mass communication and online mobilization. *Social Science Computer Review*, 20(3), 290–301.

Postmes, T., Spears, R. and Lea, M. (2000). The formation of group norms in computer-mediated communication. *Human Communication Research*, 26, 341–71.

Preece, J. (1999). Empathic communities: balancing emotional and factual communication. *Interacting with Computers*, 12, 63–77.

Prentice-Dunn, S. and Rogers, R. W. (1982). Effects of public and private self-awareness on deindividuation and aggression. *Journal of Personality and Social Psychology*, 43, 503–13.

Putnam, R. D. (2000). *Bowling Alone*. New York: Simon & Schuster.

Quittner, J. (1997). Divorce Internet style. *Time Magazine*, 14 April, 72.

Rainie, L. and Kohut, A. (2000). Tracking online life: how women use the Internet to cultivate relationships with family and friends. Available on-line at http://www.pewinternet.org

Reader, W. and Joinson, A. N. (1999). Promoting student discussion using simulated seminars on the Internet. In D. Saunders and J. Severn (eds), *The Simulation and Gaming Yearbook: Games and Simulations to Enhance Quality Learning*, vol. 7. London: Kogan Page, 139–49.

Reicher, S. D. (1984). Social influence in the crowd: attitudinal and behavioural effects of de-individuation in conditions of high and low group salience. *British Journal of Social Psychology*, 23, 341–50.

Reicher, S. D. and Levine, M. (1994). Deindividuation, power relations between groups and the expression of social identity: the effects of visibility to the out-group. *British Journal of Social Psychology*, 33, 145–63.

Reicher, S. D., Spears, R. and Postmes, T. (1995). A social identity model of deindividuation phenomena. In W. Stroebe and M. Hewstone (eds), *European Review of Social Psychology*, vol. 6. Chichester: Wiley, 161–98.

Reid, A. A. L. (1981). Comparing telephone with face-to-face contact. In Ithiel de Sola Pool (ed.), *The Social Impact of the Telephone*. Cambridge, MA: MIT Press, 386–414.

Reid, E. (1991). Electropolis: communication and community on the Internet. Unpublished thesis, Department of History, University of Melbourne.

Reid, E. (1998). The self and the Internet: variations on the illusion of one self. In J. Gackenbach (ed.), *The Psychology of the Internet*. New York: Academic Press, 29–42.

Reips, U. and Bosnjak, M. (2001). *Dimensions of Internet Science*. Lengerich, Germany: Pabst Science Publishers.

Rheingold, H. (1993). *The Virtual Community: Homesteading on the Electronic Frontier*. Reading, MA: Addison-Wesley.

Rheingold, H. (2000). *The Virtual Community*, rev. edn., London: MIT Press.

Rice, R. E. and Love, G. (1987). Electronic emotion: socioemotional content in a computer-mediated network. *Communication Research*, 14, 85–108.

Rierdan, J. (1999). Internet–depression link? *American Psychologist*, 54, 782–3.

Rimm, M. (1995). Marketing pornography on the information superhighway. *Georgetown Law Review*, 83, 1839–934.

Robinson, R. and West, R. (1992). A comparison of computer and questionnaire methods of history-taking in a genito-urinary clinic. *Psychology and Health*, 6, 77–84.

Rogers, C. (1951). *Client-centered Therapy*. Boston, MA: Houghton Mifflin.

Rosson, M. B. (1999). I get by with a little help from my cyber-friends: sharing stories of good and bad times on the Web. *Journal of Computer-Mediated Communication*, 4(4). Retrieved 10 October 2001 from the WWW: http://jcmc.huji.ac.il/vol4/issue4/rosson.html

Salmon, G. (2000). *E-moderating: The Key to Teaching and Learning Online.* London: Kogan Page.

Savicki, V., Kelley, M. and Oesterreich, E. (1999). Judgements of gender in computer-mediated communication. *Computers in Human Behavior*, 15, 185–94.

Savicki, V., Lingenfelter, D. and Kelley, M. (1996). Gender language style and group composition in Internet discussion lists. *Journal of Computer Mediated Communication*, 2(3). Available on-line at: http://jcmc.mscc.huji.ac.il/vol2/issue3/savicki.htm

Scharlott, B. W. and Christ, W. G. (1995). Overcoming relationship-initiation barriers: the impact of a computer-dating system on sex role, shyness and appearance inhibitions. *Computers in Human Behavior*, 11, 191–204.

Scherer, K. and Bost, J. (1997). Internet use patterns: is there Internet dependency on campus? Paper presented at the 105th Annual Convention of the American Psychological Association, Chicago, IL.

Schlender, B. (2000). Sony plays to win. *Fortune*, 141(9) (1 May 2000), 142.

Schlenker, B. R. (1980). *Impression Management: The Self-concept, Social Identity, and Interpersonal Relations.* Monterey, CA: Brooks Cole.

Schlenker, B. R., Weigold, M. E. and Hallam, J. R. (1990). Self-serving attributions in social context: effects of self-esteem and social pressure. *Journal of Personality and Social Psychology*, 58, 855–63.

Selfe, C. L. and Meyer, P. R. (1991). Testing claims for on-line conferences. *Written Communication*, 8, 163–92.

Shapiro, J. S. (1999). Loneliness: paradox or artefact. *American Psychologist*, 54, 782–3.

Shepherd, R.-M. and Edelmann, R. J. (2001). Caught in the Web. *The Psychologist*, 14, 520–1.

Sherman, R. C. (2001). The mind's eye in cyberspace: online perceptions of self and others. In Riva and Galiberti (eds), *Towards CyberPsychology: Mind, Cognitions and Society in the Internet Age.* Amsterdam: IOS Press, 53–72.

Short, J., Williams, E. and Christie, B. (1976). *The Social Psychology of Telecommunications.* London: Wiley.

Siegal, J., Dubrovsky, S., Kiesler, T. and McGuire, W. (1983). Cited in Kiesler *et al.* (1984).

Sitkin, S. B., Sutcliffe, K. M. and Barrios-Choplin, J. R. (1992). A dual-capacity model of communication media choice in organizations. *Human Communication Research*, 18, 563–98.

Smith, C. B., McLaughlin, M. and Osborne, K. K. (1998). From terminal ineptitude to virtual sociopathy: how conduct is regulated on Usenet. In F. Sudweeks, M. McLaughlin and S. Rafaeli (eds), *Networks and Netplay: Virtual Groups on the Internet.* Cambridge, MA: MIT Press, 95–112.

Smolensky, M. W., Carmody, M. A. and Halcomb, C. G. (1990). The influence of task type, group structure and extraversion on uninhibited speech in computer-mediated communication. *Computers in Human Behavior*, 6, 261–72.

Smyth, J. M. (1998). Written emotional expression: effect sizes, outcome, types, and moderating variables. *Journal of Consulting and Clinical Psychology*, 66, 174–84.

Spears, R. (1995). Isolating the collective self: the content and context of identity, rationality and behaviour. Unpublished Pioner grant proposal, University of Amsterdam.

Spears, R. and Lea, M. (1992). Social influence and the influence of the 'social' in computer-mediated communication. In M. Lea (ed.), *Contexts in Computer-mediated Communication*. London: Harvester Wheatsheaf, 30–64.

Spears, R. and Lea, M. (1994). Panacea or panopticon? The hidden power in computer-mediated communication. *Communication Research*, 21, 427–59.

Spears, R., Lea, M. and Lee, S. (1990). De-individuation and group polarization in computer-mediated communication. *British Journal of Social Psychology*, 29, 121–34.

Spears, R., Lea, M. and Postmes, T. (2001). On SIDE: purview, problems, prospects. In T. Postmes, R. Spears, M. Lea and S. D. Reicher (eds), *SIDE Issues Centre Stage: Recent Developments of De-individuation in Groups*. Amsterdam: North-Holland.

Sproull, L. and Faraj, S. (1997). Atheism, sex, and databases: the Net as a social technology. In S. Kiesler (ed.), *Culture of the Internet*. Nahwah, NJ: Lawrence Erlbaum, 35–51.

Sproull, L. and Kiesler, S. (1986). Reducing social context cues: electronic mail in organizational communication. *Management Science*, 32, 1492–512.

Stafford, L. and Reske, J. R. (1990). Idealization and communication in long-distance pre-marital relationships. *Family Relations*, 39, 274–9.

Standage, T. (1999). *The Victorian Internet*. London: Phoenix Books.

Stevens, R. J. (1996). A humanistic approach to relationships. In D. Miell and R. Dallos (eds), *Social Interaction and Personal Relationships*. London: Sage, 357–66.

Stone, A. R. (1991). Will the real body please stand up? Boundary stories about virtual cultures. In M. Benedilt (ed.), *Cyberspace*. Cambridge, MA: MIT Press, 81–118.

Stone, A. R. (1993). What vampires know: transsubjection and transgender in cyberspace. Paper given at 'In control', Mensch–Interface–Machine Symposium, Graz, Austria.

Stone, L. D. and Pennebaker, J. W. (2002). Trauma in real time: talking and avoiding online conversations about the death of Princess Diana. *Basic and Applied Social Psychology*, 24, 173–83.

Stone, M. (1998). Journaling with clients. *Journal of Individual Psychology*, 54, 535–45.

Suler, J. (2000). Psychotherapy in cyberspace: a 5-dimensional model of online and computer-mediated psychotherapy. *Cyberpsychology and Behavior*, 3, 151–9.

Sunday Times (2001). Office workers told to take an e-mail holiday (News Section, 4 March, 8).

Swann, W. B. Jr (1983). Self-verification: bringing social reality into harmony with the self. In J. Solsa and A. G. Greenwald (eds), *Social Psychological Perspectives on the Self*, vol. 2. Hillsdale, NJ: Erlbaum, 33–66.

Swickert, R. J., Hittner, J. B., Harris, J. L. and Herring, J. A. (2002). Relationships among Internet use, personality and social support. *Computers in Human Behavior*, 18(4), 437–51.

Tajfel, H. and Turner, J. C. (1979). An integrative theory of intergroup conflict. In W. G. Austin and S. Worchel (eds), *The Social Psychology of Intergroup Relations*. Monterey, CA: Brooks Cole.

Thompsen, P. A. and Foulger, D. A. (1996). Effects of pictographs and quoting on flaming in electronic mail. *Computers in Human Behavior*, 12, 225–43.

Thomson, R. and Murachver, T. (2001). Predicting gender from electronic discourse. *British Journal of Social Psychology*, 40, 193–208.

Tice, D. M., Butler, J. L., Muraven, M. B. and Stillwell, A. M. (1995). When modesty prevails: differential favorability of self-presentation to friends and strangers. *Journal of Personality and Social Psychology*, 69, 1120–38.

Tolmie, A. and Boyle, J. (2000). Factors influencing the success of computer mediated communication (CMC) environments in university teaching: a review and case study. *Computers and Education*, 34, 119–40.

Trope, Y. (1979). Uncertainty reducing properties of achievement tasks. *Journal of Personality and Social Psychology*, 37, 1505–18.

Turkle, S. (1995). *Life on the Screen: Identity in the Age of the Internet*. New York: Simon & Schuster.

Utz, S. (2000). Social information processing in MUDs. *Journal of Online Behavior*, 1(1). Retrieved from the WWW, 3 October 2001, from http://www.behavior.net/JOB/v1n1/utz.html

Utz, S. and Sassenberg, K. (2001). Attachment to a virtual seminar: the role of experience, motives and fulfilment of expectations. In U. Reips and M. Bosnjak (eds), *Dimensions of Internet Science*. Lengerich, Germany: Pabst Science Publishers, 323–36.

Van Gelder, L. (1991). The strange case of the electronic lover. In C. Dunlop and R. Kling (eds), *Computerization and Controversy: Value Conflicts and Social Choice*. Boston, MA: Academic Press.

Vygotsky, L. S. (1978). *Mind in society* (M. Cole, V. John-Steiner, S. Scribner and E. Souberman, ed. & trans). Cambridge, MA: Harvard University Press.

Wallace, P. (1999). *The Psychology of the Internet*. Cambridge: Cambridge University Press.

Walther, J. B. (1992). Interpersonal effects in computer-mediated communication: a relational perspective. *Communication Research*, 19, 52–90.

Walther, J. B. (1994). Anticipated ongoing interaction versus channel effects on relational communication in computer-mediated interaction. *Human Communication Research*, 20, 473–501.

Walther, J. B. (1995). Relational aspects of computer-mediated communication: experimental observations over time. *Organization Science*, 6, 186–203.

Walther, J. B. (1996). Computer-mediated communication: impersonal, inter-personal, and hyperpersonal interaction. *Communication Research*, 23, 3–43.

Walther, J. B. (1999a). Visual cues and computer-mediated communication: don't look before you leap. Paper presented at the annual meeting of the International Communication Association, San Francisco, May 1999.

Walther, J. B. (1999b). Communication addiction disorder: concern over media, behavior and effects. Paper presented at the annual meeting of the American Psychological Association, Boston, August 1999.

Walther, J. B., Anderson, J. K. and Park, D. W. (1994). Interpersonal effects in computer-mediated interaction: a meta-analysis of social and antisocial communication. *Communication Research*, 21, 460–87.

Walther, J. B. and Burgoon, J. K. (1992). Relational communication in computer-mediated interaction. *Human Communication Research*, 19, 50–88.

Walther, J. B., Slovacek, C. and Tidwell, L. (1999). Is a picture worth a thousand words? Photographic image in long term and short term virtual teams. Paper presented at the annual meeting of the International Communication Association, San Francisco, May 1999.

Warkentin, M. and Beranek, P. M. (1999). Training to improve virtual team communication. *Information Systems Journal*, 9(4), 271–89.

Wastlund, E., Norlander, T. and Archer, T. (2001). Internet blues revisited: replication and extension of an Internet paradox study. *CyberPsychology and Behavior*, 4, 385–91.

Webb, W. M., Marsh, K. L., Schneiderman, W. and Davis, B. (1989). Interaction between self-monitoring and manipulated states of self-awareness. *Journal of Personality and Social Psychology*, 56, 70–80.

Weisband, S. and Atwater, L. (1999). Evaluating self and others in electronic and face-to-face groups. *Journal of Applied Psychology*, 84, 632–9.

Weisband, S. and Kiesler, S. (1996). Self-disclosure on computer forms: meta-analysis and implications. Proceedings of CHI96. Available on the WWW at: http://www.acm.org/sigchi/chi96/papers/Weisband/sw_txt.htm

Wicklund, R. A. and Gollwitzer, P. M. (1987). The fallacy of the public–private self-focus distinction. *Journal of Personality*, 55, 491–523.

Williams, E. (1972). Factors influencing the effect of medium of communication upon preferences for media, conversations and persons. Communications Studies Group paper number E/72227/WL.

Williams, E. (1975). Coalition formation over telecommunications media. *European Journal of Social Psychology*, 5, 503–7.

Wills, T. A. (1987). Downward comparison as a coping mechanism. In C. R. Snyder and C. E. Ford (eds), *Coping with Negative Life Events: Clinical and Social Psychological Perspectives*. New York: Plenum Press.

Wills, T. A. (1992). Social comparison and self change. In Y. Klar, J. D. Fisher, J. M. Chinsky and A. Nadler (eds), *Self Change: Social Psychological and Clinical Perspectives*. New York: Springer-Verlag.

Winzelberg, A. (1997). The analysis of an electronic support group for individuals with eating disorders. *Computers in Human Behavior*, 13, 393–407.

Woll, S. and Cozby, C. (1987). Videodating and other alternatives to traditional methods of relationship initiation. In W. Jones and D. Periman (eds), *Advances in Personal Relationships vol. 1*. Greenwich, CT: JAI Press.

Wood, J. V. (1989). Theory and research concerning social comparisons of personal attributes. *Psychological Bulletin*, 106, 231–48.

Wood, J. V., Giordano-Beech, M., Taylor, K. M., Michela, J. L. and Gaus, V. (1994). Strategies of social comparison among people with low self-esteem: self-protection and self-enhancement. *Journal of Personality and Social Psychology*, 67, 713–31.

Worotynec, Z. S. (2000). The good, the bad and the ugly: Listserv as support. *Cyberpsychology and Behavior*, 3, 797–810.

Yates, S. (1996). Oral and written linguistic features of computer conferencing. In S. Herring (ed.), *Computer-mediated Communication: Linguistic, Social and Cross-Cultural Perspectives*. Amsterdam: John Benjamins, 29–46.

You, Y. and Pekkola, S. (2001). Meeting others – supporting situation awareness on the WWW. *Decision Support Systems*, 32, 71–82.

Young, K. (1996). Internet addiction: the emergence of a new clinical disorder. Paper presented at the 104th Annual Convention of the American Psychological Association, Toronto, Canada.

Young, K. (1997). What makes online usage stimulating: potential explanations for pathological Internet use. Paper presented at the 105th Annual Convention of the American Psychological Association, Chicago.

Young, K., O'Mara, J. and Buchanan, J. (1999). Cybersex and infidelity online: implications for evaluation and treatment. Poster presented at the 107th annual meeting of the American Psychological Association Division 43, 21 August 1999. Retrieved from the WWW on 3 October 2001 from http://www.netaddiction.com/articles/cyberaffairs.htm

Zimbardo, P. G. (1969). The human choice: individuation, reason, and order vs. deindividuation, impulse and chaos. In W. J. Arnold and D. Levine (eds), *Nebraska Symposium on Motivation*. Lincoln: University of Nebraska Press, 237–307.

Author Index

Subject Index